# Design Thinking and Storytelling in Architecture

PETER G. ROWE
YOEUN CHUNG

# Design Thinking and Storytelling in Architecture

BIRKHÄUSER
BASEL

To Teenie and Jenn.
To my grandpa Daddy-Long-Legs,
Tae-Gon Kim.

# Table of Contents

CHAPTER 1

# An Introduction

As a sequel to an earlier publication with much the same title, this book is an attempt to fashion a generalized portrait of design thinking ultimately as a form of storytelling primarily in architecture (Rowe, 1987). In what follows is a brief account of the book's scope, the way in which design thinking can be regarded as a fundamentally different way of knowing the world and the book's organization.

## Scope

Here design appears to be a fundamental means of inquiry concerned with making with a certain commonplace usefulness. It is also concerned with the way things should be rather than the way that they are with the latter being the domain of science and other fields, including the way our worlds have been (Simon, 1969). Moreover, design thinking can be characterized by cognitive aspects whereby it deals with 'wicked' rather than 'tame' problems, where there is no definitive stopping rule. It also places reliance on heuristic forms of reasoning essentially using rules of thumb or practical experience. There, initial hunches often matter most as they color subsequent thinking. Further it is concerned with arriving at 'satisficing' decisions rather than those that can be shown to be globally optimal. Design thinking also comes about as reflection-in-action going beyond the bounds of technical rationalism and the problem as given is rarely accepted and invariably reshaped. As such it is a case of 'knowing how' in addition to 'knowing that' even in the face of otherwise critical speculation. Generally, design thinking is seen to be both a way of making and enabling being in the world that is common within a relatively broad range of fields, at least in some respects. In most if not all, a process takes place involving empathy or listening carefully, offering a definition of what seems to be wanted, i.e. clear ideation or creation of usually novel solutions, and then prototyping and testing of solutions, including communication to others. However, even with its focus on architecture this book is not concerned with professional matters, nor with client-architect relations, nor with reception by particular groups, nor with an orthodoxy as such, even though these are otherwise worthy topics. Most but not all work described and discussed is modern and where modernity and 'contemporaneity' are seen from the perspective of path-dependent cultural trajectories and not acultural assertions. The influence of making on representation and *vice versa* is always present as is an object-oriented ontological stance to how the world is portrayed. Almost more than anything else it is a book about the creation of things and soon to be palpable scenes and the storytelling that goes on associated with the things and scenes, or more precisely again because it is about architecture, buildings or building ensembles and the propositional logics that appear to lie behind them at least sufficiently to bring them into the world. In other fields, say in business management, as will be shown, application of design thinking broadly construed does occur but also where the product in question comes about with explanations involving storytelling.

## A Way of Thinking

In several respects design thinking may be seen as distinctive from knowledge and its use in both science and the humanities. Indeed, as early as the late 1960s it was allegedly even mooted as a third way of knowing the world (Archer, 1968). For its part, science is a systematic endeavor that builds and organizes knowledge in the form of explanations and predictions about the universe. Today it manifests itself in four major fields. They are natural science, social science, formal science and applied science. Etymologically it derives from the Latin *scientia* meaning knowledge, awareness and understanding. As a way of knowing the world it dates back at least to Aristotle and his demonstrations that introduced empiricism. It was later more fully codified in the 17th century by the likes of Sir Francis Bacon. Rooted in scientific method, scientific thinking makes use of a largely standardized process by which data are gathered to test whether a hypothesis describing the universe, or world, aligns in some manner (Kuhn, 1996 and Harvard Graduate School of Education, 2010). By contrast, the humanities are academic disciplines apart from the sciences that study human society and culture. These fields of knowledge arose largely during the Renaissance from the Latin *studia humanitatis* referring to culture, refinement and education. They also involved secular education as an alternative to religious thought and usually comprised a significant historical element. Further, this broad field is distinct from science largely by virtue of modes of approach rather than purely subject matter (Levi, 1970; Walley, 1997 and Small, 2013). Also distinguished by mode of knowing, design thinking according to observers, is rooted in the talent of designers to synthesize solutions, whereas sciences and other methods are based on empirical measurable evidence and principles of reasoning. As noted earlier, it is also about the way the world should be rather than the way that it is. Its emphasis is on synthesis rather than analysis. Again, according to close observers, designerly ways of thinking set design and design thinking apart from other forms of cognitive activity (Archer, 1968; Lawson, 1980 and Cross, 2011). It is also different from systems thinking based on an insistence on synthesis rather than on analysis (Spacey, 2016). Unlike other essentially goal-oriented problem-related activities, designers create goals in creating solution concepts. In fact, it is a process of professional reflection-in-action in this regard (Schön, 1983). Therefore, they do not find solutions, certainly not in the sense of something lost. Rather, they fantasize, tell stories and invent worlds. Again, it is about what should be and about new or certainly different and imagined worlds. In this regard the propositional aspect of architecture and design is important for moving beyond critical stances and positing palpable responses. In short, design thinking is a fantastic way of knowing and enabling being in the world.

## Organization of the Book

The book is organized into six chapters. After this introduction it begins with a brief historical account of design thinking as a particular way of addressing creative problem solving in numerous fields, including architecture and related kinds

## 1 – TWO WAYS OF KNOWING

A A variant of the scientific method and B output from 'Design Thinking' of a center on the Chicago Waterfront

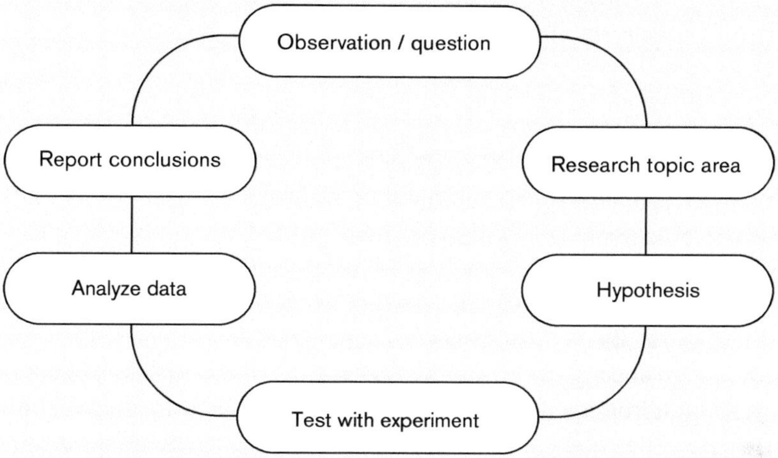


A

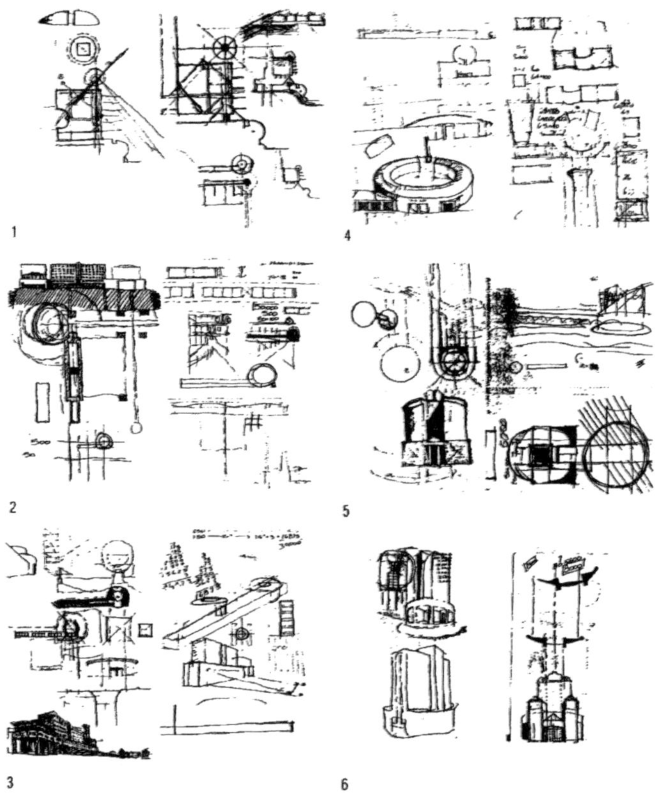


B

of design. These applications will include those that arose in business innovation in the 1970s, and then within commercial groups like IDEO in the early 1990s. Though probably dating back at least as far as Wertheimer's 'productive thinking' of 1945, design thinking in engineering and architecture began flourishing also around topics like 'design methods' in the 1950s and particularly the 60s, at least for a time. This chapter will also introduce discussion of specific topics and aspects of design thinking like: 'wicked problems', 'satisficing decisions', heuristic reasoning and various other procedures, before chronicling a worked example of an architect in action in the design of a modern chapel. The following chapter 3 will introduce the concept of 'schema' or its plural form 'schemata', including how they can be defined. Simply put, a schema is a cognitive vehicle allowing organization of experience in such a manner that an individual can recognize other experiences of a similar kind and take appropriate action. The chapter will also include discussion of how schemata have evolved particularly with reference to their overall orientation of being futuristic or traditional in the manner the 'present future' is confronted. In addition, reflexive aspects involved under the philosophical notion of 'situations' will be broached. Chapter 4 takes up particular aspects of the knowledge that goes into architecture in the sense of 'knowing that', beginning with the time-honored Vitruvian triad of 'firmness, commodity and delight'. This account is followed by discussion of modernist forms of architectural discourse up until an avant-garde reaction and drift towards hypermodernity with its emphases on specific broad aspects like programming, engineering expression, figuration in pursuit of identity, parametric design, sustainability and so on, all somewhat together although mostly sequentially. Chapter 5 returns to the cognitive realm and constructs design thinking as a framework involving situations, mental spaces, and frames within those spaces. The arrival of the digital age is also discussed, particularly in the light of representation and extended reality and artificial intelligence. Finally, chapter 6 reverts to exploration and explanation of design thinking as essentially a case of things, scenes about those things, and the concomitant storytelling that invariably goes on, replete with worked examples. Throughout the narrative is well illustrated.

## 2 – TIM BROWN'S (IDEO) DESIGN THINKING DIAGRAM
from inspiration to ideation and implementation

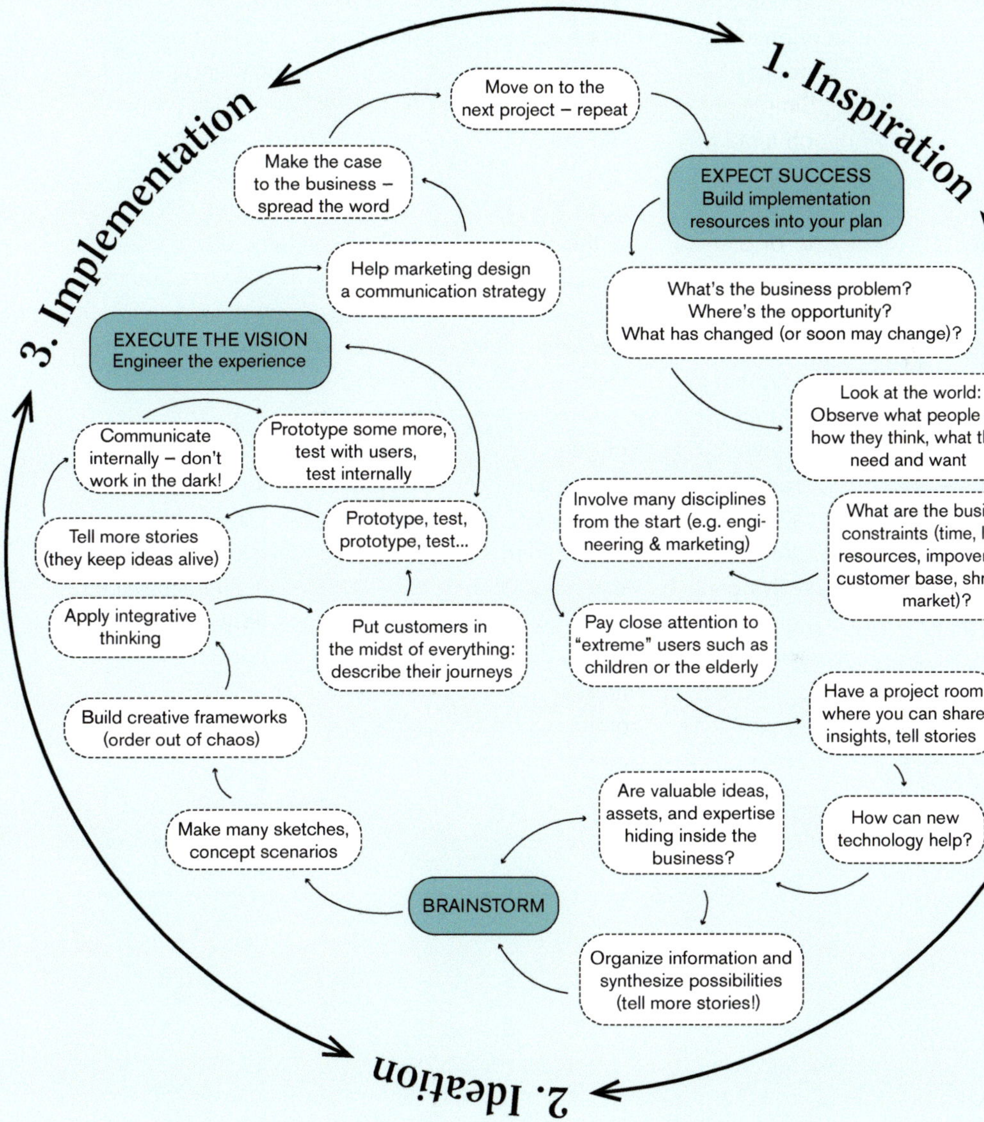

CHAPTER 2

# Design Thinking and in Architecture

By now design thinking has become rather ubiquitous in its use and encompassment. In order to lend more structure to this book's discussion, what follows here is a brief historical account of the phrase in various fields of application and emphasis. This is followed by a tightening down, so to speak, around the area of architecture and urban design and the central focus of this book. There, various definitions and commentaries will be taken up and compared across broadly agreed-upon concepts pertinent to design thinking as applied to architecture and urban design. They will include the definition of 'internal' and 'external' constraints, 'wicked' as opposed to 'tame' problems, 'satisficing' decisions and 'heuristics' or 'heuristic reasoning'. Finally, the chapter will be rounded out by a protocol analysis of a professional designer in action, illustrating the practice of design thinking.

# A Brief History

The term or phrase 'design thinking' and how it was defined and shaped has evolved since the early days of the 1950s. An early work related to the topic was Max Wertheimer's posthumously published *Productive Thinking* of 1945, that has remained relevant, particularly to contemporary ideas about schemata and knowledge structures necessary for making. Wertheimer (1880–1943) was a Czech-born psychologist and one of the founders of the Gestalt Movement. In *Productive Thinking* he distinguishes between 'reproductive thinking' which involved rote repetition and habitual ways of viewing the world from 'productive thinking' that involved novel insight-based reasoning (Wertheimer, 1945). In this distinction he was placing productive thinking against traditional logic of a syllogistic kind and classical theory of associationism (Warren, 1921). By the latter he was referring to the co-occurrence of ideas and sensations seen as a primary basis of meaningful thought in the manner, say, of John Locke (1632–1704), David Hume (1711–1776) and John Stuart Mill (1806–1873). *Productive Thinking* was also engagingly replete with storytelling in discussion of problems beingly solved creatively by the likes of Galileo and Einstein. Key elements in this contrastive mode of thinking were definition of structurally central problem features and the revelation of vectors of thought directed outside of more normal or even commonplace views and situational understandings (Wertheimer, 1945 and Steinberg, 1999).

Then, in the 1950s and 1960s, the term 'design thinking' became strongly associated with roots in the study of design cognition and design methods. There an early leader was John E. Arnold (1913–1963) an American professor of mechanical engineering and professor of business administration at Stanford University. He strongly advocated for 'inventiveness' based upon a psychology of creative thinking and imagination.

In this regard he went on to pioneer a strong school of thought at Stanford around such issues and became renowned for applying heuristics, or rules of thumb, in problem solving and generating novel solutions (Arnold, 1950). Bruce Archer (1922–2005) followed in 1968 with his dissertation at the Royal College of Art in the UK, titled *The Structure of Design Processes.* A mechanical engineer and professor in design research at the Royal College, he was among the first to moot the idea of design as a third way of knowing in the world, beside the well-established blocks of knowledge associated with the sciences and humanities.

Into the 1970s, several particular characteristics of design thinking that had emerged were more fully investigated and defined. One was the idea of 'wicked problems' that defied definitive formulation and, therefore, true or false answers. Indeed, according to Horst Rittel and Melvin Webber there were no real solutions, as such, at all to this class of problems, unlike the so-called 'tame problems' (Rittel and Webber, 1973). Rittel (1930–1990) was a German-born design theorist and professor, initially at the Hochschule für Gestaltung in Ulm, Germany, and then at the University of California, Berkeley, Washington University in St. Louis and at the University of Stuttgart's Faculty of Architecture and Town Planning. Melvin Webber (1920–2005), his colleague at Berkeley, was an American planner who also worked with Richard Llewelyn Davies in the Milton Keynes new town in the UK. Working on transportation he also introduced the idea of 'community without propinquity' (Webber, 1964). The idea of wicked problems, however, can also be traced back earlier to the work of Fritz Zwicky (1898–1974), a Bulgarian-born and Swiss astronomer who worked most of his life at the California Institute of Technology and the inventor of 'morphological analysis' (Zwicky, 1962). In the social sciences Charles West Churchman (1913–2004) an American philosopher and systems scientist referred to wicked problems as bring ill-formulated, with confusing information and where there were many clients and decision makers with confusing values (Churchman, 1967). Also, in the 1970s, Charles S. Peirce's 'Theory of Abduction' was reprised as a form of logical inference that sought the simplest and most likely conclusion from a set of observations. In other words, it revealed a plausible conclusion but did not definitively verify it and, therefore, was distinct from deduction and induction. In this respect it also comes before either other form of reasoning with the colloquial reference of having a 'hunch'. Peirce (1839–1914) was an American philosopher, mathematician, logician, and scientist, often seen as a 'father of pragmatism' (Fann, 2020).

Into the 1980s, design thinking became more fully concerned with a form of knowing in the world and as a cognitive process, especially in overt areas of design like architecture and engineering, though also beginning to branch out more broadly into other realms of professional knowledge. In this regard Bryan Lawson's *How Designers Think*, originally of 1980, sought to define a comprehensive account of design thinking with later revisions up to 2005. Lawson (1945– ) was a British architectural educator, architect and psychologist. In his work he basically broke down design thinking into three parts, as shown on figure 1. The first was 'What is Design?'

1 – FOUR CONCEPTUAL MODELS OF A DESIGN PROBLEM

A Problem space as a decision tree, B Bryan Lawson's model of actors, constraints and depictions, C Bruce Archer's stage process model and D Morris Asimow's iconic model

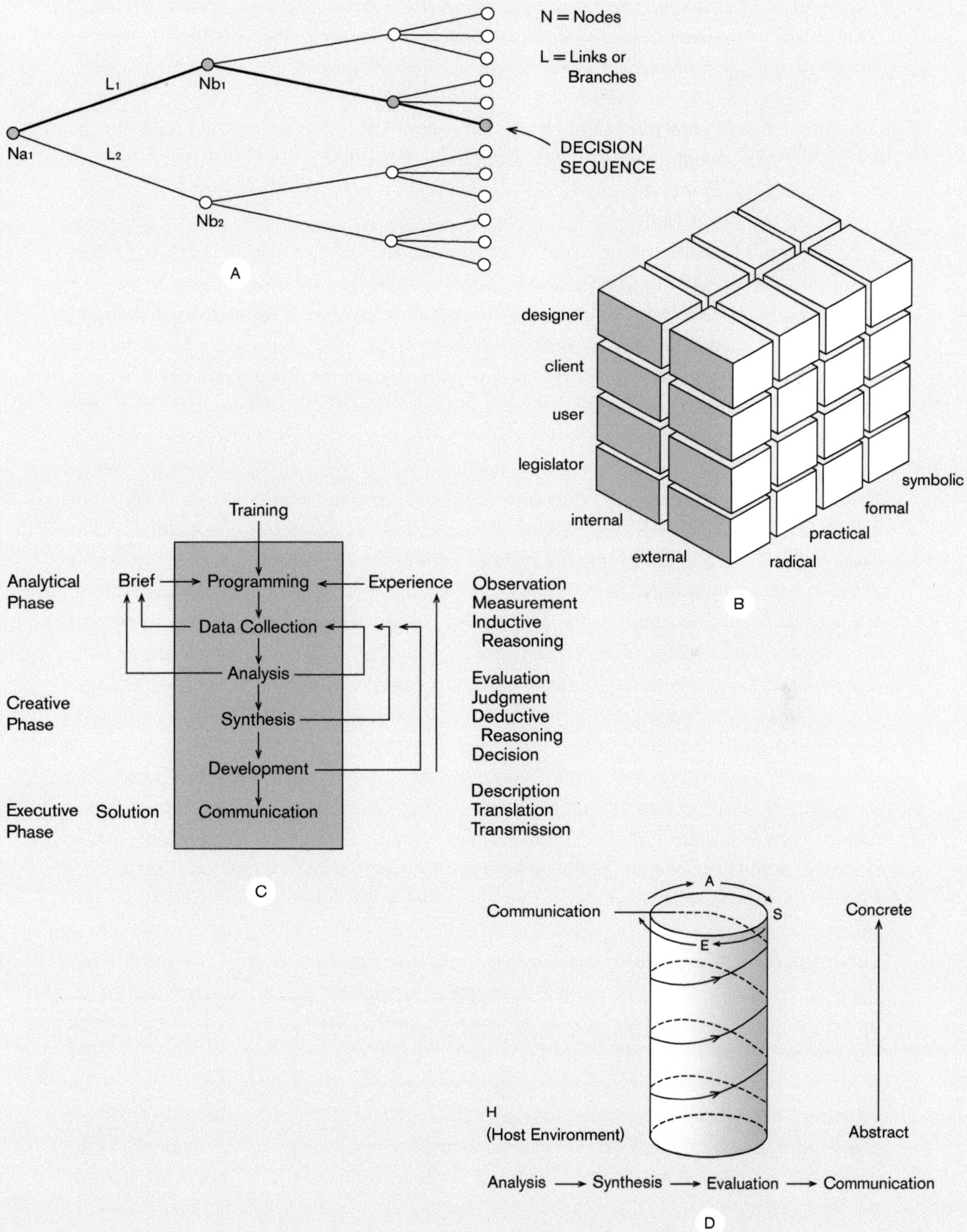

The second was 'How are Design Problems Shaped?' and the third was 'Design Thinking' in relation to the earlier model of designing that he had established. This model had three main axes: 1. a fixed state to a flexible state, reflecting legislators, users, clients and designers in that order; 2. differences between 'internal' and 'external' constraints, where internal constraints were those that were given whereas external constraints were brought to bear from the outside by designers exercising insight and experience; and 3. a characterization of problem constraints ranging from 'radical' concerned with primary purpose, through to 'formal' and 'symbolic' concerned with shape and appearance (Lawson, 2005). Clearly it is the upper right-hand side of the three-space that involves the least well-defined problematic aspects and wicked problems and 'abductive' reasoning.

Then Nigel Cross (1922–2003) took up Bruce Archer's earlier idea of design being a third form of knowing in the world, besides those of the sciences and humanities. He was a mechanical engineer and professor of design research at the Royal College of Art in the UK. In his work he identified four characteristics of design thinking. They were conceptual realization of new things; an appreciation of material culture; a use of languages of modeling; and a distinct way of knowing things (Cross, 1982). In essence he saw design as being about how things should be rather than how things are, echoing Herbert Simon in his *Sciences of the Artificial* (Simon, 1969). Donald Schön (1939–1997) followed with his classic concept of the 'reflective practitioner' and its contributions to organizational learning. Like Archer and Cross, he also broadened the scope of application to fields of professional knowledge ranging through health care, science, engineering, planning and architecture. He also established an underlying structure for 'reflection-in-action' (Schön, 1983). He was an American philosopher and professor of urban planning at MIT. In my own work, also titled *Design Thinking* of 1987, I also described and commented upon approaches to design by architects and urban designers as one in a significant early use of the term in design research (Rowe, 1987). My principal argument, however, was in the direction of Lawson's 'external constraints' or those supplied by the designer in addition to definition of the problem as given by legislators, users and even clients. In this regard I drew heavily on the Information Processing Model of Creative Problem Solving espoused by Allen Newell, John Shaw and Herbert Simon (Newell, Shaw and Simon, 1967; Newell and Simon, 1972). I was also reflecting on and bringing to bear the application of '*a priori* knowledge' to design problems in order to shed more tractable and soluble light by drawing on a schema associated with professional design education and experience (Rowe, 1982). Parenthetically, Peter G. Rowe (1945– ) is an architect, urban designer, researcher and educator.

During the 1990s and certainly into the 2000s there was a significant growth in interest in applying design thinking across an increasingly diverse range of applications, often as a catalyst for gaining competitive advantage within business sectors (Harvard Business Review, 2020). Following on from John Arnold at Stanford University, Robert McKim and Rolfe Faste taught design thinking as a method of creative action with a broad potential range of applications (Faste, 1994). In particular it was Faste's colleague at Stanford, David M. Kelley (1951– ) who founded the innovation firm IDEO in 1991. He was an American Stanford University professor and graduate from Carnegie Mellon University, Allen Newell's and Herbert Simon's academic home. In fact, IDEO in 1991 was a merger among four leading lights in design thinking, especially in the realm of product design and organization. In addition to Kelley, they included Bill Moggridge (1943–2012), the British inventor, and his Moggridge Associates in London; ID Two, also founded by Moggridge in 1969–70; and Matrix Product Design of Mike Nutall of 1983. The charismatic Tim Brown (1962– ), also born in the UK, became Chair and a leading spokesman for the group and design thinking's broad applications. In 1996 the firm was bought by Steelcase, the office furniture maker and in 1999 on ABC's *Nightline* it successfully took up the challenge to produce a new and better-designed shopping cart in a matter of five days (Brown, 2009). According to Brown, design thinking can be seen to involve three kinds of integrated modes of action divided among some 22 or so separate steps as shown in figure 2 in the previous chapter. First, there is 'inspiration' or what is the problem? This involves keen observation of people and what it is they want or aspire to, alongside how technology and business might help facilitate these wants and aspirations. Second, there is 'ideation' involving fairly constant storytelling in order to make the familiar strange and the strange familiar, but also with prototyping and testing. Finally, there is 'implementation', involving marketing design and making the business model work. For Brown, his colleagues and now many followers, design thinking is a discipline that uses designer sensibilities and methods to match people's needs with what is technically feasible and strategically viable. In making this case Brown draws on and refers to Thomas Edison, the inventor of the light bulb, but who at Menlo Park also had the far broader insight of the need for a fully developed marketplace involving electrification (Brown, 2020).

Of late, popularized and superficial applications of design thinking in so-called 'business innovation fields' has been criticized on several counts. First, giving privilege to the role of designers at the expense of a more profound and knowledgeable understanding of the communities that they serve can lead to overly conservative and less caring outcomes, sometimes actually only preserving the status quo. This is particularly the case when the key ingredient of 'empathy' in the IDEO-like formulation ignores sufficient designer reflection about the way identity and power, among other socio-cultural pressures, shape outcomes. In fact, a recent dissertation in an American business administration setting found in favor of the use of design thinking as a way of improving diversity in the architecture profession largely through the dimension of 'empathy' among other factors (Stewart, 2022). Also, highly generalized versions of design thinking run the risk of underrating discipline-specific expertise and experience so necessary to resolving many design problems satisfactorily, and the rote application of steps can depoliticize management and other practices associated with implementation (Kimbell, 2011; Vinsel, 2018 and Askander, 2018). In short, without sufficient reflection, inter-disciplinary

## 2 – CHRISTOPHER ALEXANDER'S 'CASE OF FOUR OBJECTS'

A Grouped according to shape, B as a semi-lattice and C as a tree-like graph

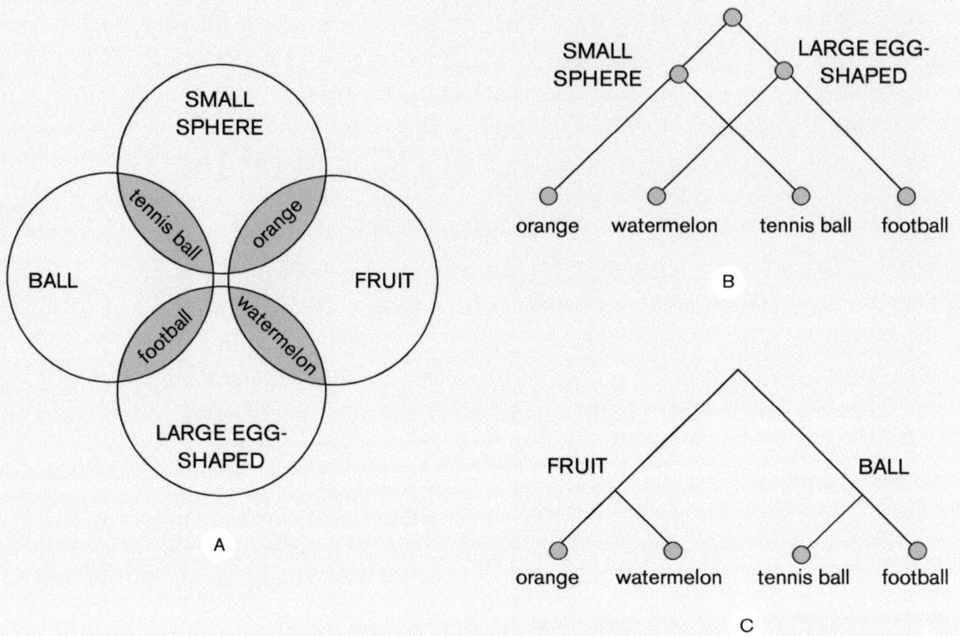


## 3 – A TWO-SPACE REPRESENTATION OF 'SCOPE' AND 'MECHANISM' DEPICTING AUTHOR POSITIONS

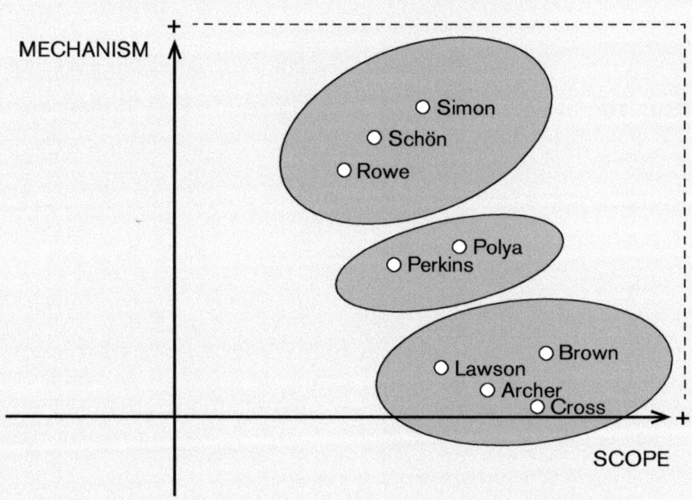

knowledge, sheer experience and even talent, the aura of design thinking runs the risk of hindering precisely what it portends for real creative innovation.

# Architectural Design Applications

Turning to work more squarely in the area of design thinking and architecture, as described earlier, several authors developed and drew on models of creative problem solving of a cognitive and activity kind. For instance, in Rowe's account, Newell, Shaw and Simon's early and pioneering work in the Information Processing Model became central, particularly in the definition and navigation through a design problem space (Rowe, 1987). This design problem model consisted of several postulates. First, there is a problem space whose elements are 'knowledge states', some sequence of which represent a solution to a problem. Second, there are one or more 'generative processes' that allow one to take knowledge states as input and starting points and produce more knowledge states as output. Third, there are one or more 'test procedures' that allow the problem solver to compare knowledge states with specification of the solution state that is not the knowledge state itself. Finally, there are further processes enabling a problem solver to decide what generative processes and which test procedures to employ on the basis of the information contained in available knowledge states. Formal representation of a problem space and of problem states in extensive form is often through a decision tree, as depicted in figure 1. Nodes *Na, Nb,* and so on, represent decision points and links *La, Lb,* and so on, represent branches and the courses of action associated with different outcomes at each decision point. A particular problem-solving approach is thus specified by a particular sequence of nodes and links beginning on the left-hand side of the tree and moving towards the right-hand side. At much the same time, if not before, a number of architectural researchers concerned with design process became involved in this kind of activity and line of speculation, also producing early work in computer-aided design (Negroponte, 1972; Eastman, 1975 and Mitchell, 1977).

Also, as described earlier, Bryan Lawson also defined a model of a design problem holistically, including those aspects that were perhaps more mundane, well-known and given at the outset (Lawson, 1980). His depiction was comprised of a three-dimensional diagram and stacking of blocks of information and knowledge that contained 'generators of design' on one axis, 'domains of design' on another, and 'function' or 'kinds of design constraints' on a third axis. In short and as shown in figure 1, the categorization of generators of design problems comprised legislators, users, clients and designers in that order. The domain of design constraints distinguished two classes as those that were given at an outset and 'internal', and those that were supplied from the outside and were thus 'external'. Finally, the kinds of constraints, as noted earlier, ranged from 'radical' and those that dealt with primary purpose, to 'practical' and those dealing with the realities of producing a design and building, to 'formal', dealing with shape and appearance and visual form, then on to 'symbolic' constraints concerned with styles and more abstract representation by the design and building.

The work of others such as Bruce Archer in his proposed model of design is schematically described in the accompanying diagram, figure 1. It was defined essentially by a sequence of activities defined or categorized according to their orientation and general types of tasks involved. Further, the process was described in a general manner, irrespective of particular circumstances. Feedback loops were also in evidence resulting in a staging of activities in a less distinct manner. Also, within the diagram a distinction begins to be made between overt behavior and the cognitive realm and also departing from a more purely behaviorist position. Nevertheless, the emphasis is still on the sequence of activities. Other depictions also emerged such as the so-called 'iconic model' of a design process shown in figure 1 building on the work of Morris Asimow (Asimow, 1962). There a chronological sequence of steps forms a vertical structure, proceeding from a definition of need, through feasibility study, preliminary design and so on, up to production itself. The horizontal planes embrace a cycle that begins with analysis and then proceeds through synthesis, evaluation and communication.

Looking across these and other models of an architectural problem space and design thinking, both similarities and differences emerge. They may be summarized in the following manner.

## Knowledge States

Generally, these states have much the same meanings and also conform to Ryle's distinction between 'knowing how' as an ability versus 'knowing that' as a factual account (Ryle, 1945). As design thinking is strongly practice-oriented the obvious emphasis is on 'knowing how', but this certainly does not occur in the absence of domain or field knowledge about architecture and urban design. Also, experience is an obvious factor in knowing how, particularly across a range of knowledge types, though also in depth within a smaller range. Lawson's prominent distinction between 'internal' and 'external' constraints corresponds more or less exactly with the Information Processing Theory's 'problem-oriented' and 'autonomous' constraints. The 'internal' and 'problem-oriented' are those that are given at some outset and initially define a problem space, whereas 'external' and 'autonomous' constraints

# 4 – CHRISTOPHER ALEXANDER'S CONCEPT OF 'PATTERN LANGUAGE' FOR A COMMUNITY CENTER
in San Francisco, California, USA

A

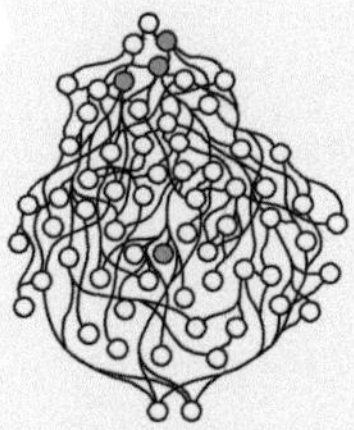

3. Size based on population
4. Community territory
7. Entrance location
11. Arena enclosure
43. Waiting diversions

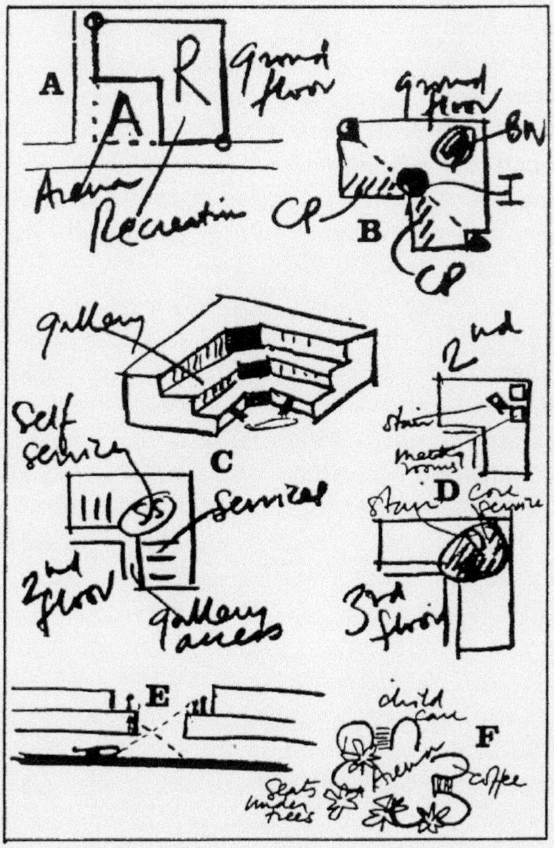


B

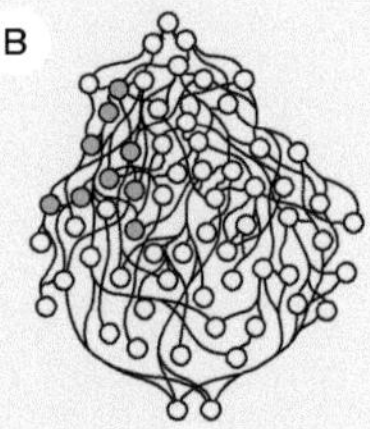

9. Arena thoroughfare
10. Open to street
16. Necklace
17. Entrance shape
24. Subcommittee watchdogs
28. The intake process
29. Outdoor seats
35. Information

C

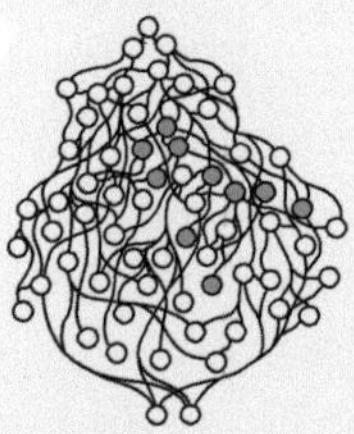

13. All services off arena
14. Free waiting
15. Overview of services
21. Self-service
22. Pedestrian density
25. Building stepped back
26. Vertical circulation
31. Short corridors
39. Arena diameter
51. Stair seats

D

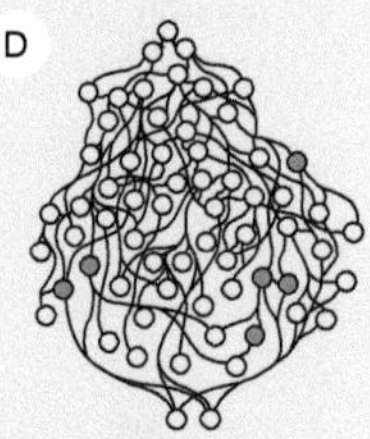

19. Core service
41. Town-meeting
47. Meeting rooms
49. Staff lounge
59. Square seminar rooms

E

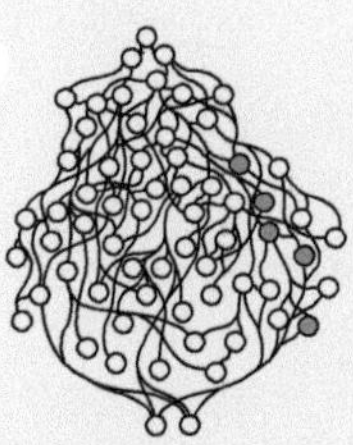

F

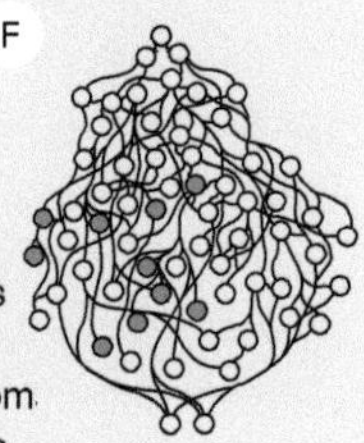

18. Windows overlooking life
26. Vertical circulation in services
33. Service layout
40. Office flexibility
56. Informal reception

20. Activity pockets
27. Self-service progression
29. Outdoor seats
32. Child-care position
38. Community wall

42. Sleeping OK
48. Barbershop politics
53. Form-filling tables
54. Accessible bathroom
57. Child-care contents

are those that are provided outside the immediate scope of a problem as given in order to progress forward in a problem space towards a solution (Lawson, 2005, pp. 93–98). In addition, the characterization of the latter into various kinds of constraints, such as 'radical' through to 'symbolic' in Lawson's design problem model more or less echo those specified in Rowe's account of 'anthropometric', 'literal', 'environmental', 'typological' and 'formal linguistic' categories (Rowe, 1987).

## Wicked and Tame Problems

Since early on in any discussion of design thinking in architecture, there has been explicit agreement that overall, it deals with wicked problems without clear stopping rules, no precise true-false answers and the necessity for 'external' and 'autonomous' constraints to be introduced. Indeed, the term was introduced as early as 1962 in fields of design thinking outside of architecture *per se* (Zwicky, 1962 and Churchman, 1967) before explicit recognition within architectural design thinking (Rittel and Webber, 1973). However, this is not to say that so-called 'tame problems' were not seen to be a part of resolving design problems. For instance, within the Lawson model of a design problem, the 'information and knowledge blocks' defined as being 'legislative through user and client' related, by 'internal' and then as 'radical to practical' in nature, no doubt involved some tame problem types for straightforward factual and even 'true-false' accounts were possible. The wickedness of design problems would seem to reside in the other domains and blocks of Lawson's model and middle segments of Archer's stage-process model of design activity and behavior (Rowe, 1987). In the case of the Information Processing Model, the underlying problem type appears to have been assumed to be wicked from the outset (Newell, Shaw and Simon, 1957 and 1967). In addition, Peirce's logical reasoning modality of 'abduction', as against 'deduction' and 'induction', shares a similar sense of non-closure and provisional veracity (Fann, 2020).

## Satisficing Decision Making

As we know from Herbert Simon's *Sciences of the Artificial*, the common tree-like shape of the representation of a problem space is most likely to be embodied within a hierarchical structure that is nearly decomposable but not fully so (Simon, 1969). In other words, the intra-connections among aspects of a problem as perceived or stated are likely to exceed a rather more recognized set of connections in a well-defined situation. This then usually requires adaptation of a messier semi-lattice representation into a more emphatic but not exact tree diagram. As Christopher Alexander (1936–2022), the Austrian-born British-American architect and design theorist, showed clearly in both simple and complicated conditions, the tree diagram did not fully capture the exact connections involved, perhaps most famously in his article "A City is Not a Tree" (Alexander, 1965). In a simple example of four ball-shaped objects, depicted here in figure 2, a shift of context from all round-shaped objects to a matter of types, namely here of balls and fruit, yields a more strictly tree-like arrangement from the earlier semi-lattice configuration. In other words, the creative leap and conversion of the overlapping characteristics of both the 'problem constraints as given' and the imposed 'autonomous constraints' constituted 'satisficing decision making', the outcome of which was neither correct nor incorrect but sub-optimal and the best available.

## Problem-Solving Procedures

Inherent in accounts of design thinking in architecture are decision-making procedures of various kinds. 'Random trial-and-error procedures', for instance, involve finding a solution to a problem in an entirely or largely unbounded manner. Usually trial-and-error procedures are made independently of results from intermediate tests. Such procedures tend to be resorted to when the magnitude of a problem is overwhelming. In the example of a jigsaw puzzle, for example, it is possible to test matched and unmatched pieces, but the outline beyond this simple matching procedure may still not be evident. In other words, solution generation takes place to a significant degree independently from the organization of the problem space after a prior trial. 'Generate-and-test procedures' are variants of trial-and-error with the important difference that the results of tests are explicitly used to guide subsequent attempts to generate solutions.

Many different manifestations of layout problems involve constant adjustment of parts to a whole in order to achieve a desired effect and solution. The phenomenon of incrementally moving from worse to better solutions and often referred to as 'hill-climbing' is also a form of generate-and-test. 'Means-ends analysis' involves an extension of the generate-and-test procedure into allowing the provision of alternative decision rules so that one can explicitly meet different kinds of problem-solving situations. Three components are necessary. They are: 1. A prescribed set of actions and means, 2. A prescribed set of goals and ends, and 3. A set of decision rules relating ends to means. In many ways N. John Habraken's concept of 'supports' and 'structures' specifies the means for individual determination of dwelling environments within a comparatively unified system of production (Habraken, 1998). N. John Habraken (1928– ) is a Dutch architect, educator and theorist involved in mass housing production in the Netherlands who also taught at TU Delft and at MIT. Finally, the purpose behind 'problem space planning' is evident from the earlier definition of a problem space and the decision tree representation of the space. Thus, planning a problem space here aims to structure the overall search process towards a solution. Alexander's hierarchical decompositional approach and his *Pattern Language* are both examples of this. In the first, a problem as given is restated in the form of numerous discrete problem statements. Then relations and connections among the statements are expressed, usually in a binary 'connected' or 'not connected' manner. Groupings of problem statements are then generated, using a cluster-analysis technique in Alexander's case, which collectively provide a map, as it were, of the problem space (Alexander, 1964). His *Pattern Language* was a further attempt to

5 – 100 WALLS CHURCH
by Carlos Arnaiz, 2013, in Cebu, Philippines

6 – TAGAYTAY CHAPEL FOR THE CHOSEN CHILDREN
by Carlos Arnaiz, 2008, in Tagaytay, Philippines

provide a heuristically based mapping of a problem space by way of interconnected specifications of desirable requirements, as shown in figure 4, like 'site area based on population' or 'windows overlooking life' for a particular class of design problem, for example (Alexander, Ishikawa and Silverstein, 1968).

## Heuristic Reasoning

Finally, heuristic reasoning involves devices that contribute to reduction in the search for satisfactory solutions for design problems and that are supplied and brought to bear externally and autonomously by designers on action. Variously defined as 'rules of thumb', 'hunches' and 'provisional procedures' (Polya, 1957; Newell, Shaw and Simon, 1967 and Perkins, 1981). Essentially, the term 'heuristic reasoning' refers to a problem-solving process in which it is unknown beforehand whether a particular sequence of steps will yield a solution or not. Indeed, it is a topic that will be taken up more fully in the next chapter titled 'On Schemata' as it is a part of schemes that are commonly used to tackle wicked problems in particular, as well as being part of the cognitive apparatus involved in creative problem solving. Also, in the case of architectural design, heuristics often take the form of representational artifacts and visualizations of the palpable 'thingness' of buildings to refer to Martin Heidegger (1889–1975), the German philosopher, and his basic concept distinguishing as it does between the shape of emptiness of a flask, for instance, and its composition and decoration (Heidegger, 1967).

Looking across these accounts a two-space might be imagined, running horizontally from relatively closed to open in the sheer scope of activities and undertakings involved in design thinking and a vertical axis moving upwards towards emphases on cognitive decision-making mechanisms, such as dealing with wicked problems, heuristic reasoning and satisficing decision making. Within this two-space the emphasis of various schools of thought or kinds and depictions of design thinking can then be plotted as shown here in figure 3. All more or less occupy the upper right-hand side or quadrant of the two-space as might be expected. After all 'design thinking' as a term or form of life in more philosophical terms is generously inclined in both scope and mechanism in dealing with ill-defined, messy and unstructured problems. Largely the term is bandied around in the realms of innovation and creativity (Harvard Business Review, 2020). However, the emphases of work by the likes of Simon and colleagues, Schön, Alexander and Rowe, for instance, is more inclined towards the mechanisms of design thinking. By contrast, the work of Brown and his colleagues, as well as by Lawson and certainly Archer and Cross in the architectural design thinking camp, place greater emphasis on the scope of applications and even the potential of it being a distinctly other way of knowing the world. In between can also be found many concerned particularly with heuristics and heuristic reasoning.

7 – STEPS IN THE DESIGN PROCESS FOR THE 100 WALLS CHURCH
by Carlos Arnaiz, 2013, in Cebu, Philippines (A) Autonomous constraints of church tradition and religious openness, (B) Conversion to a semi-lattice condition for the autonomous constraints, (C) Sources of a two-fold heuristic regarding analogies to the Mount of Olives and Stonehenge, (D) Spatial components of the two-fold heuristic and (E) Further aspects of the two-fold heuristic regarding development of the varied wall and infill structure

A

B

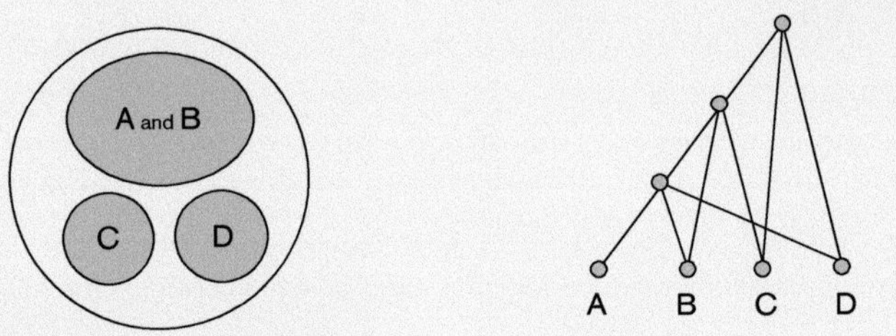


C

D

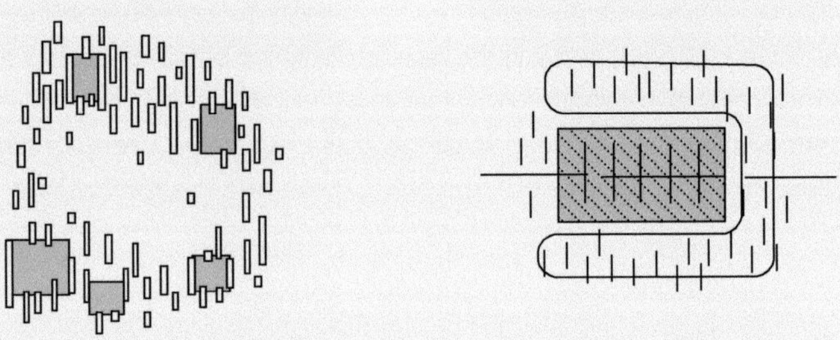

E

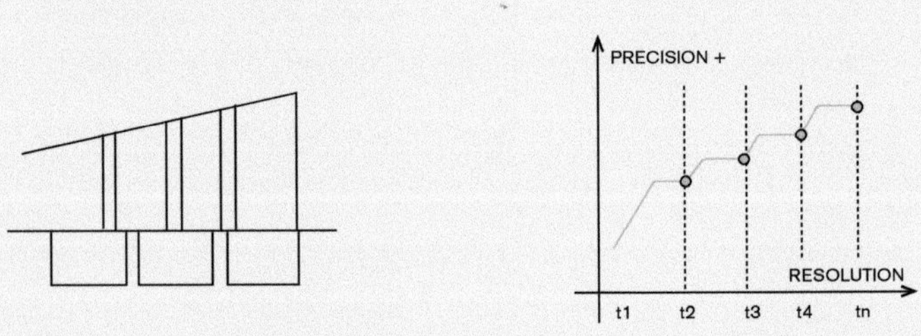

# A Designer in Action

What follows is an example of design thinking in an architectural context and according to the general outline and principles of 'The Information Theory of Problem Solving' pronounced by Newell, Simon and Shaw around 1957 (Newell, Shaw and Simon, 1957, 1967; Newell and Simon, 1972 and Simon, 1973). The building in question is the Chapel of San Pedro Calungsod in Cebu, the Philippines, sometimes more colloquially called the '100 Walls Church in Cebu'. Built in 2013, the chapel served to commemorate the canonization of Pedro Calungsod by the Vatican in 2012. In life he was a young Catholic catechist Filipino Visayan migrant who was martyred for his faith in Guam in 1672. Indeed, his death was a reaction to the catechism for Filipino Catholics that began to take hold in the late 16th century (Bersales, 2012). The site for the chapel was on a stretch of reclaimed land separated by a sea channel from central Cebu in the Visayan Province of the central Philippine archipelago. As shown here in figure 5, it is adjacent to the SM and South Road Properties commercial development, more or less on axis with the mall. In keeping with Ceburean hospitality and its numerous religious facilities welcoming locals and foreigners alike, it is a popular place for weddings. This close spatial alignment is also not uncommon in Cebu. The Chapel site itself is a compact rectangular form prone to flooding and requiring elevation above grade and thus allowing meeting rooms and other 'back-of-house' functions to be placed in a basement. This also further released the site to appear to be occupied entirely by the chapel as such. The size of the congregation to be accommodated is 800 persons and the site area is 1½ hectares (Griffiths, 2014; Fraser, 2015 and Rowe and Fu, 2022).

The architect was Carlos Arnaiz (1975– ), principal of CAZA, or Carlos Arnaiz Architects, an international architectural firm based primarily in Brooklyn, New York. He is Filipino-Colombian by background, who received his education in the United States at Williams College and Harvard University where he received his MArch degree (Hoyt, 2015). This was not his first religious building in the Philippines. While working with Stan Allen in New York he was the principal designer of the Tagaytay Chapel for the Chosen Children, located south of Manila in Luzon and completed in 2008. A comparatively compact structure, this chapel featured a prominent array of clerestory windows below the roofline which provided a substantial sense of light to the interior, somewhat in the manner of European Gothic churches (Bossi, 2009). Well-read in architecture, Arnaiz was starting his architectural career in a relatively iconic manner within a village community. The protrusion of vertical wall pilasters that created the uneven array of clerestories was also echoed on the interior and the rafters of the clear-span ceiling, as shown in figure 6. Like the later San Pedro chapel, it was painted white almost throughout.

In addition to the constraints of the site and the problem as given at Cebu, so to speak, two autonomous constraints were initially brought to bear in the design process. Within the Newell, Simon and Shaw model, autonomous constraints are those that concentrate the initial hunches, if you like, of the designer and that give initial shape, in this case, to the direction of problem space planning. At Cebu they were, first, the Gothic church tradition including a central nave, a narthex, emphasis on verticality, a choir loft and abundance of light integrated with the entire structure. The second, by contrast, was a strong leaning towards references to contemporary Catholicism in a diverse society, accentuating multiple ways in which practitioners could access the church and the faith. Both are represented in figure 7. This latter leaning, or sensibility was to also embrace religious experience but away from doctrinal concepts. In short, Arnaiz was interested in resolving the church spatial tradition in a freer and more open manner. It almost appeared as a bipolar or dialectical problem that he set himself and his colleagues.

As we know and particularly from Simon's *Sciences of the Artificial*, the tree-like shape of the representation of a problem space is most likely to be embodied within a hierarchical structure that is nearly decomposable but not fully so (Simon, 1969). This constitutes the use of 'satisficing decision making', the outcome of which is neither correct nor incorrect but suboptimal and the best available. Figuratively for the Cebu chapel at hand this 'nearly decomposed form' in figure 7 shows the site and local building technology constraints (A and B) overlapped in one set and beside the differing 'autonomous constraints' (C and D), all within some Venn-like set theoretic diagrammatic arrangement. The network graph equivalent representation, also shown here, is a semi-lattice from the four primitive informational aspects working its way up to the complete set. To continue problem solving, as there is no stopping rule implied here, this semi-lattice needs to be somehow simplified into a tree-like arrangement. In other words, to find a spatial diagrammatic arrangement that fully decomposes the arrangement of constraints through satisficing decision making, so that they are all more or less satisfied. This, like the earlier shift in context, requires the injection of heuristics on the part of the designer, where a heuristic is a rule of thumb and a bias and emphasis knowingly introduced in order to resolve apparent differences but also remaining open to continued problem solving (Newell, Shaw and Simon, 1957; Polya, 1957 and Perkins, 1981). After all, design problems are wicked problems, at least according to Zwicky's and Rittel's and Webber's characterizations (Zwicky, 1962; Rittel and Webber, 1973 and Ritchey, 2013). Application of appropriate heuristics also requires application of 'knowledge structures' that transfer a problem space via 'domain knowledge' of a factual kind, or 'knowing that', and 'structural knowledge' or an ability by 'knowing how' towards more final resolution (Ryle, 1945).

In the context of the San Pedro Calungsod Chapel, the heuristics used were twofold and involved storytelling and derived from broader narratives about spaces, the two sources of which are shown here in figure 7. The first involved imagining formal aspects of the Garden of Gethsemane, where Jesus Christ performed his last act after the Last Supper before being put to death, as was also the case of San Pedro

8 – STEPS IN THE PLANAR AND SECTIONAL DEVELOPMENT OF THE 100 WALLS CHURCH by Carlos Arnaiz, 2013, in Cebu, Philippines

(A) Plan showing alignment of walls to pews, (B) Plan indicating insertion of programmatic and wall elements, (C) Varied sizes of the walls and (D) Sectional development

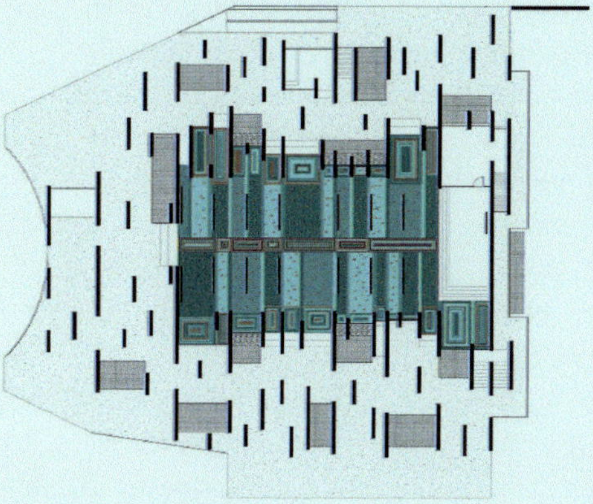

A

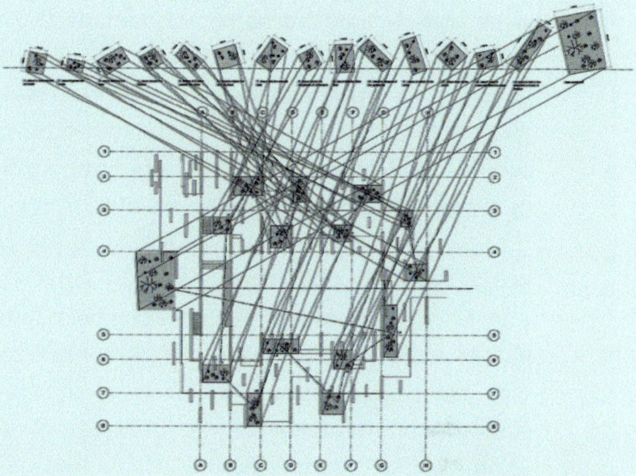

B

C

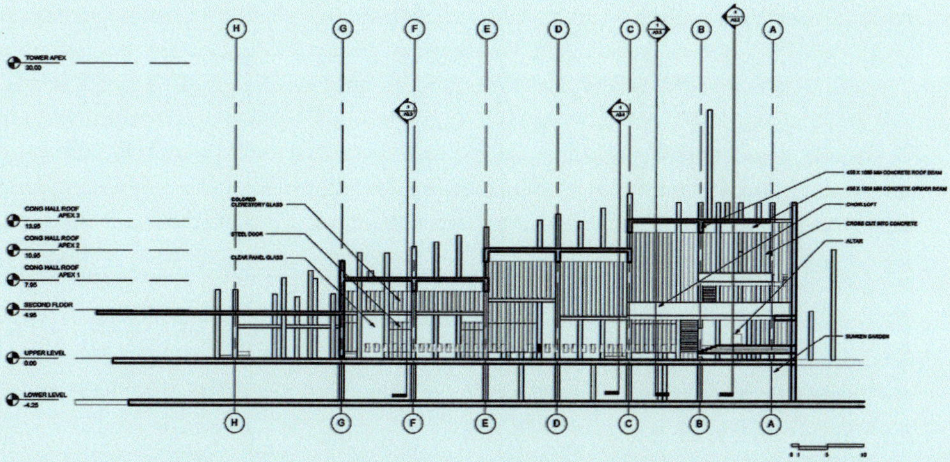

D

Calungsod. The garden is at the foot of the Mount of Olives in Jerusalem and from Hebrew suggests it was a grove or forest of trees. As interpreted and applied in this design, it was comprised of physical elements in the form of a multitude of more or less freestanding walls. A second aspect was the antiquity of the church compared to the more fleeting temporality of individual human lives and the uneven, seemingly weathered condition of the church in these regards. There Stonehenge came to mind as an uneven landscape of ruins. In fact, the design team apparently referred to their chapel as a 'modernist Stonehenge'. Application of these heuristic overlays then allowed the Gothic Church structure to be variegated and transformed into a basic seating arrangement of pews, surrounded on all sides by fragments of walls and all aligned north–south so as to produce a porous overall figure with the east–west arrangement being opaque, but also revealing more enigmatic space in-between. Further, like the Stonehenge model the walls varied in size though like the large old stones of a unitary character, as depicted in figure 7. Ergo, the resulting spatial formation allowed the desired traditional and contemporary impetuses of Filipino Catholics to be acknowledged and celebrated.

Returning to the domain and structural knowledge aspect of the Information Processing Model of Problem Solving and Gilbert Ryle's ability of 'knowing how', what is at stake is 'actionable knowledge' of a kind to be found in Donald Schön's 'reflective practitioner' (Ryle, 1949 and Schön, 1991). It also mirrors 'Schema Theory' and ideas about schemata in human knowledge acquisition and understanding that will be dealt with more fully in the next chapter. In short though, schemata both conceptually and practically represent operable stereotypes of situations in the mind's eye, so to speak, prescribing what to know, what to expect, and how to act or react. In the case of the Cebu chapel the source was clearly to be found in Christian theology and specifically in the Gospel according to Mathew 26:36–56 and similar contributions by Mark, Luke and John. The actionable knowledge or core aspect and, therefore, the schemata, namely the presence of the many walls of varying size surrounding the rectangular array of pews, derived from the tree grove of the Mount of Olives and the ruin of Stonehenge as indicated in figure 7. Its application allowed the nearly decomposed semi-lattice of constraints to be more fully decomposed as illustrated in figure 7. It involved heuristic representations that, first, abstracted key aspects of the Garden of Gethsemane and Stonehenge, namely walls of various sizes, and second spatially distributed them around an otherwise Gothic church arrangement of pews, side aisles and walls allowing for admission of light into the interior. From then on, a stage process model of similar steps ensued between reckoning with means and ends, by reframing, using heuristics involving further appropriate schemata, as indicated in figure 7.

During this aspect of the design process, several identifiable stages can be identified. First, the well-ordered rectangular central arrangement of the pews provided the north–south alignments of the walls, pulling them more into their final order, as shown in figure 8. Second with this realignment and sense of spatial order,

9 – SELECTED VIEWS OF THE 100 WALLS CHURCH
by Carlos Arnaiz, 2013, in Cebu, Philippines

other particular programmatic components of the chapel brief could be located, with, for instance, the choir loft and altar at one end and the narthex at the other. This also determined the larger vertical height of walls towards the altar than at the entrance. Third, each of the walls was different. In fact, this difference was also motivated in part by the difficulty in securing uniformity in the casting of concrete. In short, an apparent constraint was turned into an opportunity as demonstrated in figure 8. Finally, the obvious maze-like character of the wall fragments was more fully harnessed through spatial and material inflection at the level of furnishings and finishes to serve the purpose of expressing religion more fully through the mysteries and stories of individuals without the immediate legibility of the overt appearance of being a church. Just as Jesus Christ wandered through the Garden of Gethsemane, so worshippers in Cebu make their own journeys through the church, as depicted by the vignettes in figure 9. In addition, the homogeneity of the white walls and the numerous doors and spaces in between are there to remind us that there can be many paths to being drawn into the faith and with each wall being different as a manifestation of the diversity of life and yet one that also belongs to the same and singular species. In fact, according to the designer, the 100 number of walls came from a rough rounding up of the many walls incorporated during initial design into a round 100, rather than through any metaphoric or other reference to the heuristics employed in the design. In this sense it is arbitrary.

CHAPTER 3

# On Schemata

Simply put, according to Sandra Marshall in her excellent book on the topic, a 'schema' is a vehicle of memory, allowing organization of an individual's experiences in such a way that the individual can easily recognize additional experiences that are similar, can access a general framework that contains essential elements of all these similar experiences, can draw inferences, make estimates, create goals and develop plans using the framework and, finally, can use skills, procedures and rules as needed when faced with a problem for which this particular problem framework is relevant. In other words, and in plural form, schemata involve a mental framework that contains relevant knowledge and skills needed to solve a particular problem (Marshall, 1995). Moreover, they are personal in the sense of being tied to an individual's experience. Figure 1 here depicts a circumstance where a child develops the capacity to recognize a dog from a picture book presented by a parent. The essential information the child assimilates is that the dog has ears, four legs and a tail. The figure also shows two representations of schemata. One is a rough but emphatic sketch of the essence of 'house', at least in the Western and possibly American world, that simplifies the visual appearance appreciably and therefore allows for other elaborations and generalizations about the appearance and recognition of 'houses'. The other is a diagrammatic depiction of how important semantic aspects germane to a publication are organized. Then, finally, figure 2 beside Minsky's frames, shows diagrams of a 'cognitive unit', roughly equivalent to a schema, concerning Julius Caesar's crossing of the Rubicon stream in Italy before deposing the Roman Republic.

It is by John Anderson (1947– ), a Canadian cognitive psychologist widely known for his rational analysis of cognition and his hypothesis that a complex cognitive task can be broken down into a set of information processing components or 'cognitive units' (Anderson, 1983). In what follows the origins and evolution of schemata are concisely described with particular emphasis on philosophical and cognitive dimensions. A brief section dealing with what amounts to 'reflection in action' within and guided by a design situation follows. Then the chapter concludes with discussion and examples of the difference between speculative futures constantly looking forward and traditional, as well as vernacular settings, looking backward, both general kinds framing the overall orientation of schemata.

# Evolution

Historically speaking, the term 'schema' derives from the Greek *morphḗ* or the form, shape or figure of an object or thing. For Plato in the *Meno*, it embodied how to identify and define something via an assembly of common characteristics verging on a stereotype or commonplace of that thing. Socrates, in his Metaphysics and search for definition, maintained a similar view as Plato and introduced the equivalent of categories that relied on ten attributes or predicates: what, when, where, how, status, relation, position, condition,

## 1 – SIMPLIFIED AND CONCEPTUAL SCHEMA REPRESENTATIONS

A Initial schema forming by a child, B Schema of a generic house and C A semantic schema representing publication

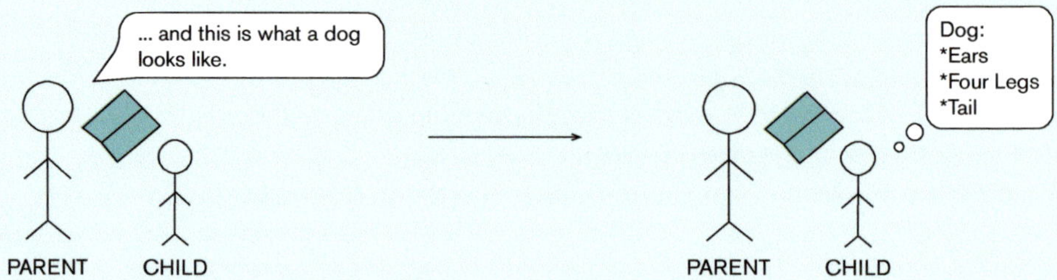


A

B

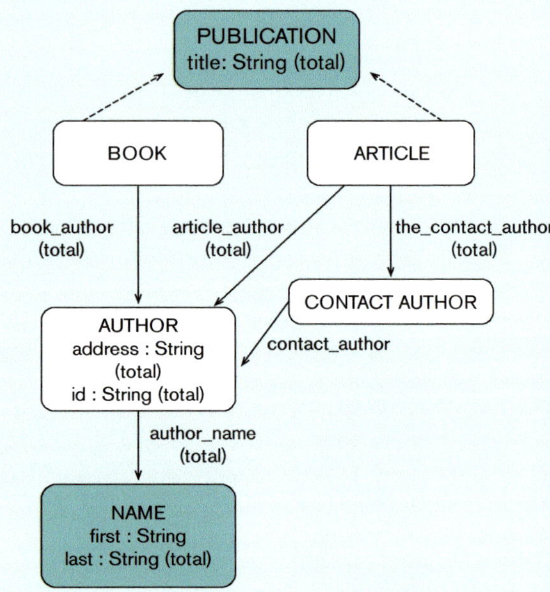


C

action and affection (Plato, 2012). What Aristotle, in turn, meant by 'form' was the essence of a thing and therefore the manner of knowing the thing (Charles, 2010).

Later in the 18th century, Immanuel Kant (1724–1804) used schemata to describe things and also turned to the description of schemata themselves. Essentially, he believed that there are concepts that exist *a priori* in the mind. For him transcendental schema was the procedural rule by which a category is associated with a sense impression. It was the link between abstract qualities and real-world things via these aspects. They were *a priori* categories, empirical information derived from sensory perception, and a link between sensibilities and understanding (Kant, 2000). Of course, the fundamental idea of Kant's 'critical philosophy' was and is human autonomy. His schema associated with sense impression though private and subjective can be discursively thought to be a representation of an external object. In addressing the issue of the relation between thinking and being he took a different approach from Gottfried Wilhelm Leibniz (1646–1716), for example, who suggested that reality was a copy of an ideal world, or from John Locke (1632–1704) and David Hume (1711–1776) in that our conceptual ideas derive from sensuous experience. Instead, Kant suggests that our conceptual thinking should be connected to reality and that our sense experience be subject to the organizing principles of the intellect. For him, "Thoughts without content are empty, intuition without concepts are blind" (Kant, 1933, p. 75).

Still later on British psychologist Frederic Bartlett (1886–1969) focused on how people remembered what they remembered, while Jean Piaget (1896–1980), another psychologist, studied the development of reasoning among aspects of thinking in what became known as 'genetic epistemology'. For Bartlett, schemata were critical to the organization of memory and when confronted with abnormal situations stories became changed to conform to schemata or what ought to have been expected (Bartlett, 1932). Piaget, though controversial, described a schema as a completely coordinated set of physical actions and cognitive functions to respond to every perceived experience that could be related to the schema. Here his novelty was the emphasis placed on action and, therefore, schemata becoming related to behavior, with assimilation and a schema altered to fit and then accommodation with a schema modified to fit experience as two operative principles. In short, subjects actively construct their worlds and are not passive (Piaget, 1952 and Piaget, 1970).

More recent research in 'Schema Theory' involved several notable figures from around the mid-1970s. They included Marvin Minsky (1927–2016), David Rumelhart (1942–2011) and Roger Schank (1946–2023). Among them Minsky became known for his 'frames', and his pursuit of higher-order explanations for how people thought. Drawing on Bartlett, frames for him were structures selected from memory when one encountered a new situation in order to make sense of it. In effect, a frame was a data structure of large, interrelated chunks of knowledge that allowed representation

## 2 – TWO CONCEPTUAL ENCODING PROCEDURES

A John Anderson's encoding of Caesar crossing the Rubicon and B Marvin Minsky's concept of 'frame system' for representing perspectives of cubes

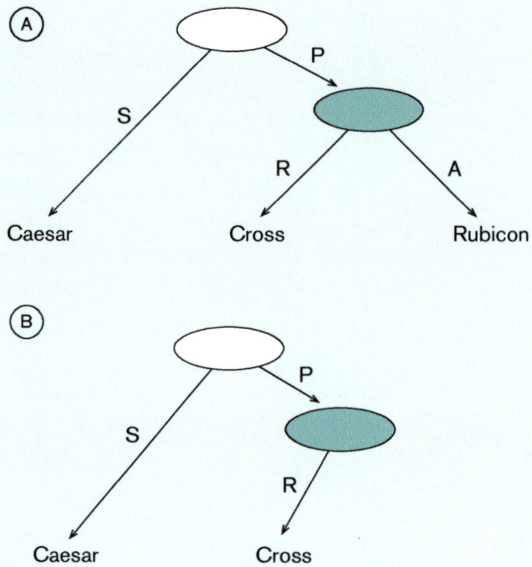


A

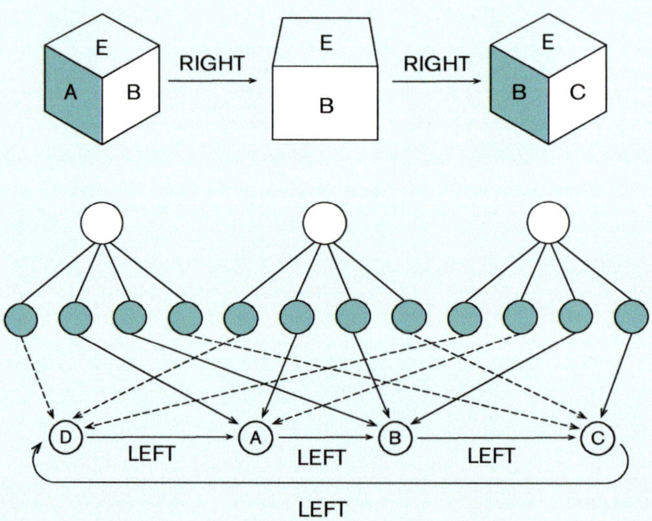


B

of stereotypical situations but also allowing for adaptation to specific aspects of those situations, as indicated in figure 2 concerning representation of a cube. Here stereotypical forms also drew loosely on Althusserian notions of cultivated beliefs, values and outcomes (Althusser, 2008). Further, frames were networks of nodes and relations with the top levels being relatively fixed but with 'slots' at lower levels with data that might be expected to match the stereotypical situation. In short, a frame was a collection of questions to be asked about a hypothetical situation, specifying issues to be raised and methods to be used in dealing with them (Minsky, 1975). Roger Schank postulated 'script schemata' as being special data structures containing a specific sequence of events in a well-interrelated circumstance (Schank and Abelson, 1977 and Schank, 1982). David Rumelhart defined schemata as data structures for representing the generic concepts stored in memory. For him they existed for generalized concepts underlying objects, situations, events and sequences of actions. They were not singular or atomic but contained specifications of networks of relations that were generally aligned with objects, and they were in some sense stereotypes of concepts. Here 'stereotype' was being used to refer to a fixed and often over-simplified image or idea of a particular type of person or thing (Rumelhart and Ortony, 1977). Further, Charles Fillmore (1929–2014), an American linguist, also used frames in a similar manner to Minsky though with regard to different subject matter (Fillmore, 1985).

George Lakoff (1941– ), the American cognitive scientist and philosopher, is well known for his thesis that people's lives are significantly influenced by the conceptual metaphors they use to conduct them (Lakoff and Johnson, 1980). For him, knowledge is organized in the mind by structures he calls ICMs or Idealized Cognitive Models, examples of which are shown in figure 3. They are also severalfold in which each is a structured whole, a *gestalt* which has varied structured principles. They are also inclusive of schemata of various kinds for dealing with different circumstances, like container schemata, part-whole schemata, line schemata, center-periphery schemata, and so on (Lakoff, 1987). Indeed, the philosopher Mark Johnson (1949– ), a contemporary of Lakoff, contributed the idea that bodily movement also came into play among metaphors and schemata, ascribing to them a source domain, a target domain, and a source-to-target mapping (Johnson, 1987). Despite all the work on language and cognition, a recent recurrent finding is that key notions cut across this work and, in fact, operate in non-linguistic circumstances as well. For instance, these include frames, analogical mapping, reference points and connections of various types. Also, the nature of mapping between domains has enjoyed sustained attention. Within this the work of the French linguist Gilles Fauconnier (1944–2021) stands out with the concept of 'mental spaces' as shown in figure 4. For him they occur among input structures, generic structures and blend structures. In effect, they are small conceptual packets constructed as we think and talk. Indeed, with Mark Turner (1954– ), a cognitive scientist, they gave rise to the 'theory of conceptual blending'. Within this, mental spaces are represented as circles within which frame structures operate, such as key aspects of 'initial mental spaces'.

# 3 – GEORGE LAKOFF'S CONCEPT OF IDEALIZED COGNITIVE MODELS

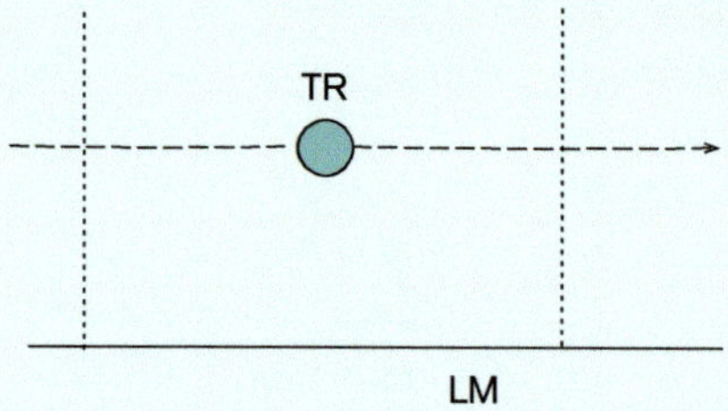


The airplane flew over the yard.
Schema 1.X.NC

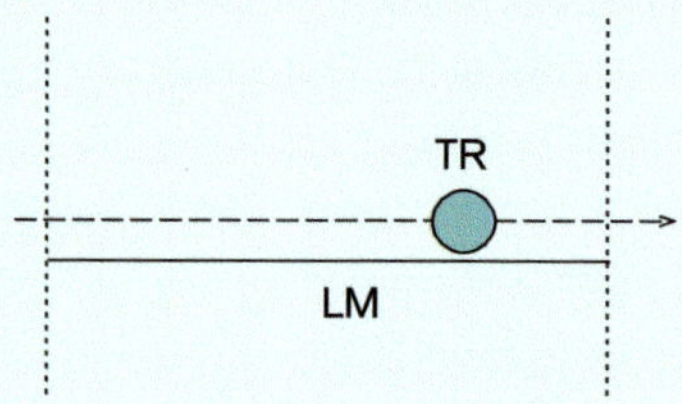


Sam drove over the bridge.
Schema 1.X.C.

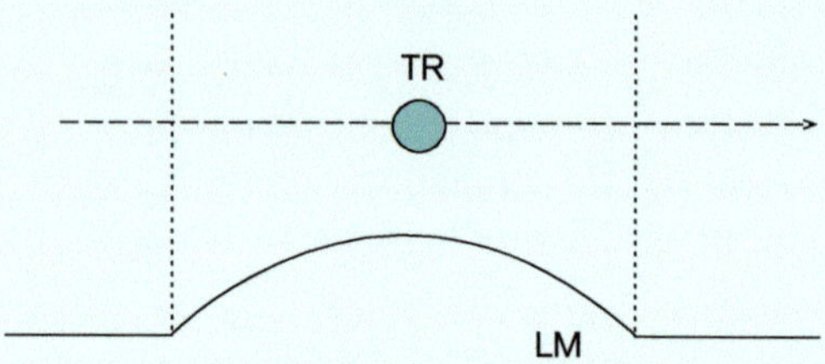


The airplane flew over the hill.
Schema 1.VX.NC

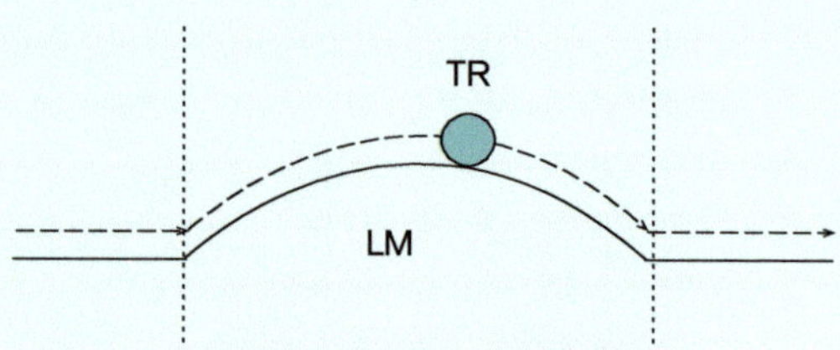


Sam walked over the hill.
Schema 1.VX.C.

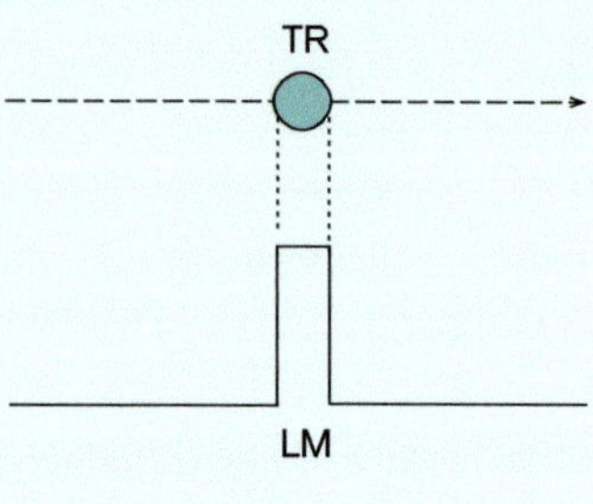


The airplane flew over the wall.
Schema 1.V.NC

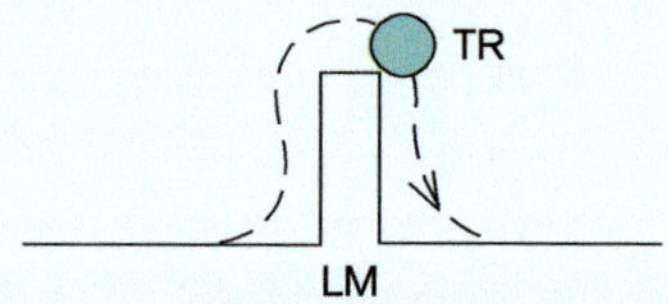


Sam climbed over the wall.
Schema 1.V.C.

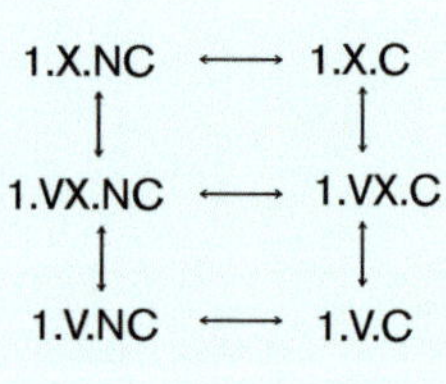


Links among schemata

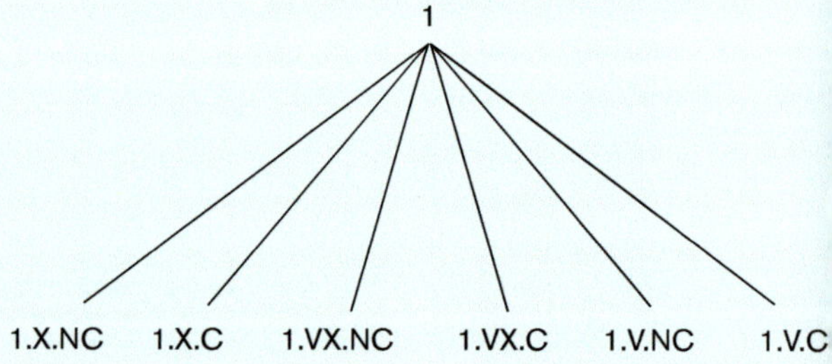


Instances of schema 1

Further, 'generic mental spaces' contain all the aspects that the input spaces have in common. In a way they are analogous to Minsky's frames and Rumelhart's schemata. The input spaces then project to another space, referred to as the 'blend space'. This then allows for cross-space mapping to occur via the 'generic space' through which inputs can be manipulated uniformly (Fauconnier, 1994 and Fauconnier and Turner, 2006).

Schemata are also involved in mental operations concerned with how meaning can be derived from non-verbal or visual arrays of material. Alan MacEachren (1952– ) is a geographer and cognitive expert in this area. He introduced the notion of 'prototype' as an abstract mental concept of a typical member of a category as an exemplar of that category via its collection of features. He also dealt with variations in the form because of, for instance, 'family resemblances', after Ludwig Wittgenstein (1889–1951) regarding genres, as well as 'fuzzy categories' and 'typicality effects' (Wittgenstein, 1953 and MacEachren, 1995). MacEachren went on to describe maps as a 'radial category', as shown here in figure 5, combining ideas of prototypes, family resemblances, fuzzy aspects and typicality. Such a mapping involved two axes with the vertical one ranging from an 'atomic level' such as a quark to a 'universal level' of scale such as a star chart, and with the other horizontal axis ranging from 'images' like a bird's-eye view of Chicago to 'diagrams' such as geologic profiles. In this formulation he drew upon Lakoff's idea of image schemata as a format for encoding information from vision and language simultaneously (Lakoff, 1987 and MacEachren, 1995). MacEachren also went on to reference the work of Steven Pinker (1954– ), the Canadian-American cognitive psychologist, and his computational theory of mind, principally around experimental subjects concerned with shape recognition, mental imagery and visual attention. In this, one fundamental insight was that the output in visual cognition is a symbolic representation or structural description of a scene, specifying the identity of its parts and the relations among them (Pinker, 1990). He also drew on *gestalt* laws of perceptual organization after Max Wertheimer (1880–1943) with regard to proximity, similarity and continuation in a scene (Wertheimer, 1938 and Pinker, 1997). This also took Pinker towards schemata which he saw as memory representations embodying knowledge to some domain consisting of a description which contained slots or parameters for as yet unknown information, very much in the direction of Minsky and others, as shown here in figure 5. Further, what he termed 'flags' are identified according to the predicates in question and in recognition of their characteristics. A matching process is then brought to bear that compares a visual description in parallel with every memory schema for a visual scene, computing goodness-of-fit and selecting the highest and best goodness-of-fit (Anderson and Bauer, 1973 and Pinker, 1990). Of course, there is a certain reciprocity involved here. For what makes a person good at reading graphic material is also bound up with what makes for easy reading. Routes for improving this relationship can be achieved via flags and processes of simple awareness, deduction and induction.

Over in the realm of General Problem-Solving Theory with the likes of Allen Newell (1927–1992), the computer and cognitive scientist, Herbert Simon (1916–2001), the political scientist, and John Shaw (1922–1991), also a computer scientist, similar rules and schema-like principles emerged in the form of heuristics and heuristic reasoning processes used to search through decision trees. To Newell, Simon and Shaw, a heuristic is any principle, procedure or other device that contributes to reduction in the search for a satisfactory solution (Newell, Shaw and Simon, 1967 and Simon, 1969). An example of goal-oriented heuristic reasoning is shown here in figure 6 (Simon, 1979). David Perkins (1944– ), a prolific scholar of thinking, was less emphatic about results. For him a heuristic is a rule of thumb that often helps in solving certain classes of problems but makes no guarantees of doing so (Perkins, 1981). Similarly, for George Polya (1887–1985), a Hungarian mathematician, the term applied again to a rule of thumb or provisional procedure that proved to be useful in problem solving (Polya, 1957). Also, others like Michael Polyani (1891–1976), the Hungarian-born British polymath, introduced the often elusive and culturally dependent character of 'rules of thumb', arguing for seeing them as manifestations of 'tacit dimensions', by this he meant knowledge involving tradition, inherited practices, implied values and prejudgments that were also a crucial part of scientific knowledge. In other words interpretative frameworks are social formations tied to their contingent factual realizations in the practice nurtured by the community of scientists at any given stage (Polyani, 1966). In all of this there also emerged limitations in human capacities for processing information, certainly in short-term memory. George Miller (1920–2012), the American psychologist, put this capacity at the number seven plus or minus two. Here he was referring to bits of information defined as the amount needed to make a decision between two equally likely alternatives (Miller, 1956).

# Reflexive Practices

Throughout this discussion terms associated with vehicles like schemata, frames and heuristics have a circumstantial and contingent quality to them. They apply in certain contexts and not necessarily in others. Moreover, acts like heuristic reasoning, for instance, where they move beyond the more objective or mechanistic realm of problem solving, begin to involve some idea of a domain, reflexive practice, or situation in the sense of the French philosopher Maurice Merleau-Ponty (1910–1961) in his discussion of the phenomenology of perception (Merleau-Ponty, 1962 and Mallin, 1979). By this term, 'situation', he meant involvement in circumstances or active concern with sets of natural, cultural and human problems. A situation occurs when an individual becomes totally absorbed in something, relates it to herself and begins to understand. Therefore, in the matter of heuristic reasoning it is not simply

## 4 – GILLES FAUCONNIER'S CONCEPT OF MENTAL SPACES

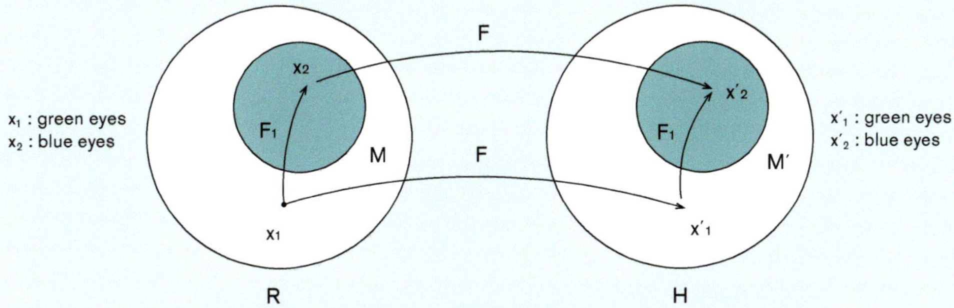


As depicted above, four spaces are involved: R ("reality"), M (the painting), H (the counterfactual hypothetical space), and M′ (the counterpart of M within H). The girl with green eyes points to a trigger in R ("the model") and identifies a target in M′ after successive applications of the ID Principle.

## 6 – EXAMPLE OF HERBERT SIMON'S CONCEPT OF 'GOALS AND FUNCTIONAL HEURISTICS'

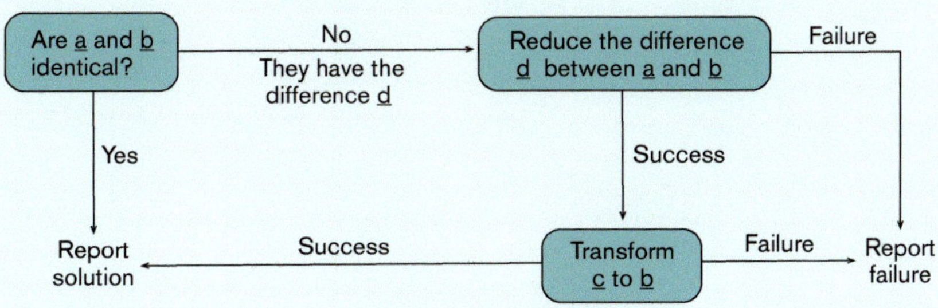


TRANSFORM A TO B

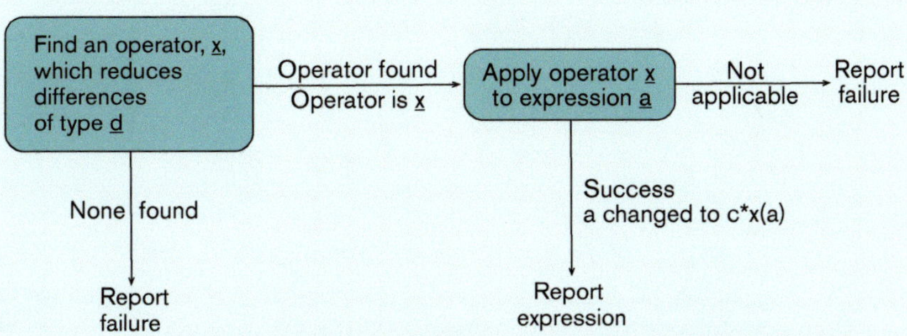


REDUCE THE DIFFERENCE D BETWEEN A AND B

## 5 – SCHEMATA OF NON-VERBAL ARRAYS OF MATERIAL

A Alan MacEachren's concept of 'radial category' and

B Steven Pinker's schema of a telephone number and graphic representation of objects

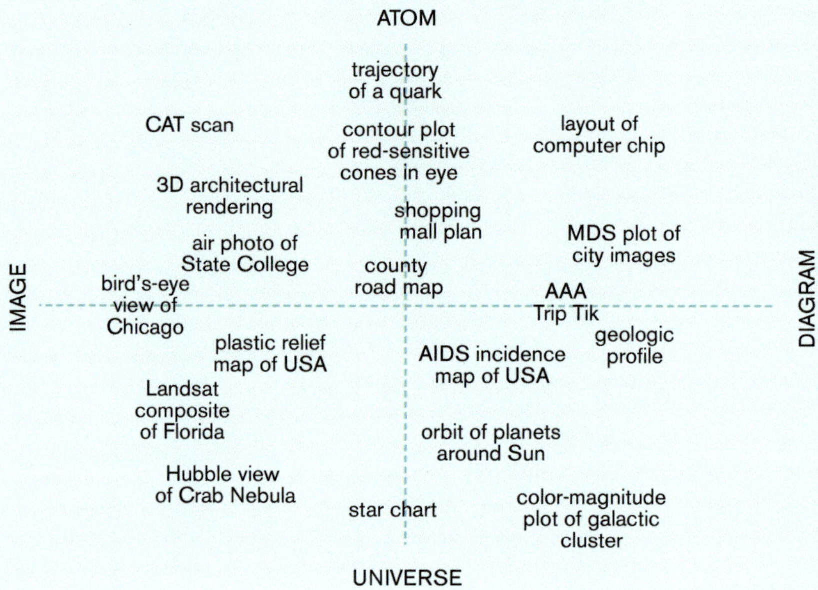


A

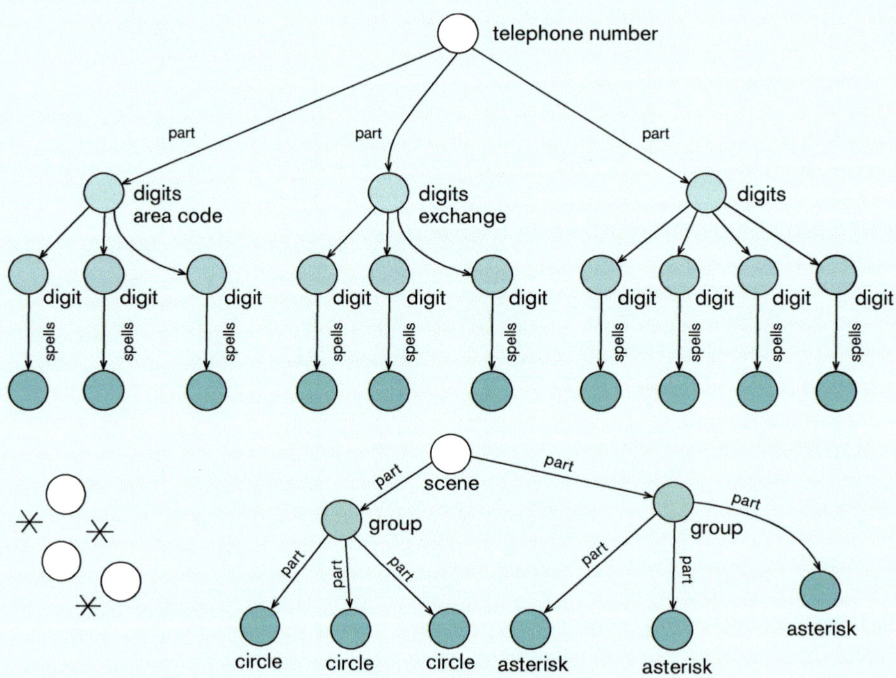


B

the case, as the information processing theorists would seem to suggest, of isolating problem-solving circumstances and settling them over against similarly abstracted sets of actions and purposes, nor is it a case of subjective idealism. The rule aspect comes into play also as an attempt is made to overcome a situation's novelty, and make sense of it, leading to the acquisition of some general principle, eventually becoming sedimented and allowing one to learn how to act in certain kinds of circumstances (Mallin, 1979). To Merleau-Ponty, when we are in a situation neither the objective realm of those things outside of ourselves nor our own subjectivity is primary. Both are found in the situation. The open-ended aspect of heuristic reasoning finds a parallel in Merleau-Ponty's definition of situations as being ambiguous. But being in a situation also occasions reflexivity by imbuing the problem with new life, as it were (Mallin, 1979).

This manner of thinking also involves philosopher Donald Schön's (1930–1997) idea of a problem-solver having a reflective conversation with a situation and the constancy of attention involved in that act (Schön, 1983). Such a conversation is reflexive in so far as the problem is not simply given but rather found by the practitioner and regarded as unique requiring a reframing of it. In Schön's case it involved a dialogue between a student and a design studio instructor when the student is having difficulty getting past a diagrammatic phase. Coming to her aid the instructor suggests reshaping a part of the site and its slope, as indicated in figure 7. This effectively recasts the design problem in a different and tractable form and is no longer simply the problem as given (Schön, 1983). Moments like this also usher in so-called 'theories of action' or praxeology, such as in the work involving quantitative approaches using fuzzy sets by the likes of Arnold Kaufmann (1911–1994), the French engineer, who worked on fuzzy or uncertain sets, among other things, including project management (Kaufmann, 1968). It also engages with concepts like 'learning by doing' and philosophical distinctions around so-called 'practical' and 'theoretical' knowledge. Probably most direct in these regards is the work of the British philosopher Gilbert Ryle (1900–1976). In his classic essay "Knowing How and Knowing That" he took what he termed the 'intellectualist' position to task by making the case that 'knowing how' is not reducible to any form of 'knowing that' and, indeed, that 'knowing that' presupposes 'knowing how'. In more commonplace terms a distinction can be made between museum possession and the workshop possession of knowledge. For Ryle intelligence involves more than acts of theorizing and is about practical knowledge in a variety of different fields or disciplines and often in a reflexive manner (Ryle, 1945 and Ryle, 1949). It also verges towards doctrines about truth and knowledge, such as those held by the likes of Hilary Putnam (1926–2016), the American philosopher, mathematician and computer scientist, in which circumstances and schemata come into being yielding a sense of relativism but one, in his case, with a small 'r' (Putnam, 1981). However, this is going too far in the present context. In summary then, a design process may be seen to be marked by a sequence of episodes or situations that are, in turn, coincident with periods of heuristic reasoning through which problems are defined and solutions sought in a reflexive manner.

7 – DONALD SCHÖN'S CONCEPT OF 'REFLECTION IN ACTION'

A Recognition of building forms in topography, B Sectional recognition and reshaping of the land to buildings and C Resulting rearrangement of the project

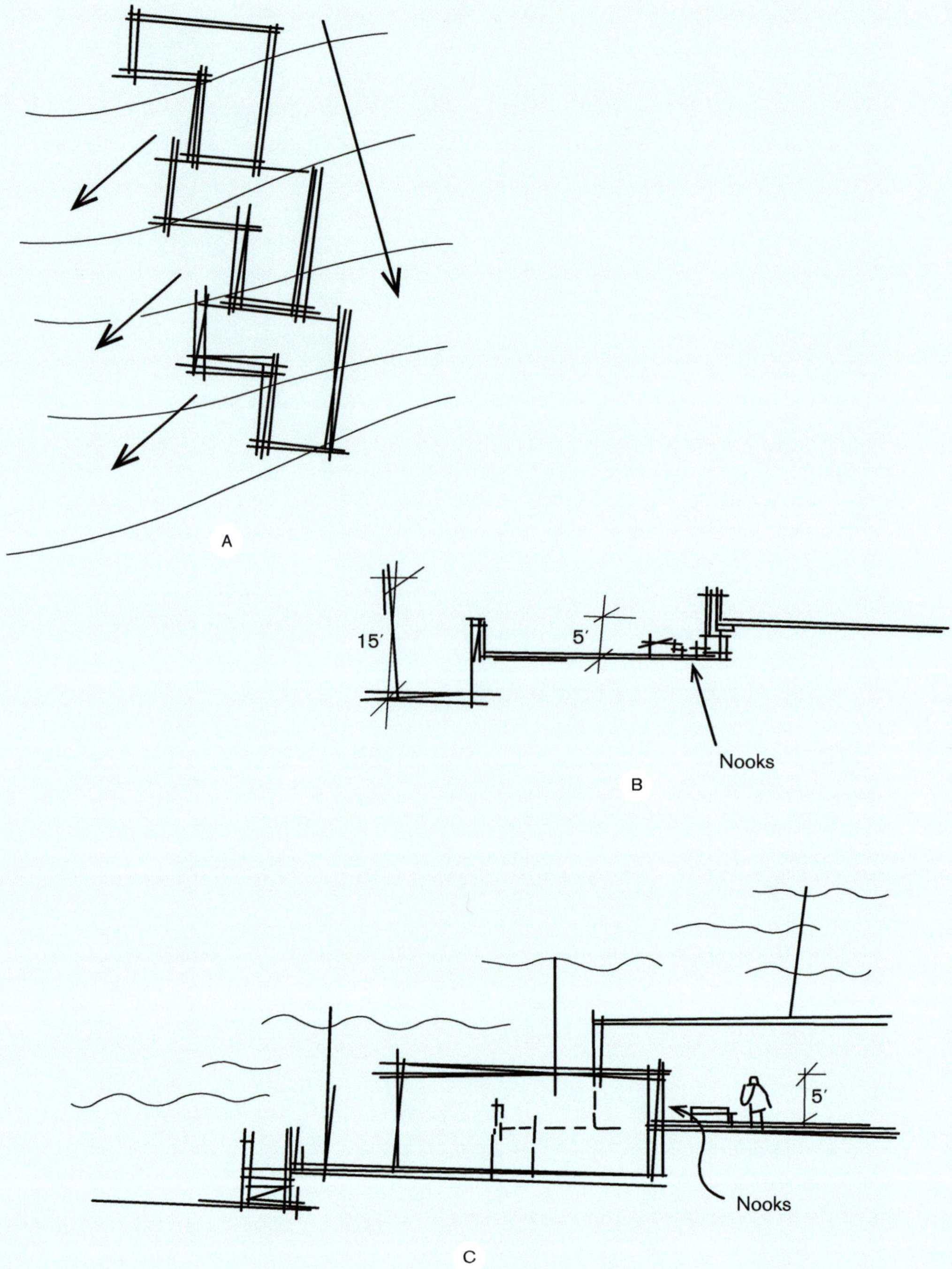

# Orientations of Schemata

As a broad generalization, schemata in architectural and urban design problem solving and design thinking are of at least two types in terms of the orientation of designers. There are those, for instance, that can be described as 'futurists' in that they constantly look to the present-future, deliberately eschewing, among other pre-occupations, observation and applying present-past ways of doing things. By contrast there are also those who are 'traditionalists', adopting tried-and-true practices from the past as a way of moving forward. Moreover, this 'futurist-traditionalist' dichotomy is relatively long-standing and also not without intrinsic cultural biases. In the East Asian ecumene, for instance, 'looking backward to move forward', as it were, has been relatively commonplace even in modern times. It recognizes the long-standing hold of tradition, strong vernacular leanings, and semblances of leveraging past practices forward to justify and give authority to present-day design activity. Among the dicta defining good and proper architecture in China, for example, since the advent of the Peoples' Republic, adages like 'socialist content and cultural form', 'modern content and Chinese form' and even today's official call to embody traditional culture and reflect Chinese peoples' aesthetic pursuits are clear episodes in point (Rowe, Wang and Chen, 2022). In addition, similar observations can be made about both contemporary Southeast Asian and South Korean architectural production (Rowe and Fu, 2022 and Rowe, Fu and Song, 2021). In the West, by contrast, art and architectural production was often strongly dictated, though not exclusively, by a search for the new and novel, certainly over the past one hundred years or so (Hughes, 1991).

## The Futurists

The term 'futurist' was first used in 1842, although its inclination had been around earlier, at least in the guise of a Christian eschatological viewpoint proposed by the likes of Jesuits such as Manuel Lacunza (1731–1801) and even earlier by Francisco Ribera (1537–1591). In this view interpretations of biblical books like Revelations and Ezekiel were literal with regard to the physical apocalypse and its global context and also gained popularity in the 19th century (Erikson, 1982 and Bohr, 2009). Then conspicuously into the 20th century there were the Italian and Russian Futurists, both artistic, literary and political movements seeking to reject the past in favor of embracing speed, technology and often violent change. In particular, the poet Filippo Tommaso Marinetti (1876–1944) and the painter and sculptor Umberto Boccioni (1882–1916) glorified modernity and sought to liberate Italy from the weight of its past (Marinetti, 1909). In architecture, there was Antonio Sant'Elia (1888–1916), who was tragically killed during World War I. He built very little but became well known and influential through his bold drawings regarding La città nuova or New City as depicted here in figure 8. In this regard he advocated raw, bare and violently colored materials in a highly industrialized and mechanized city of the future also as a narrative with lasting modern architectural influence (Da Costa Meyer, 1995). His influence even extended into movies like Fritz Lang's *Metropolis* of 1927 and, later, Ridley Scott's *Blade Runner* of 1982 (Loire, 2013). Russian Futurism was also originally a poetic and artistic movement that adopted Marinetti's "Manifesto" and also advocated cultural rejuvenation. Beginning in the early 1910s, it was originally called 'Cubo-Futurism' referring to the adoption of French Cubism in the works of the likes of Kazimir Malevich. Its demise more or less coincided with the rise of the Communists in Russia (Markov, 1968). 'Constructivist architecture' grew out of Futurism and flourished in the 1920s and 1930s strongly reflecting modern industrial society and urban space and rejecting decorative stylization in favor of mechanical assemblages of material (Banham, 1972; Frampton, 1980 and Khan-Magomedov, 1988). The term 'futurology' in a more contemporary sense was first coined in the mid-1940s by Ossip K. Flechtheim (1909–1998), a German jurist and political scientist, who proposed a new science of probability. He claimed that if futurology did no more than reveal the subset of statistically highly probably processes of change and charted their advance, it would be of critical social value. Also in the 1940s, RAND, an American nonprofit think tank, began to engage, along with several other institutions, in long-range planning, systematic trend creation, scenario development and visioning. At RAND this occurred first under World War II military contracts and then in the 1950s onwards for private corporations and institutions in the hands of individuals like Herman Kahn (1922–1983), the American physicist who also founded the Hudson Institute, and along with others more broadly in logical and political issues of forecasting (de Jouvenel, 2012). Then in 1966 Alvin Toffler (1928–2016) offered the first university course in the USA at the New School in New York on the topic of forecasting. He was an American writer and futurist known for discourses about modern technology with an emphasis on worldwide culture (Toffler, 1970). Nowadays futurism permeates many fields, emphasizing multiple perspectives, unconventional thinking and cross-cultural comparisons. Among these views, often single disciplinary and one-dimensional accounts are considered to be unsatisfactory.

## Speculative Futures

As students of the subject suggest, the field of speculative futures is seen to be amorphous and wide-ranging, engaging participants from the realms of Silicon Valley technology, for instance, to governmental organizations of various kinds, and even to Hollywood and other storytelling and film productions, all as noted earlier (Hoffman, 2022). Indeed, urban planning these days can often be regarded as a speculative storytelling exercise, often with outcomes that occupy a space between semblances of fantasy and reality. This may be said of the venerable Garden Cities Movement, for instance, and Ebenezer Howard's (1850–1928) work on the subject, as well as Bjarke Ingels's (1974– ) much later advocation of the concept of 'Masterplanet'

8 – DRAWING OF LA CITTÀ NUOVA
by Antonio Sant'Elia, 1912–1914

where already existing technologies can be pressed into action to achieve both a sustainable future and a high-quality life (Howard, 1902 and Nugent, 2020). In addition, known increases in resilience can be allegedly put down to engagement with future speculation (IPIC, 2012). As noted earlier, 'scenario building' is a prolific manner of identifying speculative futures with the important aspect of what might occur if such and such conditions and events apply, or, in short, the forecasting of a future. In another strain concerning the 'speculative design of products', Anthony Dunne and Fiona Raby advanced critical thinking with an emphasis on social, cultural and ethical considerations of emerging technologies and their role in everyday life. Founding their studio in 1994, they effectively used design and design thinking to strike up discussion and debate among designers, the industry and its public and with products like those shown in figure 9. If anything, this stance was as much about ideas as it was about the products themselves (Dunne and Raby, 2013). In yet another format, 'design fiction' has emerged, emphasizing a groundswell in transmedia practices. In the hands of the likes of Stuart Candy and Cher Potter, this is about world-building and experiential fiction as manners of making speculative futures. They also introduce and emphasize 'foresight' as an essential aspect of design thinking (Candy and Potter, 2019). 'Space fiction prototyping' as expounded by Brian David Johnson, an American futurist and professor in practice at Arizona State's School for Future Innovation in Society, is concerned with going beyond dystopic depictions of the future. This is particularly apparent in his 21st Century Robot project which aims to give everyone the ability to build hers or his own robot, an example of which is shown in figure 10 (Johnson, 2022). He also made reference in these regards to TV series of the 1960s, like *Star Trek*, in which some of today's advanced technologies like computer tablets appeared, alongside progressive social futures as illustrated in figure 11 (Hoffman, 2022). It should also be noted that future world-building has a venerable history, especially if we recall the likes of J. R. R. Tolkien's *Lord of the Rings* which expressed geographic, social, cultural and ecological alternative realities (Tolkien, 1954). More recently, Julian Bleecker (1966– ), an American artist and technologist, also moved beyond episodic future-oriented accounts and into world-building through 'Design Fiction' (Bleecker, 2009). Somewhat like an archaeologist in reverse, he would create vivid realms around creation and speculation about artifacts, often technologies, of a future world that were more palpable, 'real' and about feeling than statistical accounts and trend lines. Again, a primary aim was to stimulate imagination and engender discussion of plausible future directions and outcomes (Bleecker, 2014). Essentially the aim of 'Design Fiction' was to normalize extraordinary ideas in the near future such that they would appear to be part of a normal everyday life. Striking something of a middle ground, Bleecker and his disparate band of eighteen other designers, curators and science fact and fiction writers considered the trajectory of the big promises of the day such as those to be found in mass media, science fiction and films and to extrapolate them into the everyday life of a near future. The means they employed was two-fold. First, was to decant even the most preposterous ideas through design procedures that could exist in ordinary and normal everyday life.

9 – 'FORAGERS' CONCERNING SPECULATIVE FUTURE
by Anthony Dunne and Fiona Raby, 2009

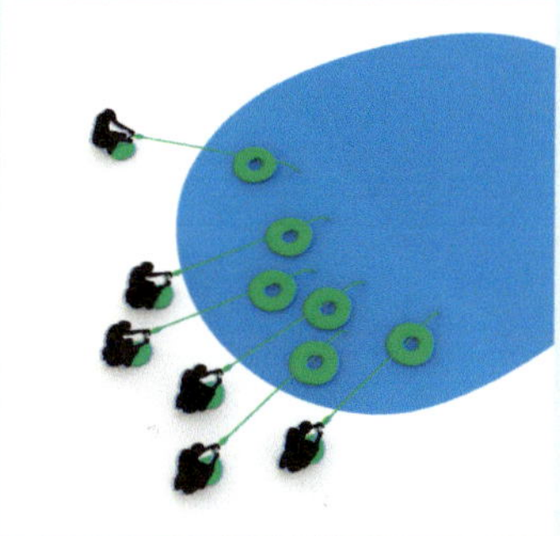

10 – JIMMY THE ROBOT
from the project 21st Century Robot by Intel and Trossen Robotics, 2014

Second, was to represent them in a catalog format called TBD1 that might exist from an everyday news stand. Here TBD stood for 'to be determined' much like TBA or 'to be announced'. Mostly product designs, the catalog presented some 136 near-term future products that could also be seen to follow the Gartner Hype Curve (Bleecker, 2014).

Within these speculative futures are also to be found particular strategies. For instance, although sight and sound are probably the main ways in which we apprehend future environments, other senses can also be constructively brought into play. When confronting air pollution, for example, Superflux, which was working in the 'Future Energy Lab' for the UAE in 2017, cleverly added the sense of smell of polluted air to their presentation, furthering the impact of their message (Zambonini, 2020). Other evocations like micronations and other geographic reformations have also often been effective. The Columbusplein Park Project and play in Amsterdam, for example, immediately comes to mind. This was a product of artist Jorge Manes Rubio's intervention and the creation of a micro-nation at the intersection of Columbusplein and Davistaart to the west of downtown Amsterdam in the Netherlands, as shown with children at play in figure 12. He was addressing the social issues of immigrants from Turkey, Morocco, Suriname and elsewhere through the creation of a park and nation of park participants in order to draw attention to their plight and to suggest a possible future for them (Rubio, 2014). In fact, the incidence of micro-nations is numerous in the world with some 67 already in existence (Ryan, Dunford and Sellars, 2006). In this context, micro-nations refer to self-proclaimed entities and their claims to be independent sovereign states within other recognized national boundaries. In addition, this issue of 'other boundaries' as a way of liberating future thinking was taken up by Rem Koolhaas and AMO in their concept of Eneropa in 2010, in order to address the important issue of energy production in Europe in the face of climate change. In their approach old national boundaries were dissolved into ones that bore on future energy perspectives, such as Solaria involving most of southern Europe, Biomassburg engaging large parts of central Europe and Hydropia involving alpine areas (Moore, 2010). Highly participatory public processes are also strategies that can be deployed effectively in the construction of speculative futures. For instance, the experience of citizens of the Leimart Park District of Los Angeles in what became their Sankofa City proposal is a case in point (Baumann, 2017). This project had begun with participants attempting to address movement system issues. Then later and as suggested earlier, collective imaginations and particularly those presented in science fiction productions like *Blade Runner* of 1982 illustrated in figure 13, for instance, or Ryan Coogler's *Black Panther* that introduced the country of Wakanda in 2018 were clear examples and also ones that presented dystopic accounts of apocalyptic futures. Indeed, if going back in time to other examples like George Orwell's *1984* and Fritz Lang's *Metropolis*, this strain of storytelling often seems to dominate futurist presentations and characterizations (Orwell, 1949 and Hoffman, 2022).

11 – FICTIONAL CHARACTER NYOTA UHURA WITH HER TABLET from 1960s production of *Star Trek*

12 – CHILDREN AT PLAY IN COLUMBUSPLEIN PARK PROJECT by Jorge Manes Rubio in Amsterdam, Netherlands, in 1981

13 – FUTURISTIC STREET SCENE FROM
THE SCIENCE FICTION MOVIE *BLADE RUNNER,* 1982
Warner Bros., directed by Ridley Scott

# Virtual Digital Twins

Generally speaking, digital twins are visual representations that serve as the real-time digital counterpart of a network, physical asset, process system or environment. Moreover, they are something that looks like and behaves identically in specific regards to its real-world counterpart. First anticipated in 1991 by David Gelernter (1955– ), an American computer scientist, through these 'mirror worlds' as he called them, the meaning of 'computer' was to be transformed into software models of some chunk of reality in vivid clarity (Gelernter, 1993). A little later in 2002, Michael Grieves, an American researcher and Executive Director of the Digital Twins Institute, introduced the concept at a Society of Manufacturing Engineers conference with application to undergird product life cycle management. In essence, this is a process of managing the entire life cycle of a product from its inception through the engineering design and manufacture, as well as the servicing and then disposal of manufactured products (Grieves, 2022). Sometimes referred to as 'virtual twins' the concept was subsequently called 'digital twins' by John Vickers at NASA in 2010. Such a twin consists of three parts. They are the physical object or process and its physical environment; the digital representation of the object or process; and the communication channel between the physical and virtual representation. This last part comprises information flows and data that include sensor flows between the physical and virtual object environments, referred to as the 'digital thread'. For instance, geographic digital twins have emerged in urban planning, particularly given the increasing appetite for digital technology in 'Smart Cities' where different types of electronic methods and sensors collect data in order to manage assets. There digital twins are visualizations usually built from conceptual models like BIM, CAD or GIS, as well as from scans of physical products as shown in figure 14. These are then related to the 'Internet of Things' connectivity collecting real-world data in real-time (Chen, 2021 and Sepasgozar, 2022). More specifically, an urban digital twin will be receiving data from sources, including vehicles, buildings, infrastructure and individuals, as well as via data captured by Smart City devices and the Internet of Things, and all augmented with the use of artificial intelligence and advanced analytics (Schrotter and Hüzeler, 2020). In the Zurich case just cited, a 3D city model was created at ETH Zurich in 2011. Its underlying terrain model was based on the real and planned building floor plans within the official cadastral survey of the city. The model incorporated some 50,000 buildings and over the years 3D spatial data has been added in response to seeking solutions to specific tasks such as pollution and environmental performance and visualization of projects to be constructed. Other cities have also followed suit (Biljecki, Stoter and Ledoux, 2015 and Batty, 2018). Moreover, these developments have been widespread internationally. In the late 2010s, Buildmedia, a local New Zealand firm specializing in 3D visualizations at various scales, created the City of Wellington's digital twin for the city's council. Using a software product called 'Unreal Engine' and data from many local sources they began locally and centrally and then moved outwards geographically. They also started with a terrain model made of discrete tiles and integrated Internet of Things services, alongside data provided by the City Council. Some 1,800 buildings were

## 14 – LAYERS OF A CONCEPTUAL MODEL OF DIGITAL TWIN CITY

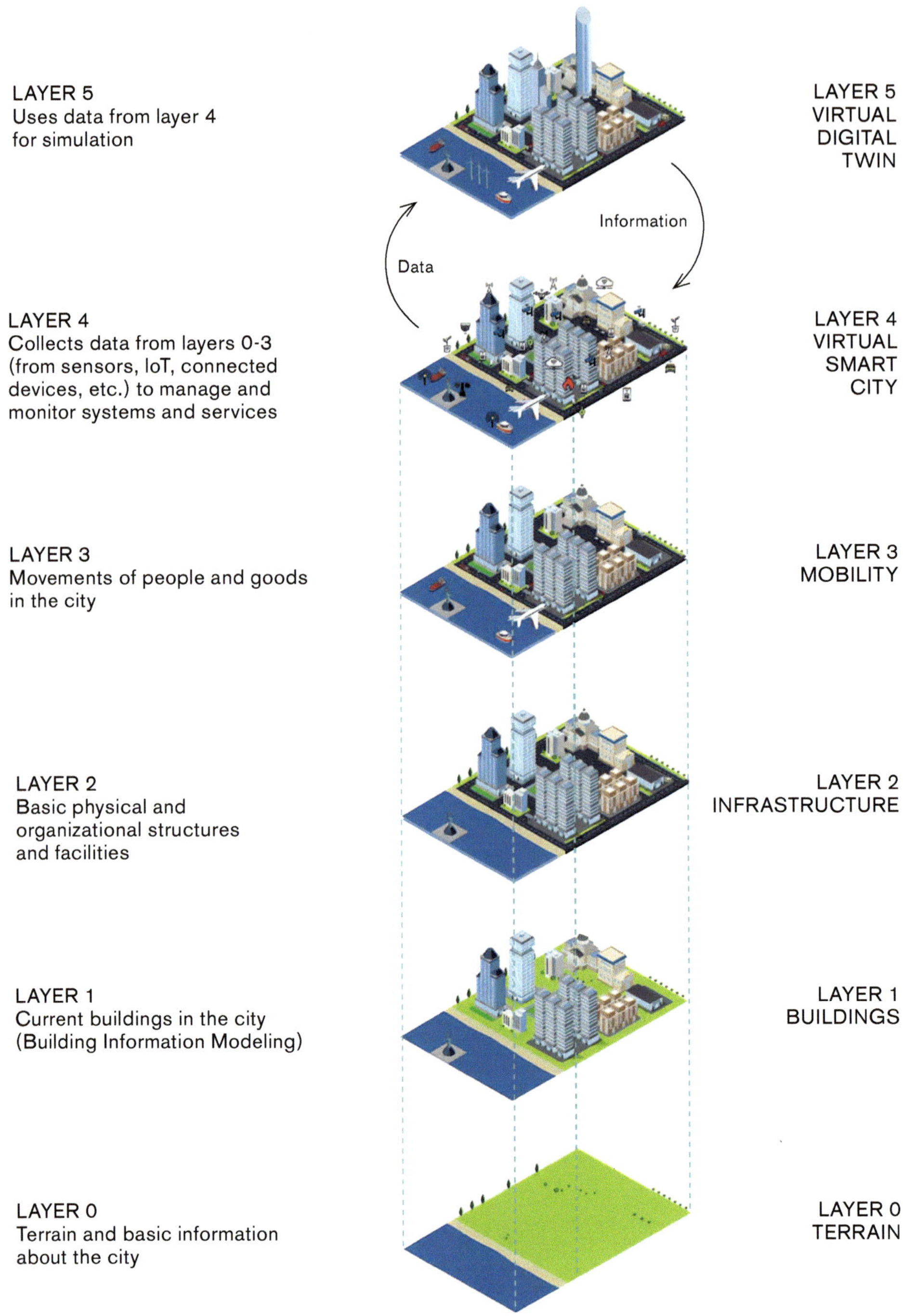

accurately depicted. In fact, the emphasis in the project was on both accuracy and realism of depiction. Subsequently, the model has been used to inform members of the City Council about projects in the city, such as transport improvements, as well as various levels of environmental performance at different locations like air pollution levels. It will ultimately become open to the public to improve transparency and enhance the participatory process of decision making (Buildmedia, 2021).

## Vernacular Traditionalists

As mentioned earlier, an alternative orientation in design thinking involves traditionalists who refer backward in outlook, as it were, in order to move forward and make buildings and architecture. Also, as noted, even today the People's Republic of China is replete with reflections of its traditional culture, not least of which involve what are called *jiangpai* communities. These are schools of artisans. Particularly in the south of China, which are sometimes also referred to as being 'artisan gangs' or 'artisan families', they are invariably led by a master craftsman with supporting workers and apprentices as shown in figure 15 (Li, 1988). At least three factors contribute to formation of the *jiangpai* in contemporary circumstances. First, geographic barriers often separated artisan communities leading to a regionalization of traditionally oriented building practice. Second, technical inheritance from master to apprentices within artisan communities led to 'learning by doing' in tune with a specific and often well codified formulation of building construction. Third, the integration of artisans forming *jiangpai* within contemporary conditions of production under the influence of government institutions have led to coexistence alongside academic and commercial institutes or similar organizations (Zhu, Chen and Li, 2022). Constructed mostly of wood, Chinese older buildings and architecture has often not been durable, requiring relatively constant maintenance and upkeep. Therefore, recording and detailing how to accomplish this over time is an indispensable aspect of traditional building. Usually this is taken up by the *zhanggan* method, which entails a pole or 'pole ruler', also referred to as a *gao-chi*, that marks the height, depth, width and so on, along with symbols for various components of a building frame, on a wooden pole with constant one-to-one dimensions as indicated in figure 15. This then allows a construction team to use the pole to measure the specific parts of a building, find the location of the joining of those parts and then assemble them accordingly. The *gao-chi* or *zhanggan*, as depicted here, is the most comprehensive of traditional building tools (Zhang and Zhu, 2005). These tools are made during the design phase and serve throughout the construction of a building. Even after completion it is usually kept under the outermost eave as a reference for further and ongoing restoration. Several meters in length, the *zhanggan* or *gao-chi* uses abstract symbols of demarcation, also as depicted here. Apart from the preservation of the confidentiality of *jiangpai* techniques, these symbols only express minimal information relevant to the construction (Yao, 2017). For instance, there are usually two types of symbols on the poles. The first concerns the types of structural elements like columns, purlins, beams and so on. The second conveys

## 15 – IMAGES OF TRADITIONAL CHINESE PRACTICE

A *Jiangpai* master and apprentices at work in Fujian Province, China, B Markings on a *zhanggan* ruler and C Daoist priest with a Lu Ban ruler

A

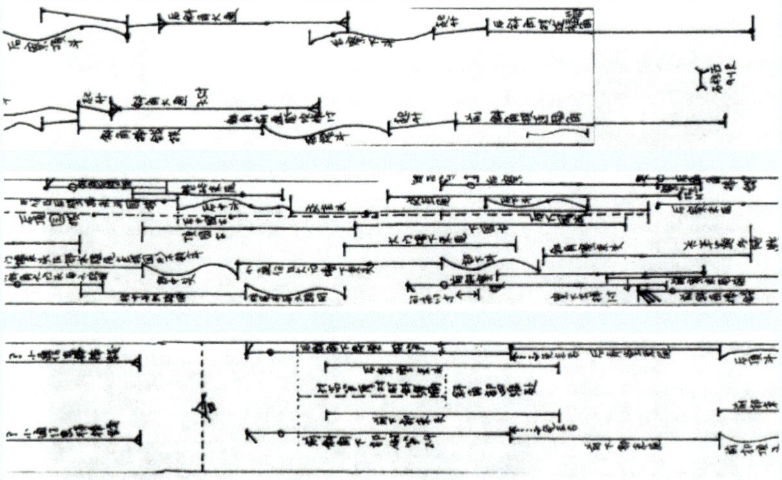

B

C

special instructions from the Master involved, noting, for example, nodal connections of specific pieces of the building frame. Generally, the more complex the structure, the more lines and symbols there are on the *gao-chi.* Written descriptions are usually glossaries of specific parts and construction terminology for communication within the *jiangpai.* Other tools are also in use, such as the bamboo ruler guiding mortise and tenon joint installation, for example. Indeed, these tools have very long-lasting use, dating back to Lu Ban (c. 507–444 BCE) the *feng shui* master and father of Chinese ancient carpentry and also the inventor of the Lu Ban Ruler, depicted here in figure 15. With different rulers for different occasions, each depicts both positive and negative measures according to the propensity to reduce negative energy and increase positive energy all within a *feng shui* system about the harmony between people and their environments (Needham, 1994). From the perspective of design thinking this artisanal approach allows material form to occur indirectly through calculation, data sifting and craftsmanship. The workflow is distinctly tool-based and calculation-driven, forming specific schema to be followed both in initial and subsequent restorative construction of architecture.

In summary then, schemata are mental frameworks that contain relevant knowledge and skills needed to solve particular problems. They are also personal by being tied to an individual's experience. They have evolved from early Greek concerns with manners of knowing things, through procedural rules by which categories of things are associated with sense impressions, on to ways of organizing memory and into full-blown 'schema theory' drawing upon 'frames' or structures in memory for making sense of new situations. Schema-like principles also emerged in the guise of heuristics, or rules of thumb, used in problem solving. Deployment of schemata also involves reflective reaction on the part of problem solvers, much in the manner of a conversation with a problem situation, during which problems are recast as stories in ways that aid further problem-solving progress. Finally, in the realm of architecture and urban design at least, schemata may be futuristic and forward-looking or traditionalistic and backward-looking in order to move forward. Recent developments in the creation of 'digital twins' have also provided more precise and real-time means for posing 'what if' questions and telling more compelling stories in real-world settings and production situations, further potentially aiding at least acceptance of creative problem solving and design thinking.

CHAPTER 4

# Knowledge Bases and Categories

In this context of architectural design and from the preceding commentary about schemata, a train of argument can be composed of inputs in the form of situations of 'design problems as given' intersecting to 'mental frames' required by situations and the 'frames' within them. Within this commentary 'situations' will take on meanings attributable mainly to Merleau-Ponty and Schön involving considerable volition on the part of a problem-solving practitioner. The character of 'mental spaces' will be after those of Fauconnier and 'frames' within them in the manner of Minsky and others containing slots for expected information for a stereotypical application. Moreover, these frames will contain knowledge of three kinds. They are: about a situation, the issues that might be raised, and how those issues might be dealt with. Generally, this will be in the form of 'if x in situation z, then apply y'. Throughout, emphasis will be placed on the visual aspects of this arrangement of situations, mental spaces and frames. The broad types and categories, particularly involved in 'generic mental spaces' will derive essentially from the time-honored definition of architecture from pre-modern beginnings like the Vitruvian triad of firmness, commodity and delight.

## Around the Vitruvian Triad

Writing near the end of the first century BCE, the Roman architect Marcus Vitruvius Pollio (c. 80–15 BCE) identified three elements or themes necessary for a well-designed building. They were what he called *firmitas, utilitas* and *venustas*, or firmness, commodity and delight. Among these, firmness was about securing a building's structural integrity. Commodity provided for utility and efficient arrangement of spaces and support systems to meet the functional needs of occupants. After Venus the goddess of beauty, venustas, or delight imparted style, proportion and visual beauty. All this Vitruvius set down in his treatise *De Architectura* (*On Architecture*) around 30 to 20 BCE (Morgan, 1914). This array of ten books began with the qualifications required of an architect or civil engineer. It then moved on to building materials, temples and the orders of architecture plus a further continuation. It then proceeded through civil buildings, domestic buildings into pavement and decorative plasterwork, water supplies and aqueducts, before finishing with the sciences influencing architecture and the use and construction of various kinds of machines in building. Clearly Roman architects were to be skilled in engineering, art and craftsmanship, pointing strongly in the direction of Gilbert Ryle's practical knowledge (Rowland, 1999).

Following this, Leon Battista Alberti (1404–1472) wrote his *De re aedificatoria* (*On the Art of Building*) between 1443 and 1452. It was the first such work to reawaken awareness of Greek and Roman classical architecture reimagined for the contemporary Renaissance city at that time. Alberti was a humanist architect and antiquarian employed in the papal administration as well as being involved in architectural projects in Ferrara, Florence and Mantua. Echoing Vitruvius, he insisted that architecture should have maximum solidity and durability and be elegant and pleasing to the eye. In fact, beauty for him was something inherent in the structure of architecture like harmony in music. He also saw architecture as a natural organism (Alberti, 1991). Another 15th century treatise by Francesco di Giorgio Martini (1439–1501) focused mainly on fortifications through rigorous drawings and established practical building norms that also gave a new actuality to classical texts (Northern Architecture, 2022). Then, during the 16th century, the character of treatises shifted towards practice. This was especially the case of Andrea Palladio (1508–1580) and his *I quattro libri dell'architettura* (*Four Books of Architecture*) of 1570 (Palladio, 1570). This was preceded by Sebastiano Serlio (1475–c. 1554) who worked in Rome during the early 16th century in his *Tutte L'opere d'architettura* (*Seven Books of Architecture*) begun in 1537 (Serlio, 1584 and Hart, 1996). This handbook confirmed the practice of transforming the appearance of existing buildings to meet the aesthetics of the Renaissance, as well as the use of antique spoils as building materials, together with practical guidance for functional and well-thought-through manners of building. In fact, it remains so well into the 19th century (Northern Architecture, 2022).

## Modernity to the Age of Discourse

Then, with movement into the 19th and early 20th centuries, commentary tended to dwell on styles, such as neo-classicism, Art Deco, Victorian and so on, as well as on revivals of one kind or another (Fletcher, 1996 and Middleton, 2003). With the arrival of modernism in the early 20th century, several schools of thought emerged, particularly around a functionalist agenda tied to the new spirit of the times and industrialization. A major proponent was Le Corbusier, aka Charles Eduard Jeanneret (1887–1965) with his foundation of CIAM or Congrès international d'architecture moderne in 1928, that flourished until its abandonment in 1959 or thereabouts (Mumford, 2000). Le Corbusier published his influential *Vers une architecture* (*Towards a New Architecture*) in 1923, setting the tone of the modern movement with a compilation of essays all published also in his magazine *L'Esprit nouveau.* For him this new architecture was to be more than stylistic experimentation by embracing the industrial age and producing an architecture based on function and aesthetics of pure functional form (Le Corbusier, 1985). He also outlined his own manifesto around his "Five Points for a New Architecture" in 1927. These were:

the use of pilotis, the free design of the ground plan, the free design of the façade, the use of horizontal windows and roof gardens. These were also published in *L'Esprit nouveau* (Weber, 2008). In Germany the Staatliches Bauhaus, commonly known as the Bauhaus, was an art and design school in Dresden and Weimar that operated from 1919 to 1933. Among others in Weimar, Germany, it also espoused a new architecture in step with the times or *zeitgeist*. Sometimes referred to as Neue Sachlichkeit, or New Objectivity, it addressed materials and the means of production associated closely with the *neues Leben* or new life. Generally, it tried to unify industrialization and mass production with artistic vision (Droste, 2019).

This strong functionalist orientation was formally concluded with the last CIAM Conference in 1959 and largely replaced by Team 10 and its shift towards principles of association, identity and flexibility along with growth and change (Smithson, 1964). Later, several American-based post-modern movements sprung up. Among major proponents was Robert Venturi (1925–2018) who challenged modernist dicta in 1966 drawing upon numerous vernacular and high-style sources to posit an architectural composition of complexity and contradiction (Venturi, 1966 and Venturi, Scott Brown and Izenour, 1972). Still others in the more contemporary era also evinced misgivings about orthodox modern architecture and associated elaborations of particular underpinnings like programming and scalar as well as surface properties. A major proponent in that direction was Rem Koolhaas (1944– ) and his several excurses (Koolhaas, 1978 and Koolhaas, Mau and Sigler, 1995). Today, with issues of a better fit with the environment of the Anthropocene, support of more sustainable mobility, promotion of digital and new material construction, and development of increased social justice, architecture is expanding within its traditional and seemingly bedrock categorical boundaries of firmness, commodity and delight (Busquets, 2022). Even before this, according to commentators like K. Michael Hays, the late avant-garde architecture from roughly 1966 to 1983 became replete with reactions against 'modernism' as such and towards an interplay of the spatial units of architecture's formal autonomy (Hays, 2010). Even figures as otherwise diverse as Manfredo Tafuri and Colin Rowe appear to have agreed that capitalism took away from architecture's social connections by way of emphasis on information, advertisement and consumption, certainly in city building. This effectively caused a disassociation from the 'real' formerly manifested in orthodox modernism and concepts like 'new objectivity' of form, function and *zeitgeist* (Tafuri, 1972 and Rowe and Koetter, 1984). This turning point, as it were, also included the likes of Aldo Rossi, Peter Eisenman, John Hejduk and Bernard Tschumi (Eisenman, 2006). Again, according to Hays, among others, this period signaled the death, so to speak, of modern architecture and architecture entering into the 'age of discourse' (Hays, 2010).

1 – THE SEATTLE CENTRAL LIBRARY by OMA, 2004, in Seattle, Washington, USA A The conceptual arrangement of programmatic blocks with spaces in between, B A view of the library in its urban context showing the programmatic blocks cloaked in a glass curtain wall

A

B

# Hypermodern Expansions

At least from the 1970s onwards, if not earlier, it can be argued that there has been a drift towards what might be called a post- or hypermodernity where a particular aspect of the time-honored triad has been exaggerated or taken as a specific point of departure. Both successively and in combination this has been expressed in narratives accentuating programming, figuration, engineering expression, parametric behavioral orientations, concerns with regionalism and place, as well as with narratives of everyday life. Programming, an aspect of 'commodity' to be sure, for instance, has moved from concerns for buildings as social condensers to synergetic contributors of diverse use programs by the likes of Koolhaas with OMA and Tschumi, as well as the unbundling of established existing hierarchies by SANAA among others. Figuration, clearly more about 'delight', also has gone from modern profiling as in Jørn Utzon's work to the use of haptic and other textures by Jean Nouvel, Farshid Moussavi, Herzog & de Meuron and Thomas Heatherwick. Engineering expression, associated with 'firmness', has gone from modern examples by Pier Luigi Nervi and Louis Kahn to expressions of complexity by OMA and Cecil Balmond, as well as Toyo Ito, among others in Japan. Parametric concerns, also about 'commodity', have shifted from even pre-modern assemblages such as the *Yingzhao Fashi* of the Song Dynasty in China to later works by architects like B. V. Doshi in informal settlements, to looseness of fit with Lacaton & Vassal as well as work by Greg Lynn, Frank Gehry and Zaha Hadid, particularly with regard to curvilinear algorithmic organic forms discussed later here. Environmentalism has found expression especially in Southeast Asia and pioneering work by Ken Yeang and, more recently, WOHA. Regionalism, that can also be seen somewhat as an aspect of 'delight' and a concern for place has moved from the universalism of modernism to poetic reinterpretation of a place, augmentation of everyday life and cultural assertions of identity by the likes of Peter Zumthor, Glenn Murcutt and Zhang Ke. These narratives of everyday life have moved from modernist assemblages of form and function to more emphatic rule-following of contextual, semiotic and geometric kinds, akin to 'delight' by architects such as Aldo Rossi, Rafael Moneo, Venturi and I. M. Pei.

While one might argue about the veracity of this particular account about categories in architecture there can be little argument about their sheer existence as such. Moreover, in this discussion of design thinking and storytelling they form the knowledge bases for the mental spaces and frames required by this thinking. Following Fauconnier, at least three kinds of mental space can be seen to exist. They are 'input mental spaces', all-important 'generic mental frames' and 'blend mental spaces' (Fauconnier, 1994). In this mix the 'input mental spaces' are the homes, so to speak of a problem as given or described. Typically, though not always, it will specify what kind of a building is involved like a church or a house, certain specifications of magnitude like floor area or accommodation volumes, the location and site for the building, and key constraints concerning cost, materials, desirable stylistic features and so on. In Schön's terms, this is not really a design problem nor the problem the design practitioner will ultimately engage in. It is yet to be defined by the practitioner along with the particular story to be told (Schön, 1983). In what follows, six of these prominent hypermodern categories are described and discussed, in principle although not fully inclusively.

## Programming

Rem Koolhaas (1944– ) is a contemporary Dutch architect and theorist often cited for his impact on design and design education (Koolhaas, 1997 and Rudin and Pellegrino, 2022). In his hands and those of his collaborators at the Office of Metropolitan Architecture or OMA, programming became a driving force in their architecture and urban design. The author of *Delirious New York* from 1978, Koolhaas observed that as skyscrapers there rose in height the less significance the original ground plane had on the internal programmatic logic of the building. His celebrated example was the Downtown Athletic Club of New York City of 1930 by Starrett & Van Vleck, that rose some 38 stories in height with each floor more or less dedicated to particular athletic-related functions. This, in turn, raised for him a questioning of parts-to-whole relationships, particularly in congested urban circumstances and also often leading to novel arrangements and combinations of activities. His Seattle Central Library of 2004 is an excellent example of the deployment of this kind of interrogation. Eleven stories in overall height, this building on an intense urban site is organized into various programs organized across five platforms and four intervening flow in-between spaces as shown in figure 1. The platforms are major programmatic components or boxes ranging downwards from the headquarters to the book spiral, to assembly spaces for meetings, to staff quarters and down to parking and play areas for kids. The four intervening spaces are reading rooms, a mixing chamber, a living room and a play area. This programmatic ensemble is then clad or almost draped in a distinctive faceted glass façade and displayed as a vertical civic space within Seattle. Another project, OMA's entrant in the Parc de la Villette competition of 1982 in Paris, turned the section of the Downtown Athletic Club on its side, so to speak, with programmatic strips organized much like the floors of the Athletic Club but now on the ground across the site. Reacting to a massive program of required accommodations that virtually obliterated the idea of a park *per se*, OMA's proposal arrested the combination of programmatic instability with architectural specificity. In effect, strips for sports were arrayed beside strips of tropical gardens and then on to playgrounds, and so on, with the intention of encouraging and supporting novel and unprecedented encounters. This mix of programmatic parts was also added to by points or 'confetti', as the designers called it, of intense activity like kiosks, greenhouses, teahouses and so on. A large existing building on the site of the former abattoir was also repurposed as a science museum (OMA, 1982 and Todorova,

2014). In later publications, Koolhaas was to deride the state of urban architecture even referring to it programmatically as 'junkspace' and declaring that modernism was fighting a losing battle with urban quantity, given places like Lagos moving from two million to fifteen million or so inhabitants in only forty years (Koolhaas, Mau and Sigler, 1995 and Koolhaas, 2002).

The winner of the 1982 competition, Bernard Tschumi, though not following quite the same programmatic solution, also proposed a project of points, lines and surfaces, of which the points were his renowned red follies, and the surfaces could be used somewhat interchangeably for different events and activities. He also authored reflections on the thinking behind this and other projects concerned with spectacle (Tschumi, 2014). In a not too dissimilar vein to the Seattle project, the New Museum or 21st Century Museum of Contemporary Art in New York City of 2007 by the Tokyo-based firm of Sejima and Nishizawa Associates or SANAA, is comprised of seven box-like volumes stacked around a central core and rising ten stories in height, as shown in figure 2. They house a variety of programs, including galleries, offices, event spaces, a café, a theater and an education center. For SANAA, function is clearly used to create the building but also, reciprocally, for the building to create the function. This is exemplified, for example, in the otherwise unused space in the air shaft between the third and fourth floors now used as a tall micro-gallery. Indeed, this reciprocity is also manifest in the overall transparency of the building and institution to its New York surroundings, despite its otherwise blank minimalist façades, and *vice versa* (Phillips, 2008 and Mole, 2016).

## Engineering Engagements

The subject of an international architectural competition in 2001, the China Central Television Headquarters Complex or CCTV_TVCC, was a *tour de force* in terms of both programming and engineering accomplishment (Rowe, 2011). Indeed, one could not have been achieved without the other and the chief author again was Rem Koolhaas with Ole Scheeren, ably assisted in the engineering by Cecil Balmond of ARUP Engineering. At the time, CCTV had become the largest media unit in the world and the project was programmed to consolidate accommodation of administrative and production facilities otherwise spread out inefficiently in Beijing and elsewhere. By one measure it was to accommodate an expansion of thirteen TV channels to over two hundred. The project occupies a site of around ten hectares, subdivided into four blocks within the central Chaoyang District of Beijing and with a total floor area of 599,000 square meters. On this site, the CCTV Headquarters of around 473,000 square meters is located adjacent to the southwest corner. It rises to a height of 234 meters and is shaped in a continuous loop housing the entire process of TV making with studios, offices, production facilities, broadcasting and so on, as shown in figure 3. Formed from horizontal and vertical sections the interlocking Z-shaped building, with its interconnected activities, offers unparalleled programmatic flexibility, overlap and collaborative potential. Another loop was

2 – THE NEW MUSEUM
OF CONTEMPORARY ART
on the Bowery by SANAA, 2007,
in New York City, USA

3 – THE MAHANAKHON TOWER
by Ole Scheeren, 2018, in Silom Central
Business District of Bangkok, Thailand

4 – THE CONCEPT OF CONTINUOUS PROGRAMMATIC LOOP OF THE CCTV BUILDING by OMA, 2012, in Chaoyang District of Beijing, China

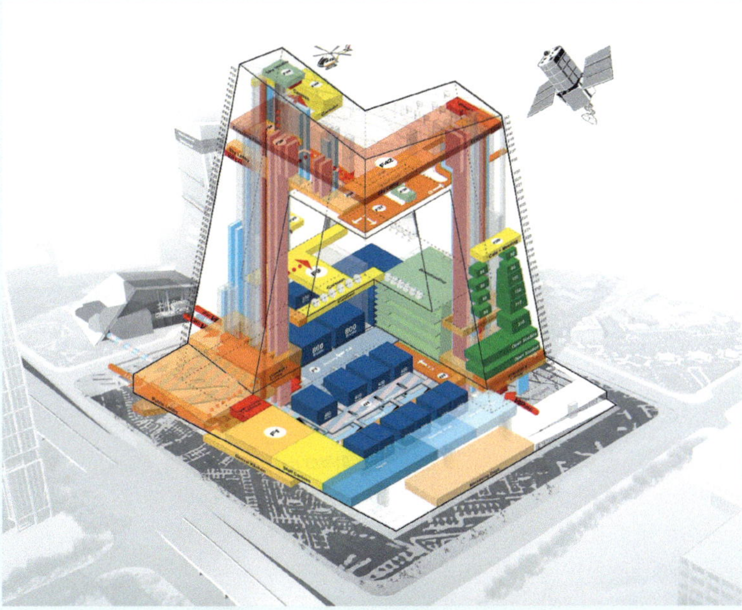

5 – DIAGONAL PATTERNS of structural reinforcement on the inner edge of a cranked segment of the CCTV Tower by OMA, 2012, in Chaoyang District of Beijing, China

also originally incorporated into the building allowing public access for visitors and providing them with vantage points for visually surveying TV production and for viewing the city beyond. Even described as an anti-skyscraper, the building was also a major accomplishment in its engineering construction and technique. Balmond and the ARUP Group developed the interlocking tower form as a braced perimeter tube structure. The cranked loop was comprised of the two leaning towers bent at top and bottom to form a continuous programmatic loop. The primary support was achieved through an irregular grid on the surface of the volumes and as a visible expression of forces traveling through the structure. The smaller the diagonal pattern the stronger the load and the greater the support, such as at the inside edge of the 90-degree crank in the loop towards the top as shown in figure 4. The braced tube also gave the building the required robustness to withstand seismic activity in the area. Before the two towers were linked, they were independently prone to wind and surface temperature variations. Actual linking of the two towers, given Beijing's weather, required it to be done early in the morning when both towers were at a uniform temperature. It also became vital that the linking take place within a few minutes, requiring mounting and final adjustment to the length of the linking elements (Rowe, 2011). Although an unabashed skyscraper of 314 meters and 77 stories in height, the MahaNakhon Tower in Bangkok of 2018 by Ole Scheeren, has a similar unconventional programmatic and structural proscription. The tower, as shown in figure 5, is carved out, so to speak, to introduce a three-dimensional ribbon of more complete building forms that extend upward from street level and encircle the building's full height (Rowe and Fu, 2022).

The Sendai Mediatheque in Japan by Toyo Ito & Associates of 2001 is comprised of library and art gallery functions and is revolutionary in its engineering and its aesthetic (Witte, 2002). Intended as a transparent cultural media center, it is virtually completely visible and transparent to the surrounding environment. Supported on six thin steel-ribbed slabs which appear to float above the street, supported on thirteen vertical steel lattice columns that stretch from the ground plane to the roof as shown in figure 6. Further each floor plan is free-form, as the structural column lattices are independent of the façade and fluctuate in diameter from floor to floor. Materially, the three major construction components are made differently. The slabs are honey-combed steel sections filled with lightweight concrete. The tubular columns are composed of thick-walled steel pipes and house all vertical services, whereas the skin is comprised of glass, steel panels and aluminum mesh (Pollock, 2001). Finally, the concept of a 'non-structure' was explored by Koolhaas and Balmond in their Serpentine Gallery Pavilion of 2006, shown in figure 7. One of the yearly architectural experiments in London's Hyde Park, theirs was an ovoid-shaped inflatable helium-filled canopy that floated above the gallery's circular base made from translucent material that glowed when lit in the dark. This walled enclosure of some 100 square meters in floor area was furnished as a café and forum for daily programs with cuboid objects flexibly allowing for different seating arrangements. The canopy above could be raised or lowered to cover the space according to the weather and the function inside (Koolhaas and Balmond with Arup, 2008).

6 – STRUCTURAL AND OTHER COMPONENTS OF THE SENDAI MEDIATHEQUE by Toyo Ito, 2001, in Miyagi, Japan

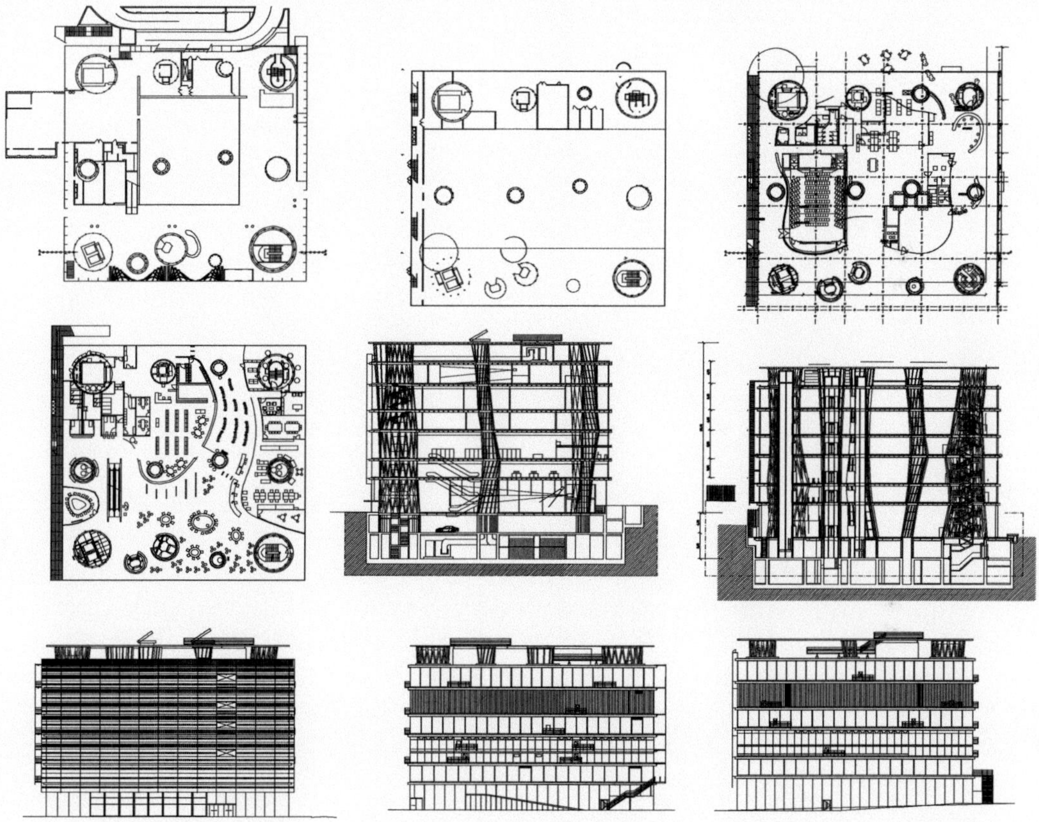

## Parametric Design

Simply put, parametric design is a method in which features, such as building elements and engineering components and even urban circumstances are created and styled based on algorithmic processes rather than through direct manipulation; it is now much a part of our digital culture (Picon, 2010 and Suzuki, 2020). Here, the term 'parametric' refers to the inputs that one feeds into an algorithm and an algorithm is a set of rules to be followed in problem solving, often concerned with general classes of such problems. Though now typically referring to the use of computer algorithms in design, early precedents can be found in the work of architects like Antoni Gaudí (1852–1926), for instance, or later Frei Otto. Gaudí's analog method employed string weighted down by birdshot weights in order to create the shape of vaults and arches, such as in the Sagrada Família in Barcelona, begun in 1882 (Rowe, 1999). Frei Otto also experimented with non-digital processes using soap bubbles among other devices to find optimal tensegrity or floating compression structures such as those used at the 1972 Olympics in Munich and shown in figure 8 (Fiederer, 2011). Tensegrity is a structural principle based on a system of isolated components under compression inside a network of continuous tension, usually supplied by cables. Richard Buckminster Fuller (1895–1983), an American architect, system theorist and inventor, was a contributor to both the theory and application of this principle (Fuller, 1982).

Within the digital world, there are two main categories of parametric models. The first are propagation-based systems that optimize certain sets of design constraints allowing forms to be found, as it were, based on these constraints. The others are constraint models in which constraints are set and algorithms are used to optimize or converge towards satisfaction of the constraints. One of the first architects to use computers for generating architecture was Greg Lynn (1964– ) an American architect. His blob and fold forms were early examples of computer-generated, propagation-based shapes (Picon, 2010). An early example is 'The Fish' or Peix Olímpic by Frank Gehry in Barcelona of 1992 shown in figure 9. Another later example but now in a large-scale building was Terminal 3 of the Shenzhen Bao'an International Airport by Massimiliano Fuksas (1944– ) of 2013, especially with regard to its elongated departure hall wrap-around façade structure with its repetitive small window openings.

Probably better known are works by Patrik Schumacher (1961– ) and Zaha Hadid (1950–2016), an Iraqi-British architect and the first woman recipient of the Pritzker Prize in architecture. These would include in China the Galaxy SOHO Mall in Beijing of 2012, the Wangjing SOHO there of 2014, shown in figure 10, and the Beijing Daxing Airport of 2019 (Rowe, Wang and Chen, 2022). Built between 2009 and 2012, the Galaxy SOHO is located in the Chaoyang central business district of Beijing and constructed for the founders of SOHO, Zhang Xin and Pan Shiyi. It was the first of three projects, also including the three blocks of Wangjing SOHO in the northeast of Beijing and the singular tower of Leeza SOHO in the northwest of the city.

7 – THE SERPENTINE PAVILION
by Rem Koolhaas and Cecil Balmond, 2006, in Hyde Park, London, United Kingdom

8 – THE OLYMPIC STADIUM
by Frei Otto, 1972, in Munich, Germany

9 – THE PEIX OLÍMPIC
by Frank Gehry, 1992,
in Barcelona, Spain

10 – THE GALAXY SOHO
by Zaha Hadid, 2012,
in Chaoyang District of
Beijing, China

11 – THE WANGJING SOHO by Zaha Hadid, 2014, in Chaoyang District of Beijing, China
A Plan configuration of the main building volumes and B The rising towers above the commercial area evoking *shan shui hua* imagery

A

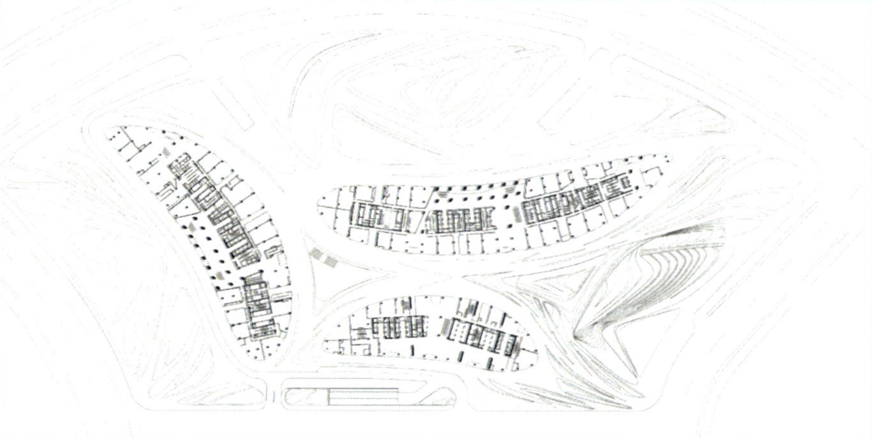

B

At close to 350,000 square meters, Galaxy SOHO is quite large. Comprised of four ovoid-shaped and continuous flowing volumes that are set apart across the rectangular site but fused and linked together by bridges as indicated in figure 10. In sum, the resulting panoramic landscape of buildings without corners or abrupt disruptions adds to the sheer fluidity and organic character of the formal composition as shown in figure 10. The upper floors are office space, whereas the lower floors and spaces in between are commercial spaces. The swirling interior courts recall the courtyard tradition of Beijing, while the towering landscape above evokes the *shan shui hua* or mountain-water art of dynastic times (Etherington, 2012). Others include the One World Trade Center Transport Hub of 2016 by the Spanish architect Santiago Calatrava (1951– ) within the reconstructed World Trade Center master plan, originally by Daniel Libeskind (1946– ). This winged structure sculpturally unifies everyday metro stops and related components appearing almost like a giant white bird about to take flight as shown in figure 12. Made from repetitive arched elliptical steel struts running parallel at street level across a site roughly 107 meters long and 35 meters wide, the winged structure rises inside above street level to about 29 meters with wings extending upwards above grade. The spaces between the ribs allow light to enter by day and emit light at night as a beacon to passersby as also depicted in figure 12 (Howarth, 2016).

## Figuration

Figuration can be defined as ornamentation by means of figures or designs often involving the use of repetitive patterns. In the physical realm of architecture, at least according to one knowledgeable commentator, such ornamentation is a product of various forces for transmitting unique effects (Moussavi and Kubo, 2008). For another, it goes beyond pleasure and, contrary to modernist messages where it is abhorred, ornament plays a crucial role in the sheer designation of a building and as an expression of social values, hierarchies and culture. Today it is also far more present than in early more orthodox modern times (Picon, 2013). It certainly played a role in conveying identity in buildings by several architects. In Jean Nouvel's Arab World Institute in Paris, France of 1987, for instance, an advanced metallic brise-soleil comprised of geometric Arab patterns cloaks otherwise rectilinear curtain-walled high-rise buildings. This complex was the subject of a competition as a part of Paris's 'Grand Projets' in the 1980s and covers a floor area of some 26,900 square meters. Its program was devised around the coming together of a relationship between Arab culture and France (Winstanley, 2011). The two buildings were located at the end of the Boulevard Saint Germain by the Seine River, itself a meeting ground of sorts in the Parisian context. The 240 panel *mashrabiya* equivalent (traditional window screening) incorporates light-sensitive diaphragms that regulate light entering the building. As shown in figure 13, regular patterns among the panels of squares, circles and octagonal outlined shapes create an Arabesque aesthetic effect and modulate solar gain within the building. A shifting geometric pattern of light is produced both day and night and on both the outside and interior of the complex, as shown in figure 14.

12 – THE ONE WORLD TRADE CENTER TRANSPORTATION HUB by Santiago Calatrava, 2016 in New York City, USA A The giant bird-like figure of the transportation hub at street level between Greenwich and Church street and B The soaring interior of repetitive panels of the transportation hub

A

B

13 – THE ARAB WORLD INSTITUTE
by Jean Nouvel, 1987, in Paris, France, showing general views of the operable *mashrabiya* panels on the façade

14 – THE ARAB WORLD INSTITUTE

by Jean Nouvel, 1987, in Paris, France (A) Arab geometric patterns on the façade's *mashrabiya* panels and (B) Interior daylighting through the *mashrabiya* panels

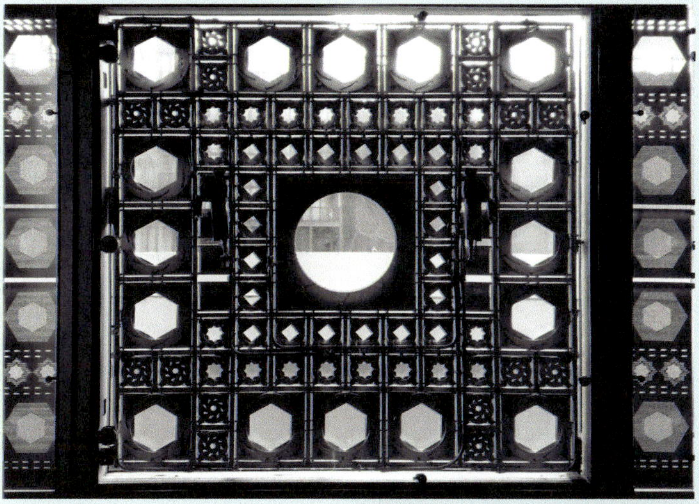

A

B

Nouvel Atelier's later design of the Louvre Abu Dhabi also involves Arab themes and the manipulation of light. The complex is located on Saadiyat Island in Abu Dhabi of the United Arab Emirates and is some 97,000 square meters of floor area in extent, making it the largest museum on the Arabian Peninsula. Designed essentially between 2006 and 2007, it was inaugurated later in 2017 (Heathcote, 2017). Programmatically it is comprised of a veritable archipelago of some 55 individual buildings, including twenty-three galleries, all composed of relatively uniform white cubic boxes and covered by a 180-meter diameter dome, as shown in figure 15. This dome is supported on four perimeter piers, each 110 meters apart and hidden within building volumes and giving the impression of a floating roof rising to some 36 meters above grade as also shown in figure 15. Further, the dome is made up of eight different layers, with four layers clad in stainless steel on the outside and four aluminum-clad layers on the inside. These layers are supported, in turn, by a 5 meter thick steel frame made of around 10,000 structural components that were preassembled into 35 larger elements and craned into place on site. Both the outer and inner layers have star-shaped outlines of varying sizes as shown in figure 16, allowing light to penetrate into and out of the interior, creating a cinematic effect as the sun progresses across the sky during the day. At night it lights up with around 7,850 stars of light radiating out into the sky. In sum, the dome evokes the rays of light shining through palms in an oasis, is a symbol of Arab architecture in itself, with the irregular arrangement of museum buildings underneath also evoking vernacular Arab settlements (ArchDaily, 2017). The Ismaili Cultural Center on Buffalo Bayou in central Houston in the United States, by Farshid Moussavi is now under construction. It is also a contemporary interpretation of Middle Eastern ornamentation, though this time Persian. Extensive use is made of verandahs and *mashrabiya*-like screens, as well as ceramic tiles. Conceived as a tapestry of stone, again it is the figuration of surface features throughout the architecture that establishes its identity, as shown in figure 17, returning to the two commentaries on ornamentation cited earlier (Waite, 2021).

The partnership of Jacques Herzog (1950– ) and Pierre de Meuron (1950– ), both Swiss architects and theorists, has also played a conspicuous role as a source of figuration, among other aspects of their work (Fernández-Galiano, 2020). Perhaps most prominent in this regard is their Beijing National Stadium of 2008, also known affectionately as the 'Bird's Nest' because of its overall appearance. This they undertook in collaboration with several Chinese participants, including Li Xinggang of the China Architects Design and Research Group, as well as the well-known artist Ai Weiwei (1957– ) as artistic consultant. Initially the stadium was the subject of a bidding process in 2001 that was decided among thirteen separate offerings. Construction started in 2001 and continued to the opening in 2008. Oval in planar shape the stadium measures some 332 meters along its longer axis and around 296 meters across its stub axis. It occupies a site of 25.8 hectares and has 80,000 fixed seats with 11,000 additional temporary seats. Of these over 200 are wheelchair-accessible. At its tallest point the structure is 68.5 meters above grade and the

15 – THE LOUVRE ABU DHABI ON SAADIYAT ISLAND
by Jean Nouvel, 2017, in Abu Dhabi, United Arab Emirates (A) Day and night views of the dome appearing to float above the museum buildings and (B) The archipelago of museum buildings on Saadiyat Island

A

B

16 – THE LOUVRE ABU DHABI ON SAADIYAT ISLAND
by Jean Nouvel, 2017, in Abu Dhabi, United Arab Emirates (A) A mock-up of a segment of the dome with exterior and interior layers and the structural steel frame in between, (B) The resulting pattern of the eight layers and (C) and (D) The interior effect of the museum with dome daylighting

A

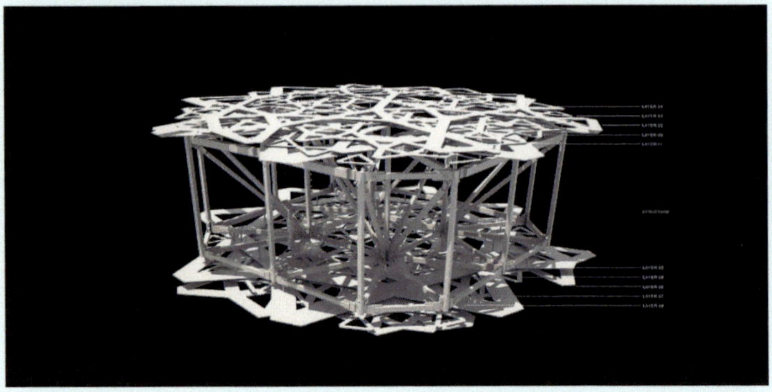

B

C

D

17 – THE ISMAILI CULTURAL CENTER

by Farshid Moussavi, 2022, in Houston, Texas, USA

A The Center in the Houston context of the Buffalo Bayou area and

B The tapestry of stone screens and walls

A

B

bowl-shaped stands afford excellent views of the playing fields from every seat as shown in figure 18. Allegedly the design originated from Chinese ceramics and the concomitant idea of the stadium being a collective building and, therefore, a public vessel and one that was also open to its surroundings. Essentially it is comprised of two major components. The first is the concrete bowl hosting the seating and the second is the outer steel frame, originally to support a retractable roof that was eliminated later. The random-looking additional steel of the outer skin was added to blend the supports into the rest of the stadium as shown also in figure 18 (Pasternak, 2008). The space between the inner bowl and outer figurative steel frame was around 15.3 meters and provided for a Piranesi-like domain for access and related venues, also as shown in figure 18. The figure of the building, however, was the exterior steel frame which was also regarded as something of a symbol of the 'New China' (Rowe, 2011). Post-Games use have included football, concerts, shopping and hosting of the closing ceremony of the 2022 Beijing Winter Olympic Games. In a similar vein, regarding the outside figuration of buildings, the Alliance Arena in Munich of 2005 by Herzog & de Meuron is also large, seating some 70,000 to 75,000 spectators and featuring an exterior skin comprised of some 2,874 ETFE-foil air panels. These have the capacity to become illuminated, as shown in figure 19, expressing for instance the jersey colors of competing teams. The stadium is the home of FC Bayern München and also hosted the 2006 FIFA World Cup event. EFTE, or Ethylene Tetrafluoroethylene is a highly corrosion-resistant and strong polymer that was first developed by Du Pont in the 1970s for aerospace use. The Alliance Arena has a square rounded-corner plan profile and also houses numerous restaurants, fast-food outlets and merchandise stores (FC Bayern München, 2015). At a far different scale, the Prada Building in Aoyama, Tokyo, Japan, of 2003 by Herzog & de Meuron is also an essay in façade figuration and imaginative compliance with local regulations as shown in figure 20 (Celant, 2003). Built in an otherwise heterogeneous area of mostly lower-rise structures, the project was relatively free, so to speak, of the need for contextual conformity. Relatively tall, at about seven stories above grade with several below, the small footprint of the building was set back to provide an adjacent public plaza. The space inside was fluid, such that more or less the whole space can be perceived rather than the more usual floor by floor. Shaped to evoke a bag, the store's vertical areas across cores and horizontal pipes are linked to form a load-bearing structure. Of more importance here, the structure, space and façade were conceived of as a single unit, characterized by diagonal crisscrossed patterns with diamond-shaped glass panes. These panes, in turn, produce the crystal-like appearance of the building while also offering views from inside to outside and *vice versa*. The use of façade figurations was not uncommon in Tokyo at the time. The Maison Hermes building in Chuo-ku central Tokyo by Renzo Piano (1937– ) and the Dior Building nearby Prada in Aoyama by Kazuyo Sejima (1956– ) of SANAA are other cases in point (Rowe, 2011).

18 – THE BEIJING NATIONAL STADIUM

by Herzog & de Meuron, 2008, in Chaoyang District of Beijing, China

A The intimate scale of spectating, B The Piranesi-like space between the concrete bowl of seating and the outer steel frame and C The figuration of the stadium's outer steel frame like a bird's nest

A

B

C

19 – THE ALLIANCE ARENA

by Herzog & de Meuron, 2005, in Munich, Germany

A An overall view of the stadium in context, B Details of the ETFE panels and C Different lighting schemes through the ETFE panels

A

B

C

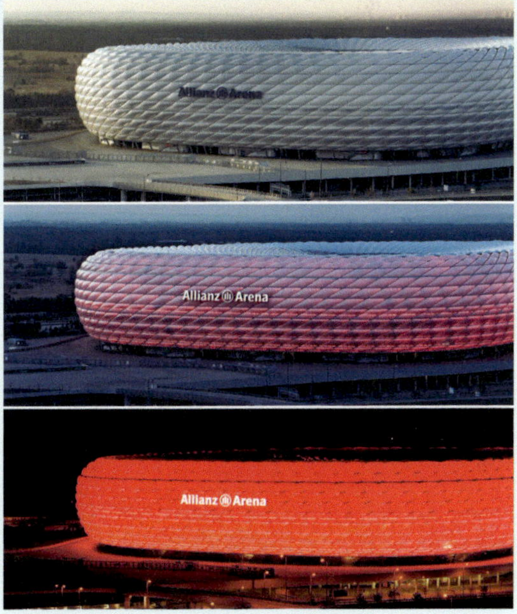

## 20 – THE PRADA BUILDING

by Herzog & de Meuron, 2003, in Aoyama, Tokyo, Japan

A A view of the Prada store in situ, B Inside and outside views associated with the Prada store and C A detailed view of the diamond-shaped glass panels

A

B

C

# Sustainability

These days sustainability in architecture and urban design is important both in very specific and broad ways. It is important certainly in the light of the Anthropocene Epoch in which we find ourselves and crises of non-renewable energy consumption, carbon proliferation and likely adverse effects of prolonged climate change (World Commission on Environment and Development, 1987). It is broad in so far as the metabolism of constructed environments impinges on a range of dimensions from resource consumption and management through waste disposal and reuse (Bacini and Brunner, 2012). It is specific in so far as particular building practices can in fact be carbon-neutral and sustained. Further work by scientific groups in the international Earth Commission identified eight key measures of planetary safety and justice of which almost all are failing to meet tipping point standards (Rockström, 2023). Looking across a range of contemporary projects in various parts of the world, at least four broad dimensions emerge. These include energy use towards carbon neutrality, water use and management, greenery and open space provision and waste management and recycling (CNN Staff, 2020). In a few instances, all four dimensions are taken up towards more complete and robust sustainability. In addition, conservation can be seen both as a means towards these goals as well as a potential pathway to fostering social justice through the promotion of accessibility and inclusion, alongside of perpetuation of culture and historic content (Baldwin, 2021). The Pixel office building of 2010 in central Melbourne, Australia, by Studio 505, for instance, was the nation's first carbon-neutral commercial building (ArchDaily, 2014). A relatively simple and coherent six story tall office building was produced within which a series of environmental systems were woven. These include an extensive green roof collecting rainwater for a water-balanced outcome, alongside a façade system of perimeter planters, fixed shading eaves, double-glazed window walls and solar panel shading. As shown in figure 21, the multi-colored pixelated exterior of the building is striking. The futuristic upswinging block of the Museum of Tomorrow of 2015 by Santiago Calatrava in Rio de Janeiro also deploys solar arrays and an unusual rainwater storage and management system. In addition, its projection into the sea strengthens the visible cultural and international identity of the city (ArchDaily, 2016). The upward-sloping Copenhill power plant and sports facility, the world's cleanest of its kind, in Copenhagen by Bjarke Ingels Group (BIG) of 2017, adds further to the aforementioned dimensions with a municipal-scale waste-to-energy plant (Baldwin, 2019). This large building in central Copenhagen is surrounded by a well-wrought figurative skin, as shown in figure 21, around the waste management facility inside that also houses the world's first steam ring generator, using excess steam to emit rings signifying a metric ton of carbon dioxide each. The complex is crowned with active recreational facilities, covering some 10,000 square meters of surface, including a ski slope, hiking trail, playground fixtures, climbing walls and simply views of the city. A 2009 corporate complex for the Suzlon wind turbine suppliers, Suzlon One Earth in Pune, India, by Christopher Benninger (1942– ), incorporates appropriate environmental technologies across all four dimensions mentioned earlier. All power is generated on-site, with 80 percent from solar and the remaining

20 percent from wind. Otherwise, it is a relatively conventional-looking arrangement of office blocks that also is carbon-neutral. Rainwater harvesting occurs throughout the site and the campus design deliberately provides public open space, as well as for on-site waste management and conversion (ArchDaily, 2014). The Bullitt Center is a 5,000 square meter, six story office building in Seattle that aspires to be one of the world's greenest commercial buildings. Designed by the Miller Hull Partnership, it incorporates, among other technologies, composting toilets, self-sufficient energy and water collection and treatment systems using rooftop arrays of photovoltaic panels and a water cistern treatment system (Porada, 2013). Finally, One Angel Square of 2012, also depicted in figure 21, is by 3D Reid Architects and located in Manchester, United Kingdom. A 32,800 square meter office facility, it was designed for maximum flexibility, with mechanical and electrical systems allowing occupiers to accommodate as needs change. Engineering features include a double-skinned façade to minimize heating and cooling. Effectively, the thermal mass of concrete employed in the building acts as a thermal sponge, passively soaking up heat and reducing the amount of energy needed to cool the structure. Consequently, there is a 50 percent reduction in energy use when compared to a comparable conventional building and an 80 percent reduction in carbon, as well as a 30 percent reduction on operating costs (ArchDaily, 2013).

## Critical Regionalism

Critical Regionalism was first coined by Alexander Tzonis and Liane Lefaivre in their essay about the work of Greek architects Dimitris and Suzana Antonakakis (Tzonis and Lefaivre, 1981). Essentially, the term refers to an architecture that strives to counter the ubiquity, placelessness and lack of identity of orthodox architectural modernism and also rejected the individualism and ornamentation of post-modern architecture. At much the same time in 1983 Kenneth Frampton (1930– ) one of the leading modern architectural historians, also saw critical regionalism as a resistive practice to orthodox modernism (Frampton, 1983). For him it was architecture rooted in the modern tradition but tied to a geographical and cultural context. It was, however, beyond simply being regionalist in the manner of vernacular architecture by deliberately mediating between the global and local languages of architecture. In doing so Frampton drew upon phenomenological arguments with emphasis on topography, climate, light and tectonic forms rather than on prevalent ideas of scenography. Two figures in modern architecture stood out for him in these regards. They were Jørn Utzon and Alvar Aalto (Frampton, 1983). Preoccupations with critical regionalism also largely predated similar inclinations in literary, cultural and political studies, such as the work of Judith Butler (1956– ), an American philosopher and gender studies author (Butler and Spivak, 2007).

Several if not numerous other architects in both the West and the East took up or embodied a critical regional orientation. Glenn Murcutt (1936– ), an Australian architect, for example, created an architecture clearly of its place and one that touched

21 – SELECTED SUSTAINABLE BUILDING PROJECTS

A Pixel office building by Studio 505, 2010, in Carlton, Melbourne, Australia, B Copenhill power plant and sports facility by BIG, 2017, in Amager, Copenhagen, Denmark, C The Bullitt Center by the Miller Hull Partnership, 2013, in Central District neighborhood of Seattle, USA and D Section of One Angel Square by 3D Reid Architects, 2012 in NOMA, Manchester, United Kingdom

A

B

C

D

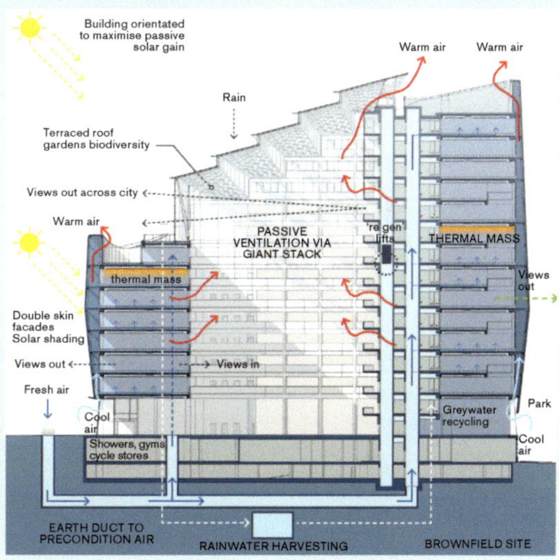

the ground, so to speak, very gently and all within the Australian landscape context. His work, like the Boyd Art Centre in West Cambewarra of 1996–1999, for instance, straightforwardly framed the views afforded by the site. The earlier Ball-Eastaway House in Sydney of 1980–1983 was raised on pillars in order to allow water to run off naturally across the site and sported a simple corrugated iron roof rounded in a manner typical of older Australian houses. Murcutt's sensitivity to environment and locality is constantly directed towards creation of forthright local architecture devoid of showiness (Beck and Cooper, 2002 and Murcutt, 2008). Another proponent, though tied more generally to life as such and in a sensuous manner is Peter Zumthor (1943– ), the American-trained Swiss architect. His uncompromising and minimalist architecture, like the Kunsthalle in Bregenz for example, seemingly derives from specific meanings he associates with certain materials and a specificity derived from plumbing a site for its form, depth and history, as well as its sensuous qualities. It is architecture, local to be sure, but also bound up with atmosphere and a phenomenological tying of architecture to life experience as such (Zumthor, 1998). Yet another group of contemporary architects that also reflect the time and circumstances of their cultural environment are those associated with China's 'third stream', distinct from State and corporate architecture (Rowe, Wang and Chen, 2022). Beginning to emerge in the late 2000s, before Xi Jinping's remonstrations about 'weird architecture' in 2016, members of this group and of the 1970s generation, like Ma Qingyun, Ciu Kai and Wang Shu began producing architecture closely demonstrating expressive convergence with Chinese values, traditional culture and senses of place. Later on, Zhang Ke (1970– ) the founder of ZAO/standardarchitecture and a prominent younger-generation architect, clearly defined his and others' 'third stream' architecture as one that was framed by essential circumstances and time of today's China, such as moderate in wealth and not glitzy, extending to a large geography and dealing with a broad diversity of local cultures. His micro-hutong project in Beijing of around 2016 exemplifies much of this sentiment. It is at once a restoration of the rundown hutong tradition in the central city but also the home of the Micro Yuan'er Children's Library and Art Center. Working closely and knowledgeably with what was there, materially, spatially and historically, the former residential site was transformed into an inventive playground and functional facility that more than met its requirements and celebrated the current moment in lane life revival (Derakhshani et al., 2021). Other architects like Li Xiaodong and his Bridge School of 2006 in Fujian and his Liyuan Library in peripheral Beijing of 2014, shown here in figure 22 also reflect this locally oriented time-place sentiment. Similar comments can also be directed to Wang Hui of URBANUS Architecture & Design and his Maritime Museum of Art of 2008 in Dalian and Hua Li of Trace Architecture Office at the Gaoligong Museum of Handcraft Paper of 2000 in Yunnan, as well as to Xu Tiantian of DnA Design and Architecture in her Lounge Bridge and other projects in rural Songyang County, China (Rowe, Wang and Chen, 2022).

22 – PROJECTS OF CHINA'S 'THIRD STREAM' OF ARCHITECTS

A Zhang Ke's micro-hutong of 2016 in Dashilar area of Beijing, China, B Li Xiaodong's Liyuan Library of 2014 in Huairou District of Beijing, China, C Hua Li's Gaoligong Museum of Handcraft Paper of 2000 under Gaoligong Mountain of Yunnan, China, and D Xu Tiantian's Lounge Bridge of 2011 across Songyinxi River of Songyang County, China

A

B

C

D

CHAPTER 5

# Situations, Mental Spaces and Other Attributes

The orchestration and doing of 'design thinking' involves at least three cognitive components, each of a general kind. Referring to previous discussions, they are 'situations', 'mental spaces' and related 'frames', or their equivalents. 'Situations' are active engagements and involvements with circumstances and in the manner of Merleau-Ponty, or in architecture of Schön (Mallin, 1979 and Schön, 1983). 'Mental spaces' are the basic structures supporting processes like input, recalling and acting (Fauconnier and Turner, 2006). While frames for their part, often inside mental spaces, allow sense to be made through stereotypical characterizations as described in chapter 3 alongside other forms of schemata. Together they combine to yield the cognitive processes of 'design thinking' especially in architecture and urban design. They also lie behind the authorship of the specific stories being told about architecture.

## Situations

To begin with and as noted earlier, Merleau-Ponty's ontology of situations essentially expresses a unity of engagement with surroundings and an individual's relation to a present milieu. Therefore, it is not to be confused with the situation of location or simply referring to some circumscribed set of circumstances in a Cartesian dualist fashion. For him, we relate to our worlds cognitively, empathetically, infinitively and practically at once. Moreover, situations are mastered via articulation and patterning in the formulation of activist dispositions. This is also innately structural as in language acquisition (Chomsky and Ronat, 1998). In addition, total absorption occurs during which both the realm of things outside us and our own subjectivity are engaged. The logic of a situation or, as Merleau-Ponty refers to situational analysis as being a kind of 'radical reflection', is closely akin to 'reflection-in-action' and 'knowing-in-practice' (Mallin, 1979).

Also, as noted earlier, Donald Schön's excursus about how professionals think in action deals with the kind of competence that is essential to professional practice like architecture and urban design. It is not entirely academic knowledge that is involved, nor unvarnished opinion (Schön, 1983). Although often tacit, knowing-in-practice also has distinctive features and limits. It also places an emphasis on professional judgment while seeking to contribute to social welfare ahead of a professional's own and employing standards of both competence and morality. An early admired manner of professional practice was what Schön called the 'Model of Technical Rationality' that derived from Enlightenment thought and resulted in 'positivism'. According to someone like Auguste Comte (1798–1857), a French philosopher, mathematician and formulator of the doctrine of positivism, there were several principles involved. First, empirical science was the only legitimate form of knowledge. Second, positivism was an antidote for mysticism, spiritualism and pseudo knowledge, as well as a program for the type of thinking that should extend scientific knowledge into political and moral realms (Habermas, 1968). In these latter cases it also emphasized a strong relationship between 'means' and 'ends' with the latter preferably fixed. World War II marked a period of ascendency for this through institutions like 'operations research' programs and professions like medicine and engineering where the ends were generally unequivocal and stable (Moore, 1970). By contrast, the challenge of problem setting under conditions that are fuzzy, ill-defined and 'wicked', referring back to previous definitions, is that we are not dealing with a technical problem *per se*, but rather one in which interactively we name the things to which we will attend and frame the context in which we will attend to them, simultaneously. This manner of acting also reveals gaps between professional knowledge and real-world practice. In this regard, Simon clearly asserted that professional practice is essentially concerned with design in the sense of changing existing situations into ones that are preferred (Simon, 1969). For Schein, professional practice is a case of divergent thinking creatively, rather than convergent thinking where the focus is on finding a single well-defined solution to a problem (Schein, 1972). In short, the model of rationality is incomplete and fails to account for practical comprehension in inevitably divergent situations. Moreover, for Schön, knowing-in-action obeys at least three conditions. First, action recognizes judgments which we know how to carry out spontaneously. Second, we are often not aware of having learned to take these actions and, third, we are likely unable to describe the knowledge which our actions reveal. Therefore, 'thinking-in-action' is something like thinking on one's feet or like improvisation in jazz. It also hinges on surprise with sudden insight, so to speak, occasioned by 'reflection-in-action' (Schön, 1983).

## Mental Spaces and Frames

Under the Theory of Conceptual Blending according to Gilles Fauconnier and Mark Turner, elements and vital relations from diverse scenarios are blended in a subconscious process that is assumed to be ubiquitous. Development of this theory began in 1993 with the citing of Arthur Koestler's *Act of Creation* of 1964 as a forerunner. In this, Koestler had identified patterns in creative activities that he termed 'bisociation of matrices' and used them to solve the riddle of the Buddhist monk (Koestler, 1964). Fauconnier's and Turner's newer version of blending came to the fore in 2002 with *The Way We Think* and as a theoretical tool was used by the likes of Lakoff and others, briefly described earlier. In relation to frames as

1 – A BASIC DIAGRAM DEPICTING CONCEPT OF 'MENTAL SPACES AS A NETWORK'
after Gilles Fauconnier and Mark Turner, 2002

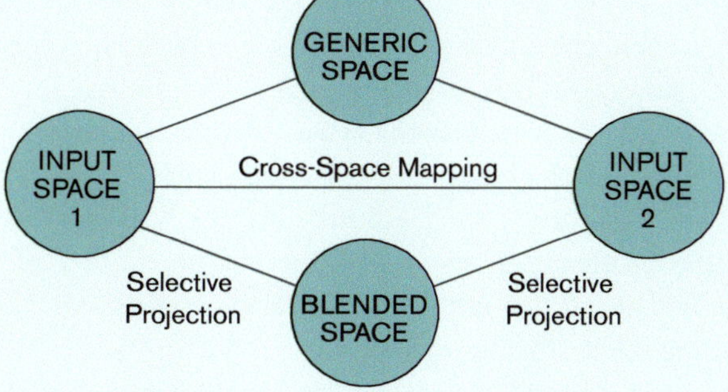


2 – THE SEQUENCE OF INPUT, GENERIC AND BLENDED FRAMES FOR THE 100 WALLS CHURCH by Carlos Arnaiz, 2013, in Cebu, Philippines:
A Initial inputs of the Gothic chapel and the Garden of Gethsemane,
B A second alignment reflecting a change in the chapel arrangement and the choice of parallel walls and C A third alignment reflecting slippage in program alignments and manners of interior daylighting

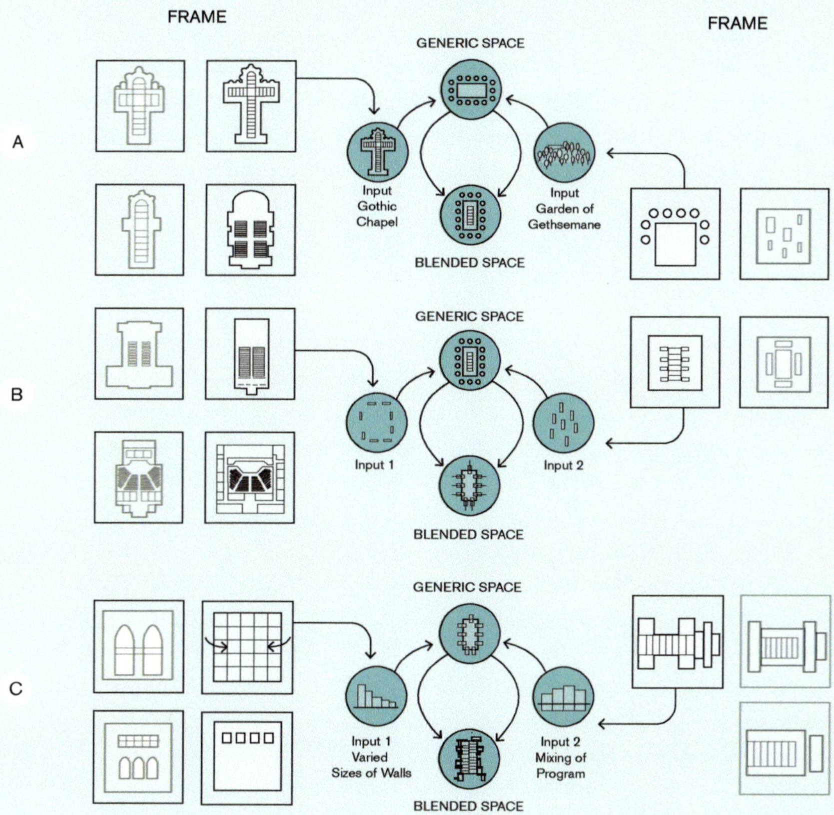

used earlier, conceptual blending involving mental spaces goes further by dealing with how frames are organized and combined. Accordingly, mental spaces are small conceptual containers used to structure processes behind human reasoning and communication. The basic form of integration involved consists of at least four separated yet interconnected mental spaces which can be modified as decisions and operations progress. They further suggest that mental spaces are generated in working memory and are connected to knowledge situated in long-term memory. As such there is a constraint in working memory within the so-called "magic number seven plus or minus two" (Miller, 1956). Among the four, here 'generic space' captures a common structure which is present in all 'input spaces' of which there are at least two. These input spaces provide the context of a specific situation or idea. 'Blended space' contains a general structure from a generic space as well as elements from input spaces that are mapped together through selective projections. Within this cross-space mapping of counterparts, various types of connections are made among the input spaces. More complicated cases can involve multiple input spaces and blended spaces (Fauconnier and Turner, 2002). A simple diagram of the network model involved is shown here in figure 1. Returning to the design of the 100 Walls Church described in chapter 2, a working example of Fauconnier and Turner's mental spaces and conceptual blending can be proposed and traced. To begin with, as shown in figure 2, a four-part arrangement of mental spaces can be made. It consists of a 'generic frame' or 'space' with a spatial structure comprised of components from both a Gothic chapel and the Garden of Gethsemane in the form of a central, relatively clear domain surrounded by objects. This in turn reflects the two input spaces of the original protocol in chapter 2 of a Gothic catholic chapel and the similar planimetric view of the actual Garden of Gethsemane. The input space of the Gothic chapel also comes from the relatively wide variety of possible plan types which act as frames or 'slots' in the sense of Minsky's and others earlier frames as depicted diagrammatically in figure 2. Planimetric views at the onset of architectural design problems are also not unusual and, given the initial inputs, probably the best way of proceeding. The fourth component of the blended space results in an open space for the chapel seating and other liturgical spaces, surrounded by an array of physical objects, like the olive trees of the Garden of Gethsemane. Further, the relatively constrained site in an east-west alignment with the SM and South Road translated readily into an overall rectangular shape for the chapel plan. In particular this is the case for the space that then formed the generic frame for a second alignment of mental spaces, addressing more specifically the architectural qualities of the church and two further inputs by the designers. First, there was representation of the many ways of engaging with the contemporary Catholic church in a more secular Philippines. This, in turn, suggested a porosity in the boundary of the chapel itself. Second there was the concomitant idea of the antiquity or long-lasting character of the church, suggesting ruins and the figure of Stonehenge.

3 – DEPICTIONS OF THE OBJECT AND SEPARATE WALL QUALITIES OF THE 100 WALLS CHURCH
by Carlos Arnaiz, 2013, in Cebu, Philippines

Remember from chapter 2 that the design team often referred to their design as a contemporary Stonehenge. Again, following the logic of the conceptual blending model, the blended space that resulted was an architectural rectangular space in plan, more or less, surrounded literally by wall elements or objects as shown in figure 2. This then further resulted in a third alignment of mental spaces with the earlier blended space. Forming the generic frame again, with two input spaces. First there was the image of freestanding walls in the ruins of Stonehenge, made up of multiple walls, and also the corresponding separation of perimeter objects and individual accommodations of the chapel as shown in figure 2 with the blended space of the actual 100 Walls Church. A further set of frames or slots also probably materialized dealing with the daylighting of the chapel as demonstrated diagrammatically in figure 2. Here, at least two important aspects pertained. One was the objective presence of the chapel from the east, the second was the open porosity of the chapel otherwise as shown in figure 3. This further easily translated into a sequence of walls all facing the same way though varying in height and width and also the inclusion of clerestory lighting as shown in figure 4. Throughout, the designers also appear to have been working from repertoires of relatively coarse-grained and typologically complete architectural components, or frames in the predominant terminology of this discussion. Then, as the overall shape and appearance of the chapel began to fall into place, the components became finer-grained and more singular in their more detailed consideration. Thus, working from broader and more encompassing design ideas down to details was the general trajectory of the problem-solving process. Moreover, this seems to be almost inevitable, once past the initial stage. Figure 5 shows a similar alignment of inputs, generic and blended frames or spaces for Bleecker's methodology deployed in the creation of TBD1 mentioned in chapter 3. After all the early rounds of generic and blended spaces essentially set the tone of design in the absence of significant backtracking. They also form the situational framework for thinking-in-action, returning to Schön and Merleau-Ponty for a moment. In the absence of difficulty such a situation exerts a significant hold over design thinking and the story about architecture being told.

Various criticisms of this model can also be discussed, alongside the duplication and mutability of different aspects of design decision making. Raymond W. Gibbs Jr., for instance, maintained that the Theory of Conceptual Blending was less a theory than a framework, owing to the sheer difficulty of testing hypotheses (Gibbs, 2000). Others, such as L. David Ritchie, have argued that the theory is unnecessarily complicated by way of explanation (Ritchie, 2004). Returning yet again to the example of the 100 Walls Church in chapter 2, the theoretical framework used there was from the Information Processing Theory of Newell, Simon and Shaw. Indeed, the interpretation was less complicated than the present framework of Fauconnier and Turner, though probably not as well suited to visual or graphic material where the act, so to speak, of blending is quite suggestive of working with visual and graphic material in resolving disparate inputs. In fact, throughout

4 – THE CHOIR LOFT OF THE 100 WALLS CHURCH WITH CLERESTORY DAYLIGHTING by Carlos Arnaiz, 2013, in Cebu, Philippines

5 – AN ALIGNMENT OF INPUTS, GENERIC AND BLENDED FRAMES FOR DEVELOPMENT AS DESCRIBED IN THE 'TBD CATALOG' OF 2014

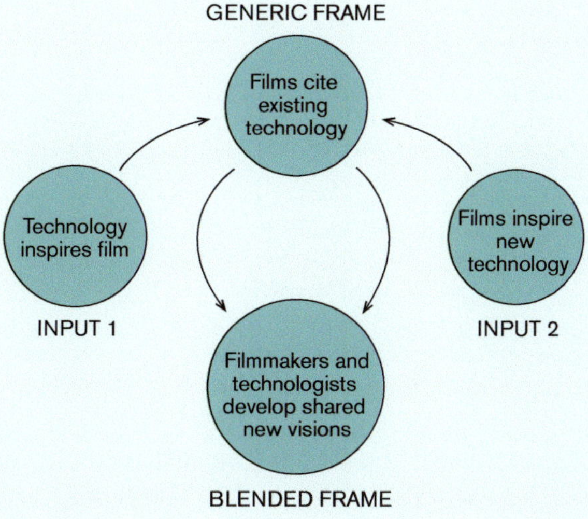

# 6 – EARLY COMPUTER GRAPHICS IN ARCHITECTURE

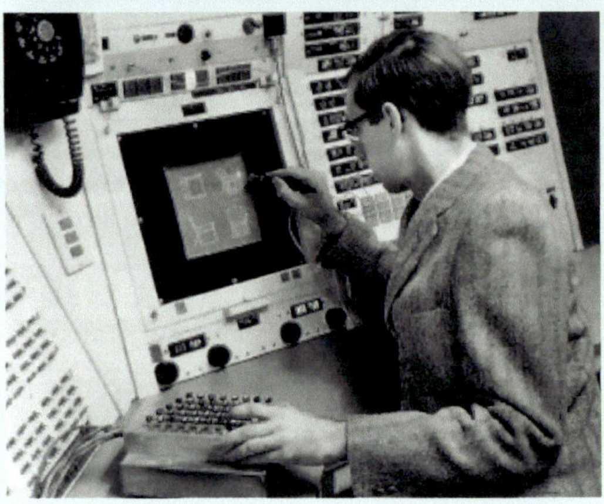

this and previous descriptions of schemata, there is considerable overlap among otherwise different theories and frameworks as noted earlier. In summary then, creative problem solving of the type under discussion does appear to be a matter of blending or otherwise associating together different and often disparate inputs. Moreover, there is almost always present an array or repertoire of relatively discrete architectural elements as frames or slots like the chapel floor plans, from which choices are made by designers in action. This further suggests that experience on the part of a designer can be a relatively conspicuous advantage and explains also why different designers have their own repetitive strategies, proclivities and styles (Moneo, 2004). In the 100 Walls Church daylighting was accomplished through clerestory lights in much the same manner as the earlier Tagaytay Chapel for the Chosen Children by the same designer as shown in figure 6 of chapter 2. This also suggests that the repertoire of design strategies for a particular designer might be large but not infinite.

Following on from the general train of discussion in chapter 4, Rafael Moneo's account of eight contemporary architects reflects his belief that the recent period was one of reflection and critical discourse rather than one of elaborations of systematic theory (Moneo, 2004). Certainly, Robert Venturi's *Complexity and Contradiction in Architecture* was a personal reflection on and about architecture (Venturi, 1966). Indeed, Moneo's account begins with James Stirling (1926–1992) followed by Venturi in the 1960s followed by Aldo Rossi in the 1970s (Stirling, 1975; Venturi, 1966 and Rossi, 1982). These probing attitudes were then followed by a desire for theory to precede practice, especially in the work of Peter Eisenman (Eisenman, 2006). Then there was a reversion to architecture explicable in itself and through Álvaro Siza (1933– ) and Frank Gehry as the dominant figures of the 1980s (Testa, 1996 and Goldberger, 2017). This was further to be followed by Rem Koolhaas and his non-intellectually prejudicial accounts of the necessity for development (Koolhaas, 1978). More or less coterminously, Jacques Herzog and Pierre de Meuron asserted the almost transcendental nature of elemental solids and minimalism (Mack, 2020). Apart from detailed reconstructions of how these architects designed, Moneo's account demonstrates how different periods are often dominated by particular points of view and broad modes of design thinking. As with other creative pursuits there often is a temporal fashionableness involved. It also showed that these trail-blazing architects adhered to their own repertoires of design thinking and styles of practice.

# The Digital Age and Other Attributes

Although the precise onset of the digital age is difficult to pin down exactly, we seem to know when the first large-scale electronic calculating machines like ENIAC were invented at or soon after the end of World War II. Other ingredients of the modem computer also came along around the same time and even earlier, if we take into account contributions by the likes of Herman Hollerith (1860–1929) and the US Census of 1890, Claude Shannon (1916–2001) and his "Mathematical Theory of Communication" of 1948 and Alan Turing with his test and the Turing Machine. It was sometime later, however, before the first effective network came online with the American SAGE system in the 1960s. Events were all rather interrelated and incremental (Mahoney, 2011).

## Architecture in the Digital Age

With regard to architecture, however, it was not until the late 1960s and early 1970s that the international scene was marked by attempts to relate architecture to what became an increasingly pervasive computer culture (Picon, 2015). Rather quickly thereafter and especially during the 1980s and into the 1990s, significant developments in computer applications bearing directly on architectural design and the stories that could be told began to change the field. Certainly, by the 2000s, many if not most design activities had come under the spell of the digital age. Computer-aided design software, after the early turning point in the direction of graphic interaction between a designer and a computer with SKETCHPAD at MIT in 1963, significantly reduced the need for draftspeople by the 1980s and 1990s as shown in figure 6 (Mitchell, 1977 and Gero, 2011). Simultaneously, universities adopted software that quickly became ubiquitous in design studios and other academic settings. Geometric modeling, enabling the construction and representation of free-form curves, surfaces, and volumes arose in CAD and Computer-aided Manufacturing environments by the later 1990s, followed by three-dimensional printing. In fact, this last term, coined in 1995, involves a process for making solid objects from digital models, as we know. More pervasive still, the World Wide Web and Internet came on with a rush by about 1992, after developments as early as the beginning of the 1970s and about the time of the PC computer, with far-flung computing networks (Ryan, 2010). In sum then, at least five areas were either directly enabled or saw major digital contributions in architecture, as illustrated in part by figure 7. The first and perhaps most widespread was in representation, ranging from increasingly sophisticated graphics packages to intelligent CAD applications and crossovers into three-dimensional modeling. Despite some lacunae in compatibility in a crowded field this substantially changed the way in which the design world could be viewed and imagined, certainly in terms of media. A second area was integrative efficiency via digital platforms like building information modeling of otherwise separated tasks, trades, and even disciplines. A third area was in building performance assessment, particularly in lighting, climate control, and various forms of resource consumption and programmatic functionality. A fourth area was parametric modeling and the uses of applied geometries to the surface and other features of architecture including matters of fabrication, like those pioneered by the likes of Frank Gehry and Permasteelisa, again in the late 1990s. Finally, a fifth and more recent area involved rapid prototyping, harnessing the capabilities of technical developments, like digital printing and three-dimensional modeling married to other constructional mechanisms, to allow integrated proofs of concept for building components and other devices to be quickly fabricated and assembled (Hamblen, Hall and Furman, 2001). However, seen from a more fundamental perspective involving core properties of human information processing embracing fuzzy and even wicked problem sets, the impact of the digital age on design thinking, as such, is probably less clear. To be sure, designers can accomplish more tasks, some only imaginable in the pre-digital age, and often carry them out more quickly. At a superficial level at least, graphic facilities have been increased, as have understandings of various architectural means and their effects. Moreover, certain domains of imaginable possibility have become opened-up and made more commonplace, largely through expanded modeling capacities. Certainly, access to all manner of structured information has largely moved from the static repositories of libraries of various kinds and become enabled quite literally from a designer's desk. Concomitant advances in communication have altered the manners of teamwork and, in many cases, made it more inclusive by way of different knowledge and skill sets, as well as from the perspective of those actively participating in real time from far-flung places. Nevertheless, the essential task of designers to resolve what at first appear to be incommensurate constraints with regard to issues and terms of reference towards potential and satisfactory final outcomes, remains. So do the necessities of actionable knowledge, often increased by professional experience and shaped by acquired heuristic repertoires. As in the more distant past, such as with the invention and deployment of perspective and related means of seeing, imagining and representation, a major paradigm shift in architectural design has certainly occurred or begun to occur, but the ineffable characteristics of design problems and of design thinking also appear to have remained.

## Matters of Incompleteness and Precision

Now, looking over the cognitive side of design thinking, two other essential properties emerge, namely what can be termed, for want of better words, 'incompleteness' and 'precision'. Indeed, design thinking is a process that trades on the presence of both and, fundamentally, the balance between both for continued problem-space structuring. There must be, for instance, sufficient incompleteness along the way in order to prompt useful and novel forms of further heuristic reasoning pushing

7 – SOME DIGITAL CONTRIBUTIONS TO ARCHITECTURE

A Representation, B Integrative efficiency, C Performance assessment, D Parametric modeling and E Rapid prototyping

A

B

C

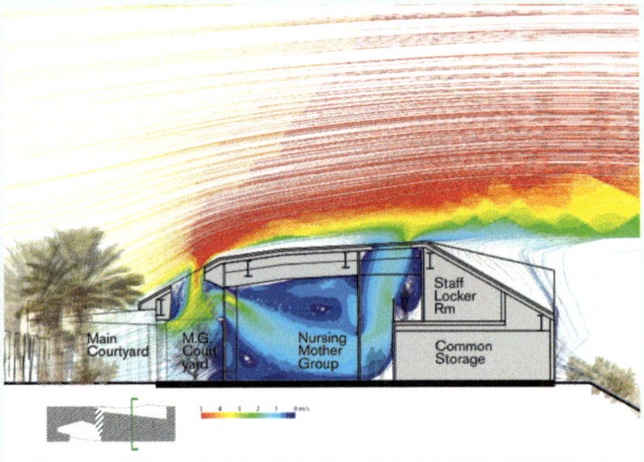

D

E

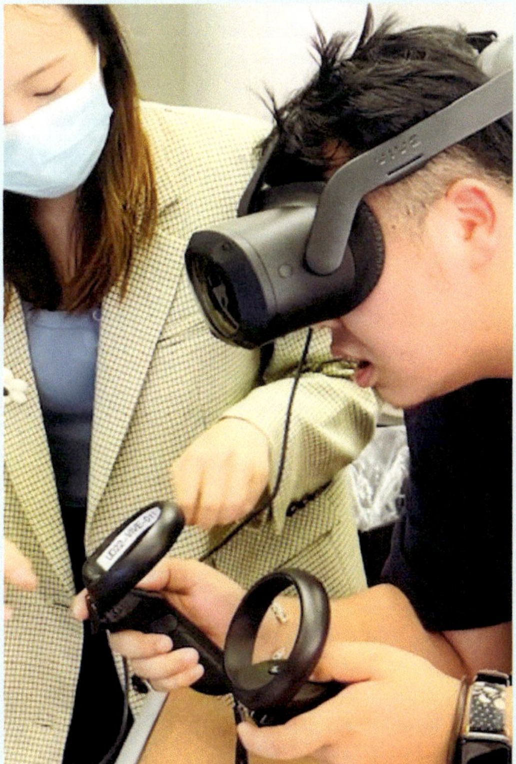

8 – USEFUL GUISES OF ‘INCOMPLETENESS’ AND ‘PRECISION’

A Clear definition of parts and wholes, B Sufficient prompts towards productive problem solving and C Reduction of problem space to two unknowns

A

B

C

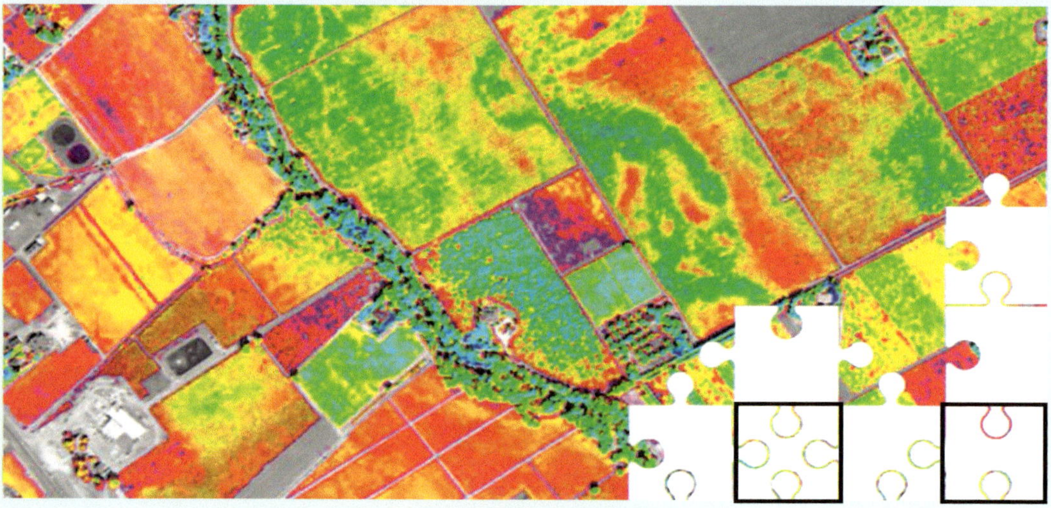

towards potentially better outcomes, as illustrated in figure 8. It also follows somewhat tautologically from the properties of wicked and ill-defined problems described earlier. On the other hand, clear definition or precision is also necessary in order to be able to recognize and understand successive stages of problem structuring and to ensure success in narrowing the search for satisfactory outcomes. Too much incompleteness severely hampers and even dooms problem-solving activity, and too much or false precision promotes premature and, therefore, probably highly sub-optimal outcomes. In all of this, incompleteness manifests itself in a number of guises. First, there is the lack of full closure from a specific decision rule aimed at reducing the difference between the properties of a proposed outcome and those that would seem to meet an aspirational set. This may be instrumental in the manner in which a problem space is initially defined, as well as occurring during subsequent rounds of information processing. In any event, it is very useful by initiating and helping to define subsequent heuristic operations. Second, the lack of clear stopping rules and essentially an awareness of bounded rationality and the open-ended aspect of problem solving encourages if not obliges further problem structuring and a narrowing of a search. Third, and as a corollary to the second guise, an inherent understanding of the lack of strict correctness and objectivity in outcomes may lead to lackadaisical problem-solving behavior – a sort of 'anything goes' on the one hand – but also be a boon to more rigorous and higher-minded aspirational search on the other, when pushing on to do better. Fourth, incompleteness in material representation also has its positive uses. Suggestive aspects of sketchy drawings, for instance, are usually more open to and can prompt reinterpretation and further construal than those that are somehow more finished and complete. Recognition and understanding of innate biases in particular media and representational techniques and, therefore, their incompleteness, can also lead to constructive rethinking and realignment of design thinking. Without being overly repetitive, incompleteness, as intended here, is productive because it enables, by allowing the furnishing of useful information at disjunctions, for continued search and restructuring of problem-spaces. This, in turn, comes about through more complete inclusion of constraints and their auxiliary conditions in a directed and coherent manner, at least in the mind's eye of a designer. Also, incompleteness, here, should not be confused, of course, with fogginess or 'not having a clue'. Incompleteness suggests enough shape to be provocative in moving forward. Precision, by contrast, is both useful and necessary by operating almost in the opposite direction. First, clear views and understandings of aspects of a problem-space structure often allow for conversion into well-defined problems where goals and ends towards them become more immediately apparent. This, in turn, leads to a truncation of the overall problem-space search. Second, various forms of incompleteness also immediately beg the issue of precision by posing questions of what is needed to be more precise and, therefore, where to look next. Here, the sheer reciprocity between incompleteness and precision is clearly productive in moving design thinking forward. Third, high levels of precision in goal-set definitions in the first place can be suggestive of potentially productive avenues of reasoning and heuristic choice. This goes back again to the potential power of prejudices, hunches, and moments of subjective insight, as well as entrainment of certain schemata. Mostly they would seem to trade on reasonable and comfortable degrees of certainty to be seriously entertained and deployed. In older stage-process models of creative problem solving, this phenomenon also speaks to the recommendations of time spent on fact finding and problem scoping. Finally, the more complete the resolution and, therefore, definition of persistent constraints, *ceteris paribus*, the higher the degree of certainty about having reached at least a satisficing outcome, if not one that is more globally optimal.

## Extended Reality or XR

Extended Reality or XR is an umbrella term encapsulating 'augmented reality' or AR, 'virtual reality' or VR and 'mixed reality' or MR as well as everything in between. Within this rubric MR was introduced by Paul Milgram (1952– ), a professor emeritus in the Mechanical and Industrial Engineering Department at the University of Toronto and some colleagues in 1994 (Milgram and Kishino, 1994). Milgram and his colleagues formulated and proposed a manner of classifying and discriminating among some seven forms of mixed reality and the world of XR in general. First, they described the Mixed-Reality Continuum or a 'Reality-Virtuality Continuum', as they called it (Milgram, Takemura, Utsumi and Kishino, 1995). As shown here in figure 9, this continuum runs between real environments on the right-hand side to the left-hand side of fully virtual environments through a middle zone between real and virtual. Here, 'virtual' is expressed in a digital format and is usually a model of some real-world object. Along this continuum, the seven types of display concepts constituting Mixed Reality were located. These include: 1. Monitor-based, non-immersive AR displays upon which graphic images were overlaid; 2. The additional use of head-mounted-displays (HDMs); 3. HDM-based AR systems incorporating optical see-through devices; 4. HDMs of AR incorporating video see-through; 5. Monitor-based Augmented Virtuality (AV) systems with computer graphic substratum employing superimposed video reality; 6. Immersive or partially immersive AV systems with computer graphic substratum employing superimposed video or texture mapped reality, and finally 7. Partially immersive AV systems which allow additional real-object interactions such as 'reaching in' and 'grabbing' with one's hands. The authors also note that additional classes or types have been delineated but that they limited themselves to the primary factors characterizing the most prominent of MR displays.

More complete classification was then referred to a three-space comprised of EWK or 'Extent of World Knowledge' and how much is actually known about objects and the world in which they are displayed. This is arrayed against measures of reproduction fidelity of which there are at least two. The first is RF or 'Reproduction Fidelity' *per se*, and the relative quality with which a display is able to produce or reproduce the actual or intended object displayed. The second is EPM or the 'Extent of Presence Metaphor' and the extent to which the observer is intended to feel 'present' with the displayed scene. For instance, highly immersive environments tend to have strong

9 – THE CONCEPT OF 'MIXED REALITY' OR 'REALITY-VIRTUALITY CONTINUUM'
after Paul Milgram et al., 1995

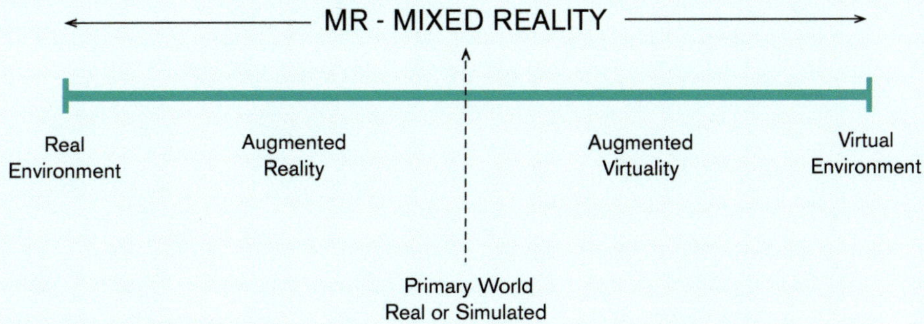


10 – A THREE-SPACE OF 'EXTENT OF PRESENCE METAPHOR (EPM)', 'EXTENT OF WORLD KNOWLEDGE (EWK)' AND 'REPRODUCTION FIDELITY (RF)' FOR SEVEN MODES OF MIXED REALITY
showing A Highly immersive environments have strong presence metaphors, B Reproductive fidelity formed by head-mounted optical alternatives and C Extent of world knowledge is relatively independent

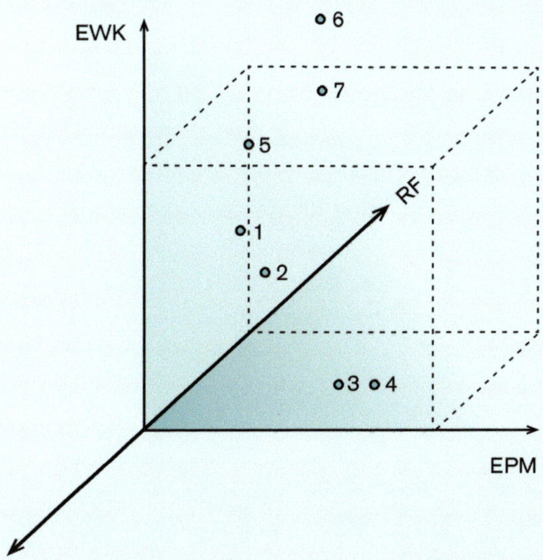


1 = Monitor-based Video + CG Overlay
2 = HMD-based Video + CG Overlay
3 = HMD-based Optical ST + CG Overlay
4 = HMD-based Video ST + CG Overlay
5 = Monitor/CG-world with Video Overlay
6 = HMD/CG-world with Video
7 = CG-based world with Real Object

presence metaphors, such as types 2, 3, 4 and 7 in the earlier examples (Milgram, Takemura, Utsumi and Kishoni, 1995). This three-space is shown diagrammatically here by figure 10, with EPM along the x-axis, EWK along the y-axis and RF along the z-axis. Further depiction and categorization of XR applications has also been undertaken, especially with regard to building operations of various kinds. There, both the volume and rapidity of automated contributions has risen appreciably since the early days of the 1990s and the Internet. In one such survey there were 24 of 88 contributions from 2018 in 37 different publications (Casini, 2022).

Within the business community the interface between humans and machines has come under scrutiny in the light of digital transformations and the arrival of Augmented Reality or AR. A doyen of competitiveness in business practices, Michael E. Porter (1947– ) a university professor at the Harvard Business School, is among the insightful recent commentators. According to him, among others, this interactive process began as far back as the 1800s with the advent of various mechanical and electrical enablers of human decision making and production. Indeed, the British historian of science, Rupert Hall (1920–2009) declared that the late 18th century was the turning point in time at which the curve of diminishing returns from pure empiricism dipped to meet the curve of increasing returns from the applied sciences and engineering (Hall, 1962). Much later according to Porter and colleagues, by the 1960s computerization of processes had begun in earnest, such as those already described and discussed in the realm of architecture and design. The business impact was one of productivity enhancement. This was followed in the 1990s by the Internet and further application and, by the 2010s, of embedding the I-of-T or Internet of Things technology within products themselves. One dramatic example of this is the ultra-contemporary tractor and a combination of geo-positioning and other digital applications to reduce the sheer amount of waste in agricultural cropping. In short, as this article insists "every organization needs an augmented reality strategy" (Porter and Heppelmann, 2017). More specifically in the realm of architecture and urban design, a continued and amplified presence of XR technologies appears to be both practical and likely, particularly in the sheer visualization of new construction proposals in existing circumstances or backgrounds; the highlighting of site and surrounding area attributes impinging negatively and positively on what might be called the environmental performance of building proposals such as the presence of brownfields, flood-prone areas, zones of high transportation accessibility, areas of socio-economic improvement and so on. In fact, without necessitating going to the extreme ends of Milgram et al.'s continuum or three-space, fruitful areas of digital and AR application are becoming visible and used (Wang, 2009; Broschart and Zeile, 2015 and Chen, 2019).

Now, at this important interface between humans and machines lies AI or Artificial Intelligence, an area that has also been rapidly developing. Moreover, according to some commentators it shows similarities in its evolution with the industrial digital revolution (Makridakis, 2017). However, it dates back at least to the pioneering work of Alan M. Turing (1912–1954) the English mathematician, computer scientist, logician, cryptologist and philosopher. In 1936, he developed the idea of the Universal Turing Machine, a forerunner of the modern computer and in 1950 he invented the Turing Test to tell whether a machine could be intelligent like a human (Turing, 1950). This test, called 'The Imitation Game', involved a human judge conversing only in written text with a second human and a language-using computer, each hidden away in separate rooms. The point of the game was for the computer to converse in such a human-like manner with the judge that the judge could not tell the second human from the computer. The second human also tried to convince the judge that he or she was human. To date no computer has passed the test reliably and often. Then in 1956, the term Artificial Intelligence (AI) was coined allegedly by John McCarthy (1927–2011), an American computer scientist and cognitive scientist. The occasion was the Dartmouth College Summer Research Project organized by McCarthy. Also participating were Herbert Simon, Marvin Minsky and Claude Shannon (Veisdal, 2019). McCarthy himself was to continue to contribute to this new field, especially in the area of human-like forms of AI and notions of common sense (McCarthy, 1959). More recently commentators have attempted to classify artificial intelligence in several ways. The first is according to aspects of human capacities. There are at least four categories that can be discerned. The first involves 'Reactive Machines' providing automatic responses to limited sets of inputs, something like IBM's Big Blue and chess. A second is 'Limited Memory Machines' with a capacity to learn from historical data to inform subsequent responses, such as chatbots. Today this appears to be where the majority of newer AI have reached. The third is 'Theory of Mind Machines' which remains either a concept or work in progress and involves machines being able to discern needs, emotions, beliefs and thought processes, the last being taken up earlier by Herbert Simon et al. in their General Problem Solver (Simon, 1995). The fourth is a fully 'Self Aware Machine' that has evolved to a point that is completely human-like and remains hypothetical. A second classification involves technological approaches of three types: ANI or Artificial Narrow Intelligence; AGI or Artificial General Intelligence and ASI or Artificial Super Intelligence beyond human cognitive capacities (Hassan, Silva, Unger, Tajmazinani and MacFeely, 2020). These authors also joined into the debate as to whether we should seek AI in a full-blown sense or remain with AI and intelligence augmentation in line with present applications. As can be seen today's LLMs or Large Language Models, Foundational Models and Generative Transformer-based models have provided chatbot formats, often based on huge data sets and often at great cost. Nevertheless, they are also an almost inevitable successor to the Web browsers and search engines that began in the 1990s, moving now beyond 'search' and into 'curatorial' functions. It now seems likely that bodies of knowledge will be split up and become the subject of specific chatbots, including areas of architecture and urban design. Moreover, it also seems likely that the prohibitive barrier of the need for gigantic data sets on which to base the models will give way to more elegant approaches (Behera, Bala and Ray, 2021).

## 11 – CHARACTERISTICS OF QUALITY IN DESIGN THINKING

A Efficiency and enablement in the design problem-solving process,

B The capacity of maintaining palpable thingness in the designing process

A

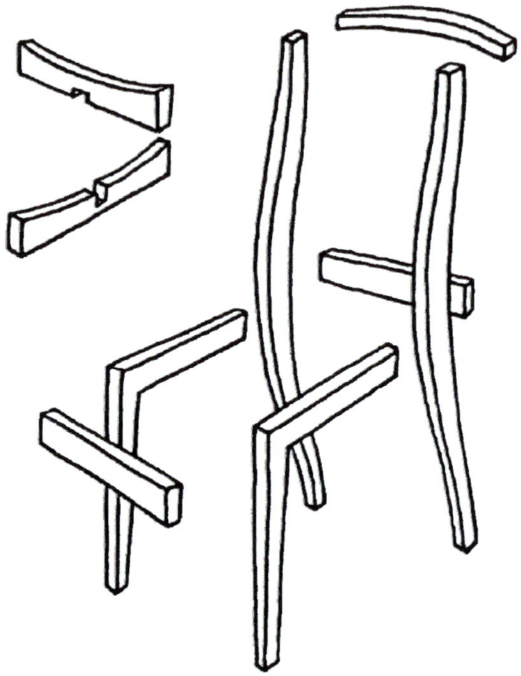

B

## Useful Aspects of Design Thinking

Returning more squarely to the topic at hand concerning the influence of the digital age, it becomes evident by way of the alterations that can take place in the balance between the essential properties of incompleteness and precision in the process of design thinking. Indeed, the more immersive the process, at least up to some point, the more likely the possibility of alteration. In this regard, of importance is how quality in design thinking is to be understood for which there are at least two lines of consideration, as illustrated by figure 11. First and perhaps most pragmatically, quality can be assessed in terms of efficiencies in the problem-solving process, of narrowing down problem-space searches and of minimizing the capacities and resources required. Also, and as a corollary and probably more fundamental would be enhanced enablement of the generation and consideration of outcomes during the unfolding of a design process and particularly those that were formerly daunting or undoable. Second, and always important, is improved incorporation of knowledge immediately in design thinking about relative performance efficiencies of outcomes and integrative complexities, as well as improved access to domain knowledge in general. Also, there is the capacity of maintaining palpable aspects of thingness more present in a design process, in both a common place and Heideggerian sense and for more of the time, in the interests of poetic properties and aspirations (Heidegger, 1967). Towards these sorts of ends, there are at least four areas where products of the digital age appear to have made considerable contributions to design thinking and, potentially, to its quality. Moreover, in many cases, they impinge on this balance and relative presences and degrees of both incompleteness and precision in design thinking as illustrated in figure 12. The first area involves aids in productive exploration of conceptual and technical vagaries that begins with a greater variety of readily available representational techniques and with higher degrees of precision. Here one immediately finds a range of graphical techniques, an easier capacity to move from planimetric and sectional presentations into three-dimensional modeling among any number of rendering techniques and *vice versa*. Effectively, what this new precision and rapid pursuit of completeness can provide is better and more concise definition of poorly considered aspects of potential outcomes, alongside of those that are less so. This, in turn, provides potentially better and more comprehensive guidance in further structuring of problem-spaces. In other words, this is a case of definition leading to revelation of incompleteness and then on to more directed problem-space search, followed again, and so on. This overall capacity also allows sub-problems to be more broadly bracketed into otherwise well-defined problems with relatively certain outcomes. Clearly, conspicuous instances of high degrees of integration, almost by definition, can be found in the application of software packages and systems. A second area of contribution derives from the sheer iterative power of generate-and-test procedures and similar parametric manipulations made possible through computational techniques, including those of a formal kind, that significantly broaden the scope of developing a plausible array of satisfactory outcomes. By definition this then opens up or widens the conditions of bounded rationality even if ultimately the condition continues to persist at some level.

To some extent, arriving at a clearer view of suitable stopping rules might also be enhanced by observing a broader array of outcomes, although there is no in-principle guarantee that this would be the case. As demonstrated earlier, in reasonably advanced forms of parametric design in architecture, especially those using unusual and otherwise difficult geometric formulations, aspects of this kind of contribution allow concepts to be represented and explored that were essentially undoable before, even if they could be imagined. Indeed, in design, the entire area known as architectural geometry has blossomed and assumed a conspicuous role because of computing and associated representational software. Moreover, this is quite apart from similar strides in areas of computer-aided manufacturing and prototyping that lie outside of this particular discussion about design thinking. A third area of contribution is broader access to information along with higher degrees of accuracy, scope, and technical sophistication in the evaluation and assessment of outcomes. This essentially involves and applies to the testing aspect of generate-and-test strategies. Nowadays, comprehensive digital design environments incorporate specific well-tried methods for evaluating various aspects of building performance, layout, structural and material efficiency, as well as various cost and resource consumption parameters. Here, it is often not so much that the methods were unknown before, but that easy application of numerous tests were intractable outside of the use of computational procedures in digital environments. The relevance to the quality of design thinking is at least two-fold, including improved efficiency and raised levels of certainty and understanding around the phenomena being assessed which, in turn, can be reflected in better guidance for further problem solving. Finally, a fourth and closely related area of contribution comes by way of the enhancement of ready access to information across many aspects of problem-solving activity, along with increasingly better research capabilities and simulation techniques. If nothing else, there have been notable improvements in certain areas of domain knowledge, primarily concerned with building materials, components, and performance, as well as in the other broader direction concerning knowledge of the behavior of more complex interactions and more complete building visualizations. The modeling of lighting, thermal performance, wind flow, and other aspects of environmental response to buildings is a clear case in point. In summary, then, we have potentially improved capacities for manipulation, iteration, assessment and 'informational search'. Also, looking across these four areas of contribution, raised levels of 'definition' and precision seem to be highly likely within problem-space structures, providing for more focused further problem-space structuring and the narrowing of searches for better outcomes. Conversely, returning to the reciprocal relationship intended here between incompleteness and precision, productive expansion of identifiable yet conceptual and technical vagaries, areas of imprecision and uncertainty enables further and potentially more profound levels of problem-solving activities. Moreover, both conditions take place against a background of domain knowledge that in itself has been significantly improved (Rowe, 2017).

12 – FOUR DIGITAL-AGE CONTRIBUTIONS TO DESIGN THINKING IN ARCHITECTURE A Variety in available representational techniques, B Sheer iterative power of generate-and-test procedures, C Broader access to information bearing on design and D Improvement in domain knowledge via research and performance simulation

A

B

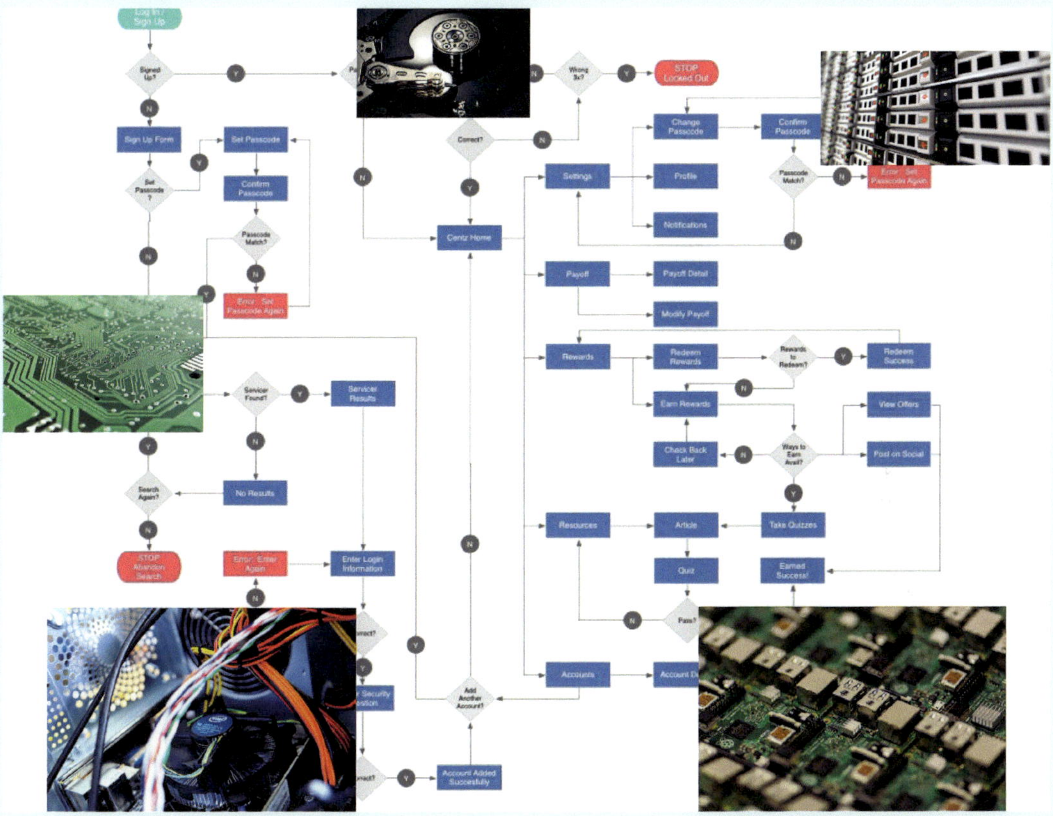


C

D

CHAPTER 6

# Scenes and Storytelling

Finally, this chapter will attempt to synthesize various aspects of 'design thinking and storytelling' in architecture, based on preceding chapter discussions of the mechanisms and subjects, so to speak, of design thinking, especially in architecture, including knowledge bases, schemata and situational mental spaces and frames. It will also start by acknowledging that design thinking is concerned with what should be in the world rather than the way that the world is. Second, the orientation of design thinking may be towards the present-future or towards the present-past as well as in between. Third and in line with creating what should be, the outcomes of design thinking should be broadly valuable in topical focus and, for instance, about sustainable environments in the Anthropocene, the availability of social justice and the perpetuation of cultural preservation. Fourth, specific instances of design thinking revolve around 'scenes' and the 'stories' associated with those scenes. As noted earlier, a scene might be a situation or commonly occurring circumstance, like an issue of business advancement or, more specifically in architecture, one of creating a culturally identifiable building or urban complex. Of course, storytelling is a social and cultural activity of very long standing. In addition to traditional forms, such as folk tales, legends, myths and so on, storytelling has represented history, evolving cultural norms and educational experiences. It is also often involved in the passing on of values and can be regarded as an aesthetic enterprise and one that proposes alternative futures (Cassirer, 1953; Cassirer, 1965 and Bruner, 1986).

## Narrative Qualities

A narrative is a form of storytelling that allows one to come face-to-face with situations. With roots in the Latin verb *narrare*, narrative is the organization of real and fictional events into a sequence revealed through the telling of the narrative. As such it also can and does involve rhetoric, with figures of speech or similar, like metaphors, tropes, allegories and so on. Aristotle's *Rhetoric* is an ancient Greek treatise on the art of persuasion dating from the 4th century BCE (Bizzell and Herzberg, 2001). Generally, three modes existed. They are 'pathos' and appealing to an audience's empathy, 'logos' and an appeal to the logic of arguments being advanced, and 'ethos' resting on the sheer credibility of the narrator. In writing about 'narrative architecture', Nigel Coates (1949– ), a British architect and academic, was pointing to an architecture that went beyond the more usual modernist context-use-narrative triumvirate, or response to utility, as well as simply being stylistically distinctive. He was seeking to describe, in short, a mental space where architects need to understand how people interact and know their environments. He also saw narrative as a category of rhetoric and also with the necessary persuasive aspect of Aristotle. However, unlike most other forms of narrative its linearity dissolves in architecture as the spatial dimension dominates. It has a connotative, or associative quality that is not denotative. Coates even goes so far as to map out a method of three distinct kinds of narrative architecture. They are binary narratives involving a parallel identity beyond function, a sequence narrative derived largely from the laying out of spaces from one situation to another, and biotypic narratives involving relatively small environments occupied by communities of organisms in a mutually beneficial microworld (Coates, 2012). Similarly, in a study by the Gensler office, storytelling and narratives in architecture was discussed in some detail. Firstly, the basic themes were identified, including the characters to be involved as users and visitors, followed by the image or physical appearance of the building, then the backstory of the project about its location, context and relevant history and then on to the theme, or underlying principles to be involved. The study then goes on to show why so-called 'McBuildings' fail as simply bad or as 'one-liners', followed by an exhaustive set of steps around how architects, ideally, should create narratives (Studio Guide, 2023).

## The Quality of Design Thinking

Returning to several points made in chapter 5 regarding the quality of design thinking and storytelling in architecture and even how it might be assessed, it needs to be regarded both as a process and in terms of the success and quality of its outcomes. First, in the former regard, it should be efficient as a problem-solving undertaking. Most probably this will involve allowing problem spaces in the context of the Information Theory of Problem Solving, for instance, to be concise with little to no backtracking. It may also involve the deployment of specific procedures to enhance the overall process including techniques such as parametric design. Second, there must be the necessary and sufficient degrees of incompleteness and precision, again returning to chapter 5, for creating a rich array of pathways towards outcomes. In essence, this involves the rewriting, as it were, of the problem as given in a useful and reflective manner. Here at least two approaches appear possible. The first and not uncommon one involves identifying and deploying specific building technologies and materials in a design-compatible manner. The second involves more purely the precise spatiality of constructed environments, beyond location and site, as well as other approaches in between. Third, there is the need for a capacity to truly evaluate and assess outcomes and in so doing use well-known analytical techniques to do so. This need for performance-based as well as propositional assessment of design, places emphasis on knowledge bases and categories discussed in chapter 4, as well as adequate methodological and often empirically based procedures.

## 1 – A SCHEMATIC ILLUSTRATION OF DAILY LIFE IN 'PARIS 15-MINUTE CITY'

1. Parking space transformed into terraces and gardens
2. A peaceful street for pedestrians and bicycles
3. A garden below your home
4. Safe routes for children
5. Increased local services

Data does matter. Fourth and finally, there should be a maintenance of a strong focus on the thingness of the work in hand, in a Heideggerian sense, and also beyond mere utility and style. Finally, the story being told must be compelling.

# Some Cases of Design Thinking

What follows are several cases of design thinking in architecture which illustrate these qualities. Moreover, they are drawn from a contemporary topical array of storylines that are seemingly fashionable today if nothing else. The first involves sustainability in the Anthropocene and two projects aimed squarely at metabolic improvements of built form. The second deals with an issue of social justice and relief from homelessness in a large American city. The third is a tale about geometry and the figure and form of architecture, while the fourth concerns traditional artisanal architecture as a manner of making and knowing how.

## Tales About Sustainability

As early as 2001, Bertrand Delanoë, the Mayor of Paris, France, initiated many social and environmental reforms, later to be taken up by Anne Hidalgo who succeeded him into what became known as the '15-Minute City'. First coined by La Sorbonne Business Professor Carlos Moreno, this concept challenged the dominance of private cars in cities, promoted bicycling and resident-focused development, along with proximity, daily and seasonal life that would be located close-by and no more than 15 minutes away (Gongadze and Maassen, 2023). Figure 1 gives some semblance of what a major street in Paris might look like, including scenes of people working, recreating and just going about their daily activities. During this period the Clichy Batignolles ZAC (Zone d'aménagement concerté), also known as the Clichy Batignolles Eco-Quartier, was conceptualized, with work beginning in 2002. It is comprised of 54 hectares of what was once an SNCF railroad yard also near the Périphérique highway surrounding Paris and to the north. Intentionally and tellingly from a social point of view, the site is more or less on the border between the old Haussmann Paris and the peripheral *banlieue*. The project was built to give a glimpse of the low-carbon future that so many climate plans envision, including those in France. As shown in figure 2 in a plan coordinated by François Grether, it was also comprised of a 10-hectare Martin Luther King Park designed by Jacqueline Osty, which also marks the old 19th century gate to the commune of Clichy and, of course, the leader of the American civil rights movement. The overall plan accommodates 3,400 residences,

2 – CLICHY-BATIGNOLLES ZAC, 2002, 17TH ARRONDISSEMENT, PARIS, FRANCE
A Site before the development of the ZAC,
B Site after the development of the ZAC, C Site plan coordinated
by François Grether and D Views of buildings within the ZAC

A

B

C

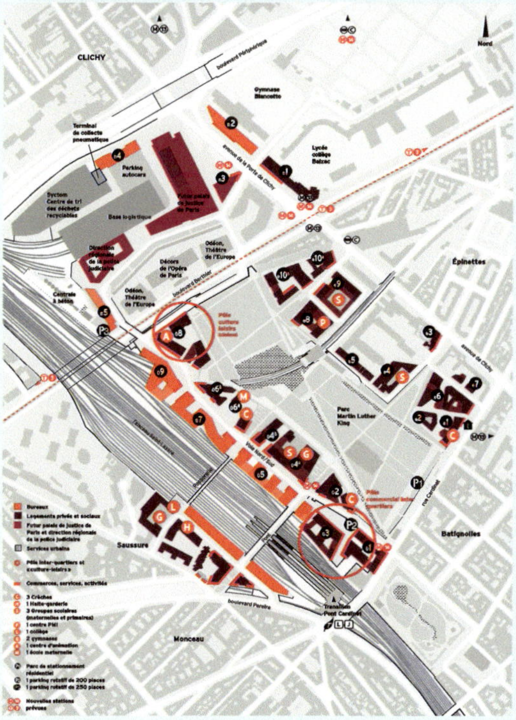


D

140,000 square meters of offices, 31,000 square meters of commercial space and 38,000 square meters of public facilities. In addition, the Court Building of Paris by Renzo Piano is also located on the northern side of the complex and is made up of some 120,000 square meters of space (Julien, 2016 and Shmurak, 2018). The scene as depicted in figure 3 and suggested by figure 1 is of a mixed-use, socially diverse, biodiverse, environmentally responsive community working towards carbon neutrality and built around an extensive park that also supports the community's environmental and social agenda, and thus, so to speak, the design was executed.

The Clichy Batignolles ZAC uses several technological strategies for achieving its environmental objectives, several of which are illustrated in figure 4 and, therefore, the story's emphasis focuses on their application. Most of the heating is provided through a project-wide geothermal system which, in turn, reduces the amount of carbon released into the atmosphere. Some 35,000 square meters of solar photovoltaic panels affixed to buildings also offset off-site energy use substantially. In addition, greening of buildings acts as insulation as well as hosting higher biodiversity within the community. Vacuum tubes convey waste from buildings to a site within the project where it is compacted, thus reducing the volume needed to be transported off site as well as concomitant carbon emissions from heavy trucks. The Martin Luther King Park is replete with stormwater capture and management amid ponds, canals and other water conveyances. Biodiversity is enhanced through the rich array of planting in the park, as well as from various intermediate scales of vegetated open space within the community. The mixing of uses is also promoted, particularly within the vertical sections of taller buildings, and housing has been expressly made available to students and lower-income residents, alongside market-rate dwellings. Collectively working towards carbon neutrality and biodiversity is clearly being recognized within the community. Sensors and other devices are distributed in order to register progress in these directions encouraging residents and workers to become engaged in efforts of this type.

Using a stock flow model the material, water and energy flows associated with the constructed environment of the ZAC can be identified, originating in the natural sources of the geosphere, biosphere and hydrosphere and then constituting a metabolic picture of the community's physical environment (Wolman, 1965 and Bacini and Brunner, 2012). These flows, in metric tons per year or appropriate equivalent, are then traced forward through production of materials like limestone, cement, steel timber products, and so on. From these estimates, using mostly local available data, flows associated with buildings and other aspects of constructed environments can be made, leading on finally to waste production and management. Representation of these flows can be readily made in the form of Sankey diagrams, where the width of a flow depicts its equivalent relative volume of material, water or energy (Schmidt, 2008). As shown in figure 4, the material flows for the Clichy Batignolles ZAC were estimated to be 1,023,477 metric tons per year. Of this most came from the geosphere (74 percent) followed by the hydrosphere (17 percent)

# 3 – SOME ECOLOGICAL MANAGEMENT COMPONENTS OF THE CLICHY-BATIGNOLLES ZAC, 2002, FRANÇOIS GRETHER, 17TH ARRONDISSEMENT, PARIS, FRANCE

A Geothermal heating and solar panels, B Waste management and compaction to reduce truck loads, C Vertical mixing of uses, D Components of increased biodiversity and living with nature and E Another component of biodiversity at a smaller urban scale

A

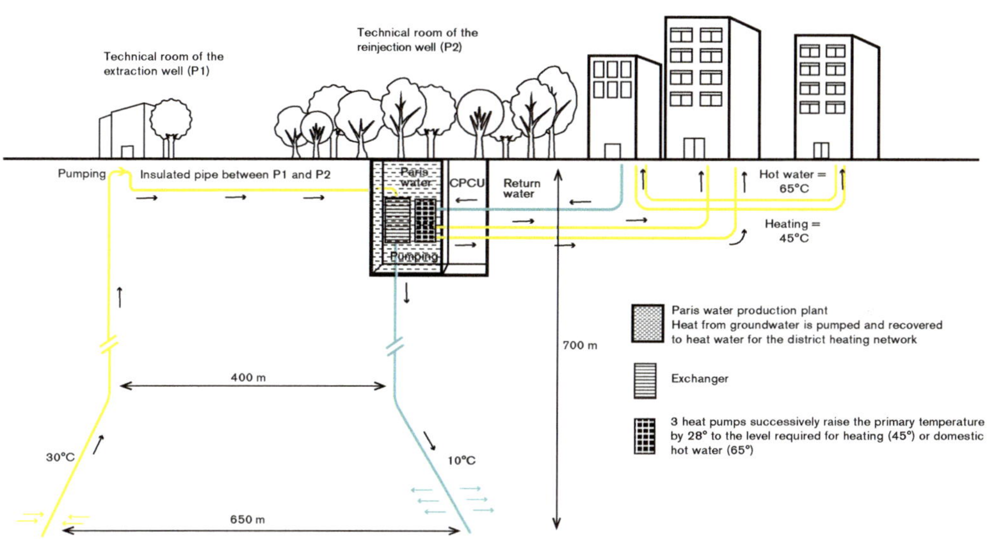


B

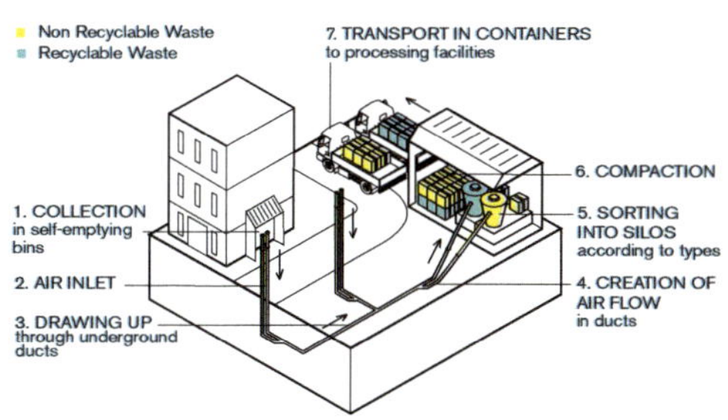


C

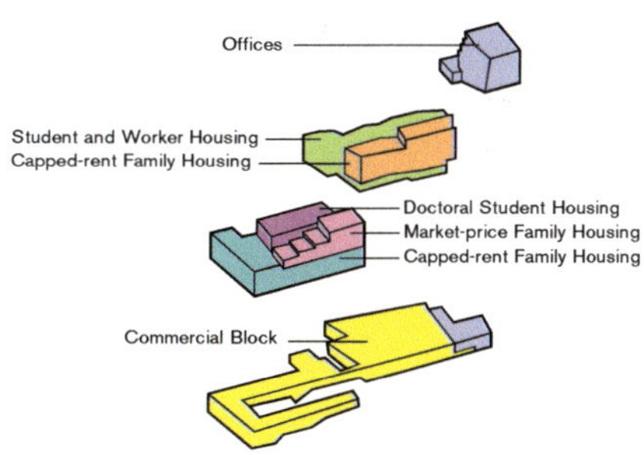


D

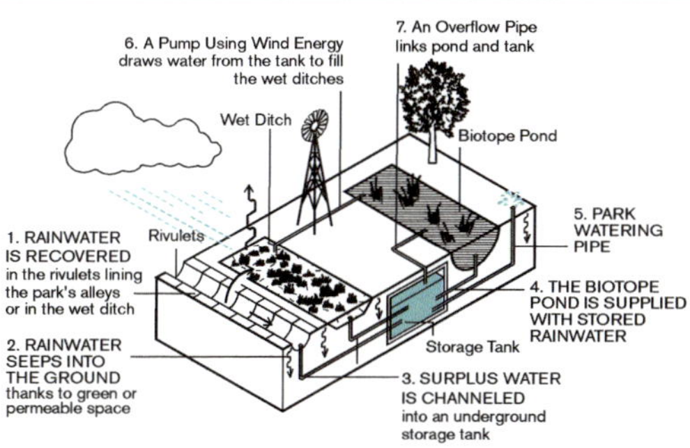


E

# 4 – SANKEY DIAGRAMS OF THE CLICHY-BATIGNOLLES ZAC, 17TH ARRONDISSEMENT, PARIS, FRANCE

Ⓐ Material flows, Ⓑ Water flows and Ⓒ Energy flows

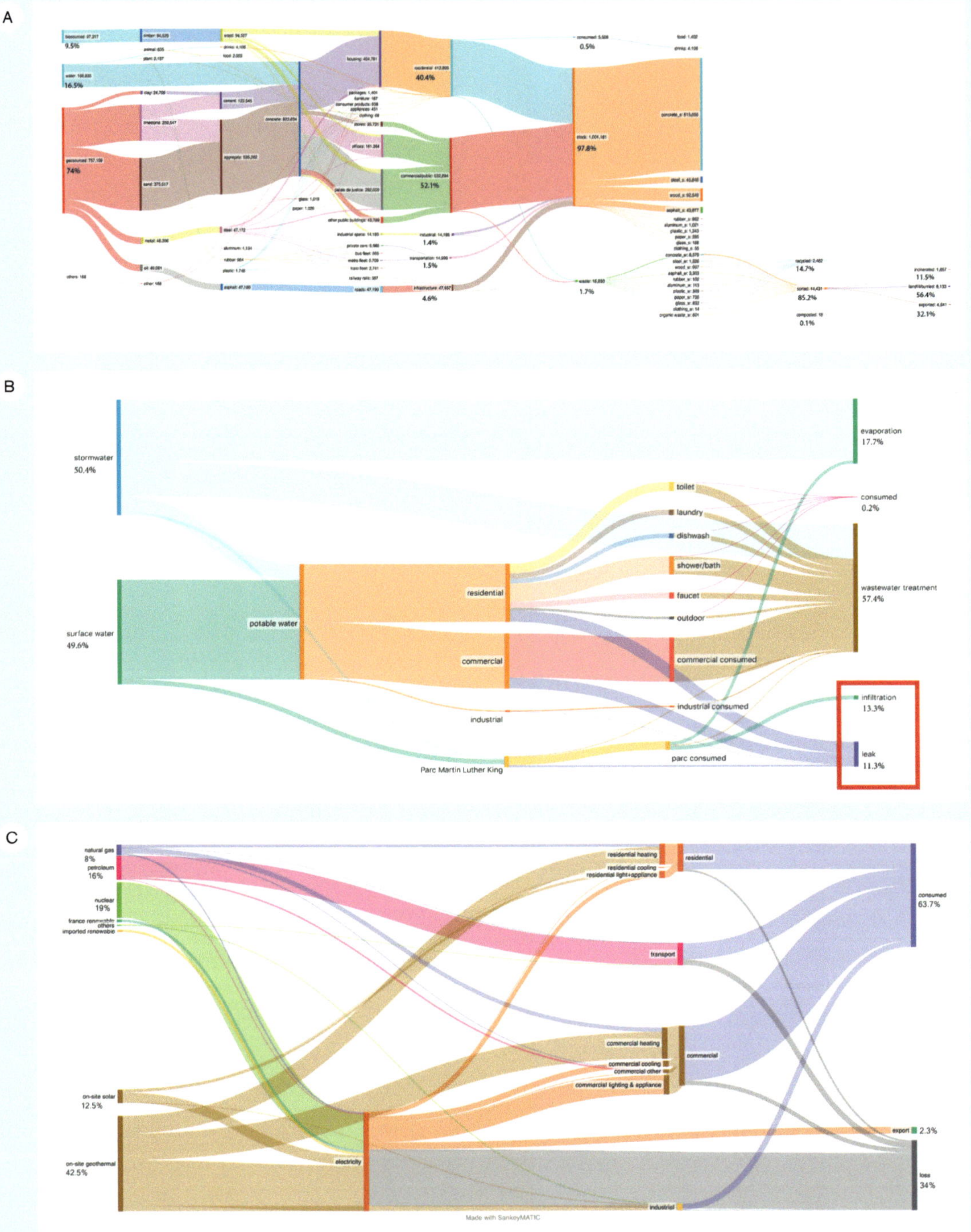

# 5 – SANKEY DIAGRAM OF MATERIAL FLOWS FOR THE DEDHAM, WESTWOOD AND NORWOOD ZONE

on the periphery of the Boston Metropolitan Area, Massachusetts, USA

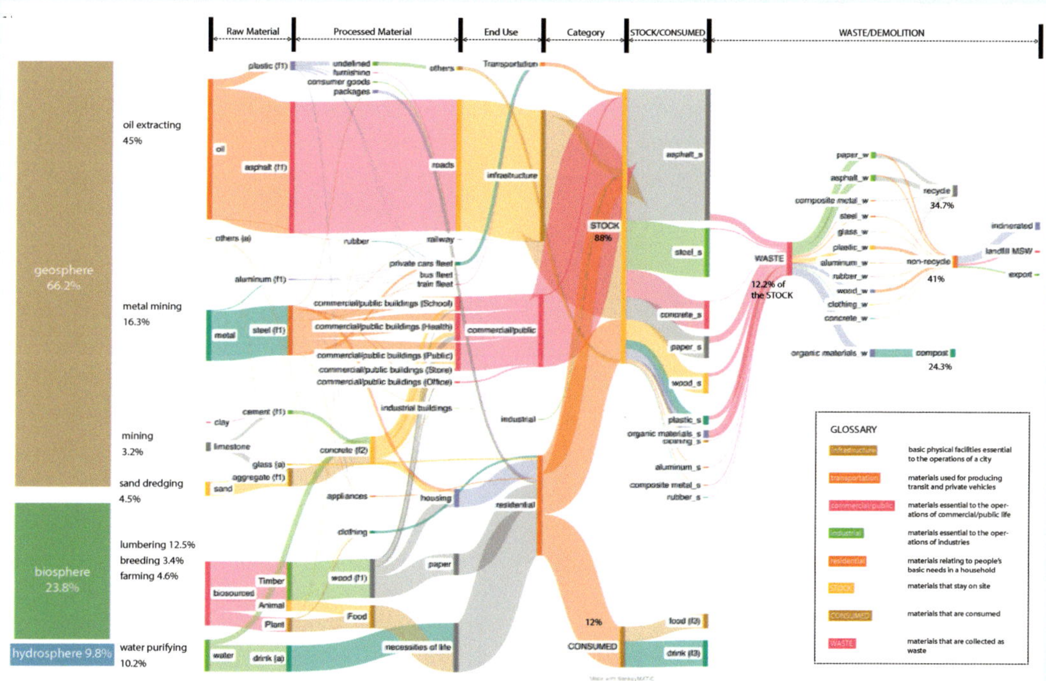

and a further 9 percent from the biosphere. With regard to project end uses 52 percent was for commercial and public facilities, 40 percent for residential use and only around 6 percent in transportation and infrastructure. Remember that one of the chief aims of this story was the reduction of the presence of motor vehicles. The level of waste was also comparatively low at less than 2 percent of overall flow and of which 15 percent was recycled. With regard to water flow, again as depicted in figure 4, about half was drawn from stormwater management and the other half from surface sources. Not surprisingly, most was used for residential purposes, with some 17 percent lost to evaporation and 11 percent to leakage. Performance in the critical area vis-à-vis carbon or energy use was encouraging, with fully 52 percent coming from on-site geothermal and solar sources, again as shown in figure 4, with only 24 percent from non-renewable fossil fuel sources. Again, consumption more or less mirrored the relative proportions of use and was, therefore, accessible to the intended collective mitigation efforts. Overall, the story about sustainability at Clichy Batignolles in Paris was heartening, as well as pointing the way for other similar undertakings. If nothing else it stresses the need for multiple strategies, each to some extent involving a design orientation alongside technological compliance. Returning to the problem space involved, it quickly boiled down to mental spaces, frames and networks focused on how to fit otherwise technological approaches into building and urban design outcomes.

A case in a very different domain of settlement co-existence can be found in the American-style automobile suburb, such in the Boston metropolitan area within Dedham, Westwood and Norwood located on Route 128, encircling the periphery of the city and built as a part of the Federal Government Highway Program initiated during World War II (Rowe, 1992). Here the story begins with the observation, from figure 5, that fully 42 or so percent of the material flow of the constructed environment is roadway and paving. In relative terms that is undeniably high, particularly when compared to other more compact domains of settlement coexistence, like Clichy Batignolles in Paris. This scale can also be put down, at least partially, to the wastefulness of relatively low-density yet accessible residential development, no longer completely functional commercial activity and parking requirements most easily affordable at grade, alongside of massive highway and intersection construction within the Dedham, Westwood and Norwood communities. Also striking are the material flows in the amount of daily consumption and waste production, most of which is not recycled (Rowe and Guo, 2023). Another feature of the site area is the presence of natural forest and ecological preserves associated with the Neponset watershed and the patchwork character of intervening settlement areas shown in figure 6. From a contemporary perspective these naturalistic elements seem to be in danger but also offer approaches to appropriately intervene and change the general landscape towards one where paving is actively diminished in favor of strongly landscaped corridors or even shifts towards agricultural production and something of a return of the landscape to its former use (Kain and Allison, 1986 and Friedman, 2007). This challenge was taken up poetically and practically as depicted in figure 7.

Initially a scene was emblematically associated with an ecological mend for the edges of existing suburbia by way of what were termed 'green stitches' and 'gray needles'. Placement of both resulted in a selective design intervention involving dense greenways and water courses running downhill from the typical suburban single-family housing lots towards the Neponset River corridor below. In addition, structured car parking was proposed but also in an architectural manner that called attention to the location of these structures across the site and thus further signaled the diminution of paved areas for private vehicle use through prominent collectivized programs. Overall, though, the telling of this story was less about diversification and placement of technologies towards advancing sustainability as it was urban design harnessing an alternative emphasis on ecological landscapes and a certain reliance on poetry rather than utility.

## Tales About the Relief of Homelessness

The City and County of Los Angeles in the United States are experiencing significant problems of homelessness, particularly with populations suffering from mental health conditions and substance abuse. In fact, they are among the highest numbers and rates in the USA. In Los Angeles County, homelessness in 2022 was estimated to include some 69,144 people, while in the City of Los Angeles about 41,900 people experienced homelessness, all according to the Los Angeles Homeless Service Authority. Roughly speaking, this is 17 percent or so more people living in tents, vehicles and makeshift structures than a couple of years ago (Homeless Initiative, 2022 and Levin, 2022). Though around only about 1 percent of the total population, these numbers and rates are higher than in other large US cities. In 2022, the amount in the City of Los Angeles was 1.1 percent and in the County of Los Angeles 0.7 percent. This County figure is higher than in San Francisco, for instance, at 0.9 percent of total population and significantly higher than Boston in the US Northeast at 0.2 percent. These data also take into account that during the pandemic that began in 2019, Federal assistance and local aid policies actually kept more people in their homes, relatively speaking. Nowadays, generally relief from homelessness comes in at least two basic forms. The first is through long-term assistance that provides more or less permanent supportive housing paid by participants with a housing subsidy with case management and supportive services. It has proven to be a relatively successful approach. The second is transitional assistance in order to help stabilize people with mental health issues and substance abuse. These approaches are both different from emergency shelters that are mostly very short-term and crisis-oriented. Usually, transitional housing can last for six months to three years and requires a signed lease, sublease or occupancy agreement (SAMSHA, 2023). Each of the two projects described and discussed here applies to either long-term assistance in the case of the Star Apartments in Los Angeles' Skid Row, 2014, by Michael Maltzan, or to transitional and supportive housing at Vignes Village, also in Los Angeles, 2021, by Carlos Arnaiz, the principal of CAZA in New York and introduced earlier in chapter 2. Both projects deploy significant components

## 6 – GENERAL ENVIRONS OF DEDHAM, WESTWOOD AND NORWOOD ON THE PERIPHERY OF THE BOSTON METROPOLITAN AREA

A The Neponset Watershed and ecological preserves and B An aerial view of existing land uses

A

B

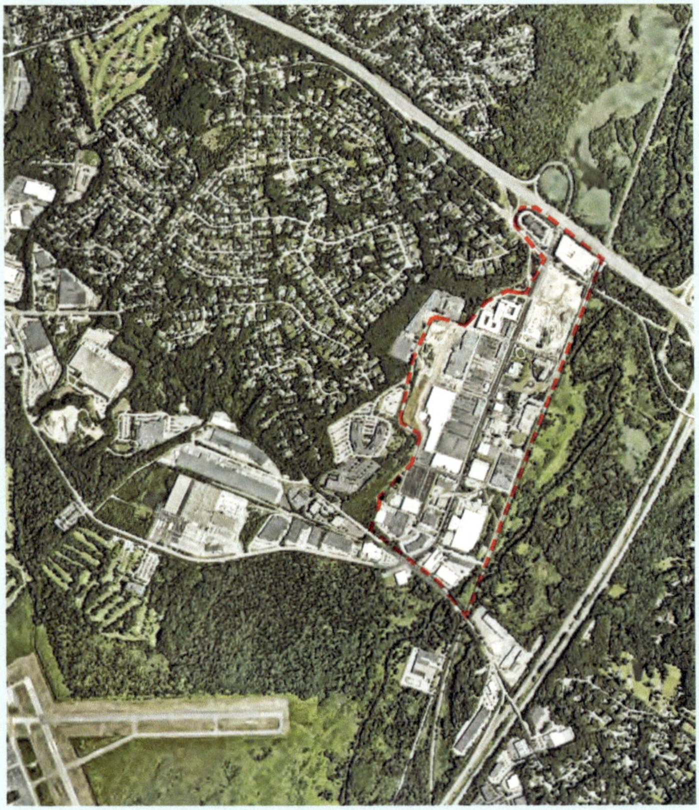

7 – 'GREEN STITCHES' AND 'GRAY NEEDLES' – A PROPOSAL FOR THE NORWOOD SITE by Ben Parker and Priyanka Kar, 2023

A The concept of 'green stitches', B The concept of 'gray needles', C Site environs and D Axonometric of proposed design intervention

A

B

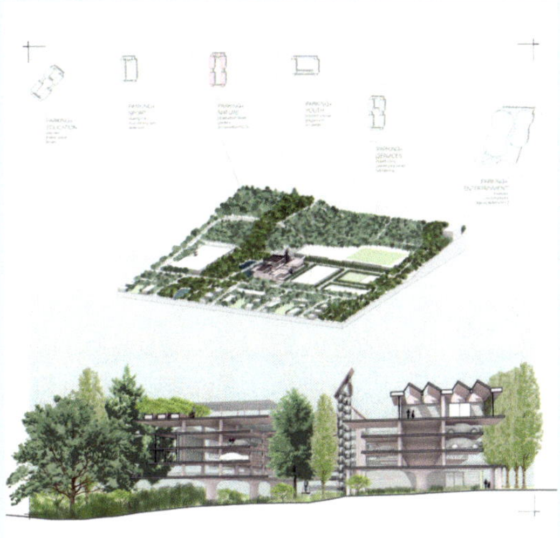

C

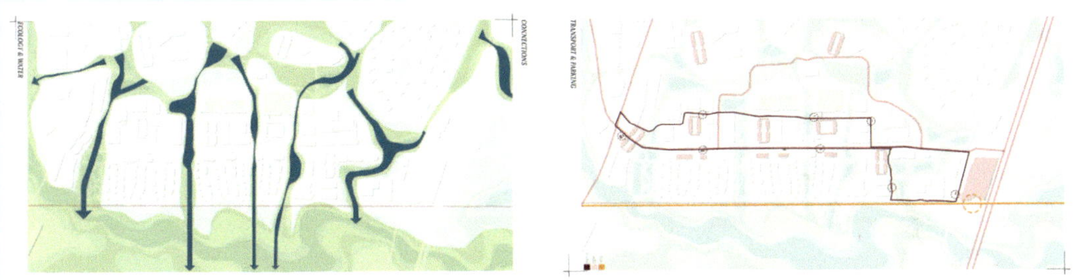

D

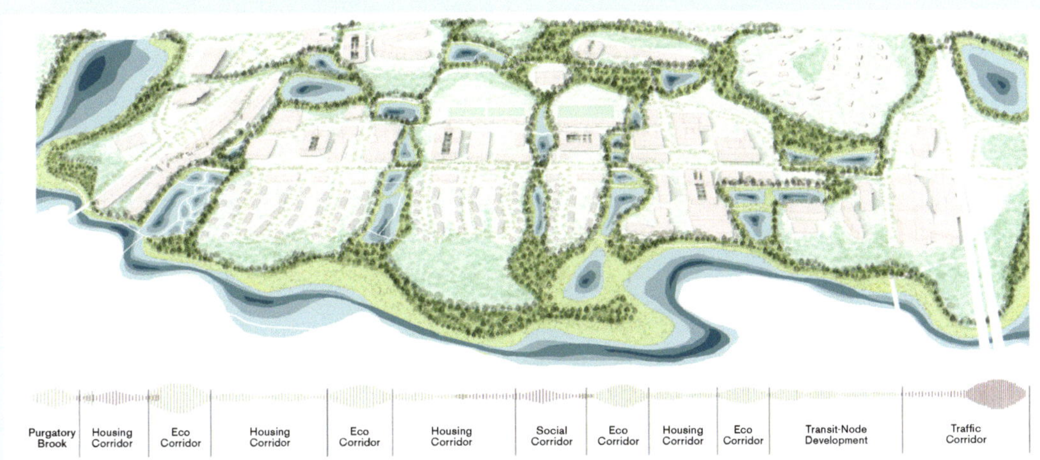

of prefabricated housing produced by the same company, Guerdon Enterprises in Boise, Idaho. Vignes Village is close to the Los Angeles River, a broad area of considerable homeless housing encampments, that accounts for approximately 22 percent of the United States' homeless population (Foster, 2021 and Garcia, 2023).

Michael Maltzan (1959– ) is an American architect and principal of the firm Michael Maltzan Architects which he founded in 1995 after moving to Los Angeles in 1988 to work in Frank Gehry's office. The Star Apartments of 2014 are one of at least six housing projects, including several others for the Skid Row Housing Trust, under its stated mission to provide permanent supportive housing so that people who have experienced homelessness, prolonged extreme poverty, poor health, disabilities, mental illness and/or other addictions can lead stable lives in wellness (Skid Row Housing Trust, 2023). The Star Apartments are located on East 6th Street near downtown Los Angeles and also house facilities for the Los Angeles County Department of Health, among its resident support amenities. The complex occupies almost a full city block and is comprised of 102 dwelling units with an average size of 35 square meters. It is six stories tall and incorporates about 8,000 square meters of occupied space. This space, in turn, is divided into three components. The first, at ground level, is the existing commercial uses on the site, which were stripped back to form a podium for the rest of the building. Then there are the housing units above, with the gap between consisting of a horizontal community space. This was made up of a community kitchen, art rooms, a library, recreation facilities and health and wellness resources. As shown in figure 8, the dwellings themselves are grouped into boxy ensembles with open patios between them. They are all made from prefabricated units, the first of their kind in Los Angeles. Fabricated in Boise, Idaho, the pre-made units were craned into place on site, using the lower levels as building infrastructure. The advantages of the use of prefabricated units were severalfold. First, there was insufficient room on site to adequately stage regular construction. Second, prefabrication speeded up the construction phase with some associated cost savings. Third, the factory-built units offered relatively uniform high quality of workmanship and energy-saving tight envelopes, alongside ready inclusion of energy-efficient appliances and far less on-site construction waste requiring removal. Writing later about the Star Apartments among other projects, Maltzan argued strongly for the need for 'social transparency' by which he seems to have meant primarily making a city's different populations visible and of which the occupants of the Skid Row housing are certainly one. He also went further to make the point that the architecture of housing was a powerful way of representing the city itself (Maltzan, 2016). In these regards, knowingly or not, he was certainly harkening back to an architecture beyond simply both utility and stylistic distinction discussed earlier.

Before going into the details of the Vignes Village project, it should be noted that procedurally it involved at least two architectural efforts, including the use of shipping containers on the part of NAC Architecture, Los Angeles, and the pairing of a prefabrication with a proprietary parametric model to optimize unit layouts, known

8 – THE STAR APARTMENTS

by Michael Maltzan Architects, 2014, on Skid Row, Los Angeles, California, USA
A The project in situ, B Street-level view of the project, C The horizontal level of community facilities within the project and D A sectional model of the project showing infrastructural support elements

A

B

C

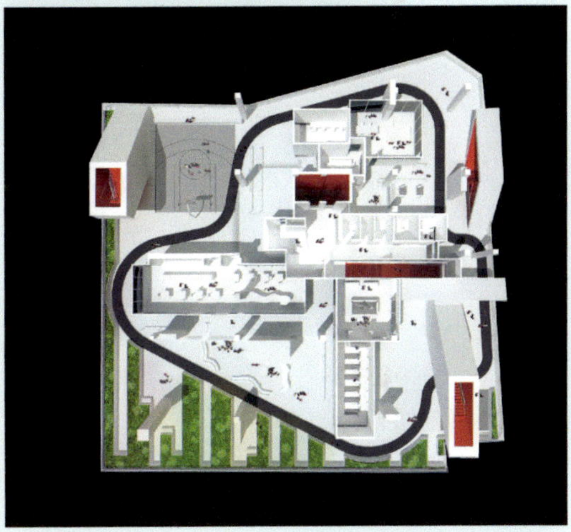

D

9 – ASPECTS OF THE MODUFY PARAMETRIC MODEL DEVISED by CAZA in New York A Underlying decision tree and flow chart, B Grasshopper script overview, C Software integration into AI model and D Volumetric permutations of the model

A

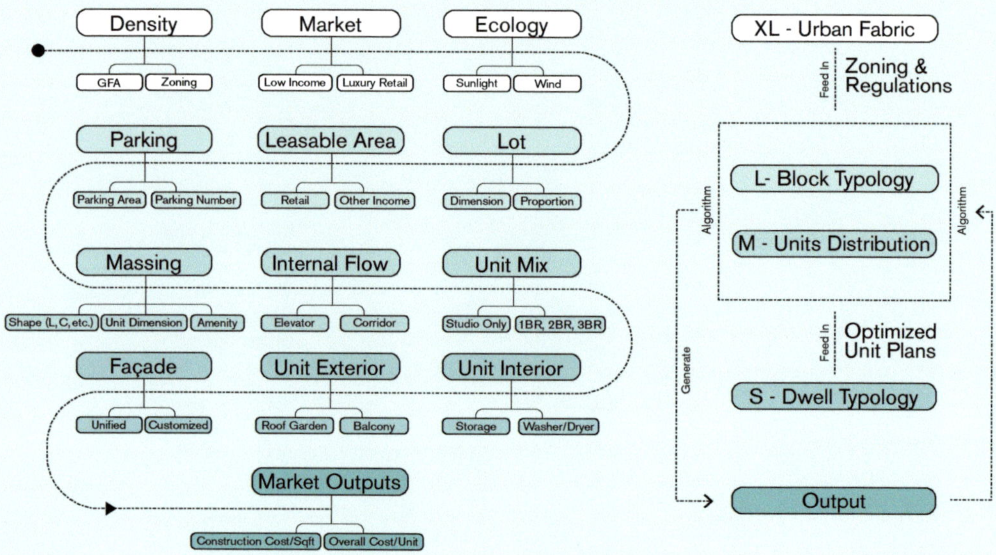


B

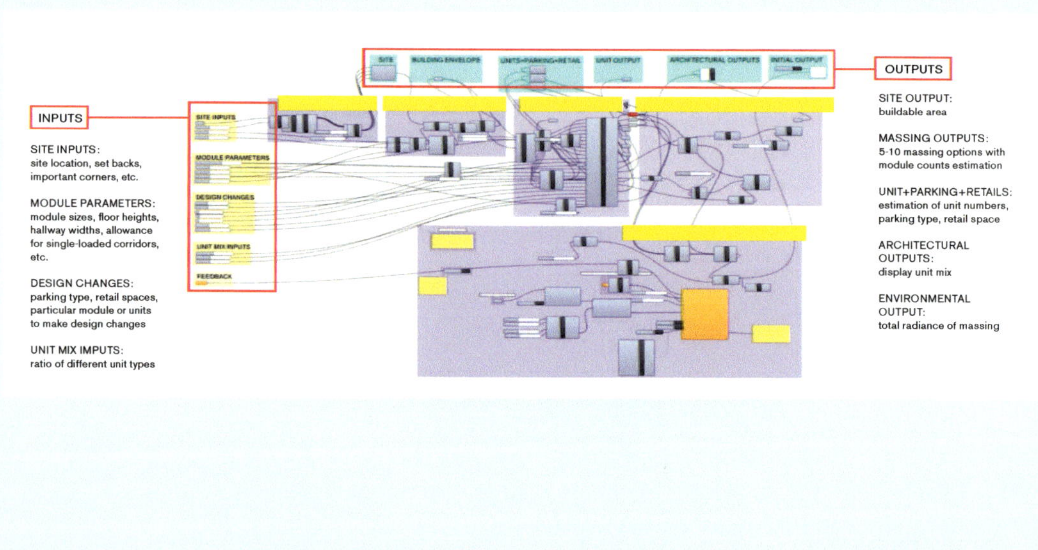

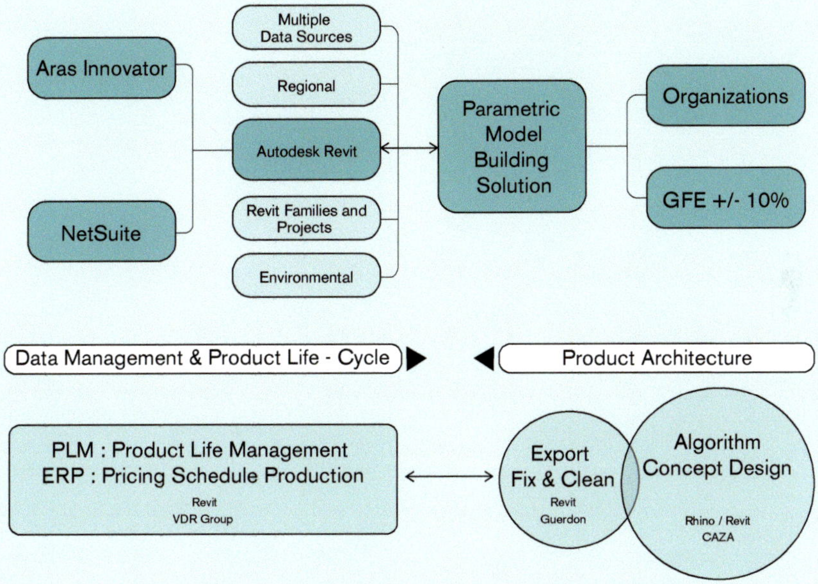
Aras Innovator
NetSuite
Multiple Data Sources
Regional
Autodesk Revit
Revit Families and Projects
Environmental
Parametric Model Building Solution
Organizations
GFE +/- 10%
Data Management & Product Life - Cycle
Product Architecture
PLM : Product Life Management
ERP : Pricing Schedule Production
Revit
VDR Group
Export
Fix & Clean
Revit
Guerdon
Algorithm
Concept Design
Rhino / Revit
CAZA

C

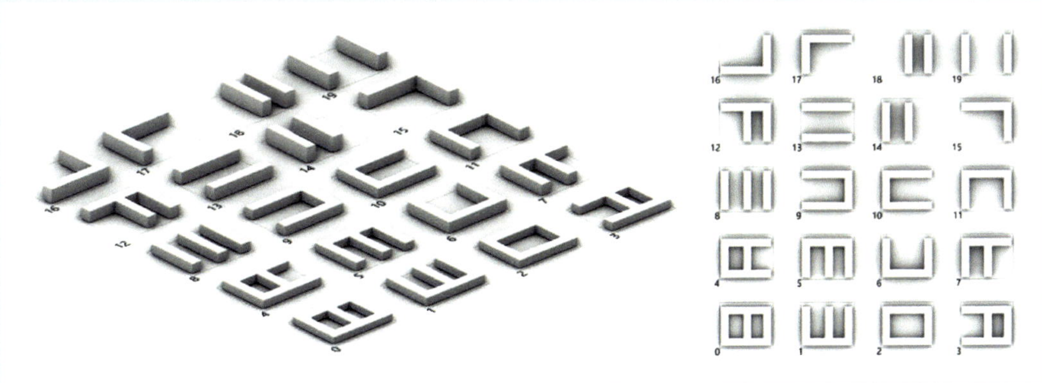

D

10 – RECREATIONAL HOUSING PROJECT by CAZA, 2022, in Steamboat Springs, Colorado, USA (A) General site and location, (B) Site and its immediate urban context, (C) Parameters of sun and wind and (D) Optimized mix of housing units using the Modufy parametric model

A

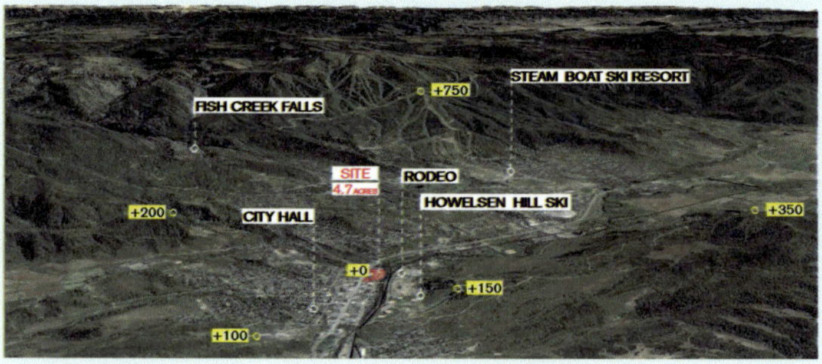


B

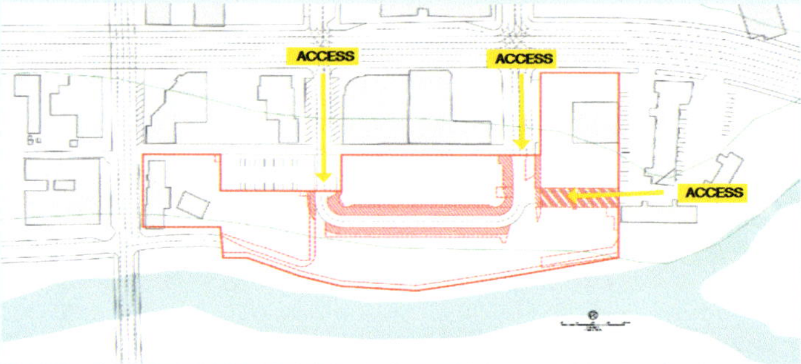


C

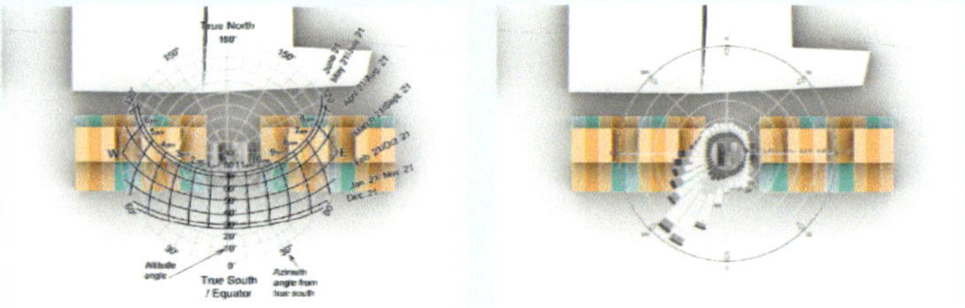


D

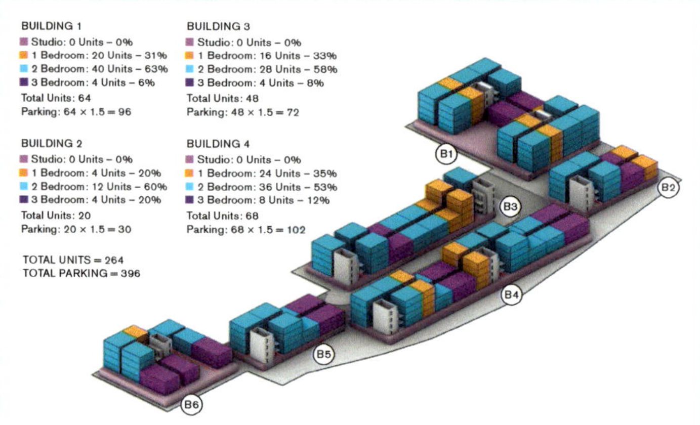

as 'Modufy' devised by CAZA Architects. This latter model development came on the heels of some earlier work with Guerdon Enterprises in Boise, Idaho, concerned with prefabricated ADUs or 'auxiliary dwelling units' and has been deployed in several different kinds of housing circumstances, including transitional housing. Some basic aspects of algorithmic development are shown in figure 9. Indeed, Modufy has now become a separate corporate entity using artificial intelligence together with modular design and building prefabrication to help deliver housing projects at a variety of scales. At the core of Modufy's approach is parametric Grasshopper scripted coding that allows modules, according to prefabrication specifications, to be combined as dwelling units and for various other code requirements, like access, vertical rise and solar orientations to also be incorporated. By altering different parameters, optimization occurs based on mixes of dwelling unit types. Figure 10 shows a typical sequence of spatial layouts, in this case for a recreational housing project in Steamboat Springs, Colorado, of 2022. The Vignes Village site consists of two projects, side-by-side on an irregularly shaped lot in downtown Los Angeles. The first is the Hilda I. Solis Care First Village, named for the Chair of the Los Angeles Board of Supervisors and designed by NAC Architecture, Los Angeles, under the direction of Michael Pinto and Bernards, a building construction and management company. The second is the accompanying wooden prefabricated units and community and administrative building by Modufy with CAZA as architects. The first phase Solis facility is located on the Alhambra-Vignes upper corner of the site, as shown in figure 11. This project is comprised of essentially two roughly parallel bars of dwellings made of three stories of stacked shipping containers containing some 232 dwelling units and with access via open corridors and stairs as shown in figure 13. Both blocks have ADA-compliant units as well as standard units. No attempt has been made to disguise the shipping containers. Indeed, they are brightly painted in yellow and orange bringing a colorful liveliness to the project. Each container contains two units with 12.5 square meters each of available space. Each is also well equipped with a bed, microwave, mini-fridge, flat screen television, as well as a private bathroom. All are separately ventilated and heated and cooled (Sharp, 2021 and McKnight, 2021). Areas between the buildings are well landscaped, including outdoor seating and spaces for pets that might accompany residents. Separated by a fire access road as shown again in figure 11 is the Modufy project at the corner of Vignes and the railroad tracks. This is comprised of four bars of dwelling units more or less lined up in parallel and essentially in two forms of sleeper modules, as depicted in figure 12. They are made of Guerdon prefabricated units, providing on the order of 300 beds in somewhat more commodious accommodation, again with private bathrooms and ADA-compliant as well as standard units. An administration and community building is located adjacent to the dwellings comprised of nine Guerdon prefabricated units covering about 630 square meters. Within the facility there is a laundry, a dining hall, an adjacent preparation kitchen, a laundry and offices for staff and service workers, also as illustrated in figure 12. Praised for the efficiency and relative low cost of construction, these approaches to homeless housing seem likely to be repeated in Los Angeles and the West Coast (Smith, 2021).

This likelihood has also led, as it might, to a repeatable modular way of thinking about transitional housing provision to further design speculation by the likes of CAZA and Modufy. As shown in figure 12, a prototype on a single acre square site is depicted incorporating much the same assemblage of three story dwellings, a community and administrative center and ample green space and even market gardens for residents. What does seem clear from these stories about homeless housing is that prefabrication and modular units, combined imaginatively with other support facilities embracing a wide range of uses, alongside purposeful green space, offer considerable and useful opportunities to help resolve a serious social problem.

## Tales About Geometry and Work on Language

A fundamental aspect of architecture has been and is the inscriptive practice of drawing as a form of knowledge production. It is the equivalent of an extended discourse in writing although offering its own particular insights into the practical activity of making architecture. Indeed, drawings can be seen as scores to be reenacted, so to speak, and some kinds like axonometric, isometric and parallel projections in general provide readable three-dimensional images that can also be measurable, as illustrated in figure 14. According to some authors these date back as far as the 4th century BCE in the West and are of longstanding as well in East Asia (Scolari, 2012 and Lucas, 2019). Returning to the comments by Hays in chapter 4 concerning the late avant-garde of the 1960s through 1980s, architectural modernism came under severe scrutiny and replacement, particularly in a later manner often described as 'deconstruction' or post-modernism (Papadakis, Cooke and Benjamin, 1989). Writing at the time, one of the luminaries of the movement, Peter Eisenman (1932– ), an American architect, theorist and educator, chided architecture for lagging behind science and philosophy in failing to fully scrutinize and assess the veracity of disciplinary underpinnings, and particularly traditional dialectics like form and function, structure and ornament, and figuration and abstraction (Eisenman, 1989). Accepting these dialectics as a kind of location or *topos*, Eisenman argued for 'atopia' in reaction to them. In his own architecture and especially his house projects of the 1970s, like House VI of 1975, for instance, he incorporated considerable spatial disorientations, such as the glass slot on the outer wall of the bedroom and continuing through the floor more or less forcing sleeping arrangements to be divided. Otherwise, as shown in figure 15, it stood on its wooded site like a piece of abstract contemporary sculpture (Perez, 2010). Also, as illustrated in figure 15, other houses followed as well as institutional complexes like the Wexner Center for the Arts at Ohio State University of 1989, which has been referred to as the "museum that theory built" (Goldberger, 1989). Replete with a strong grid system mimicking the urban grids of Columbus, Ohio, where the complex is located, an axial rotation was introduced into the museum that also creates a spatial tension and interstitial ambiguity in the building (Langdon, 2014).

11 – PLAN OF THE VIGNES VILLAGE SUPPORTIVE HOUSING PROJECT by NAC Architecture and CAZA, 2021–2022, in Downtown Los Angeles, California, USA

## 12 – PREFABRICATED UNITS

at Vignes Village by Modufy and CAZA, 2022, Downtown Angeles, California, USA
A Layout of the sleeper modules, B Layout of the community and administration building and C Typological study of the supportive housing for a square single acre site

A

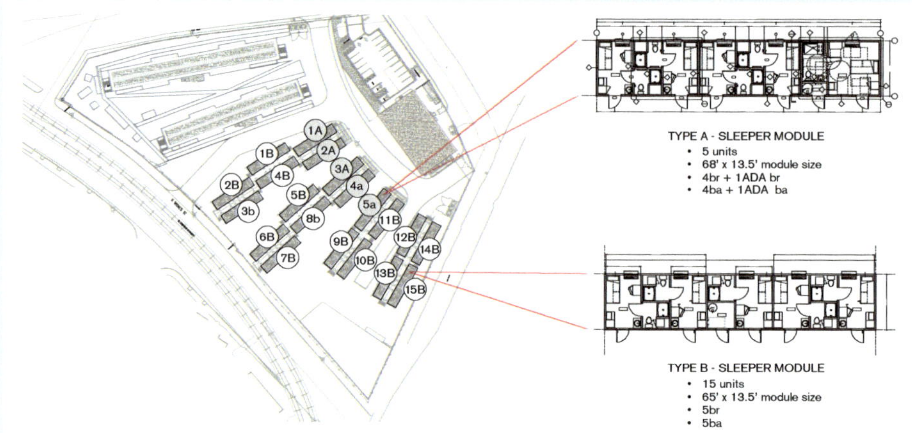


B

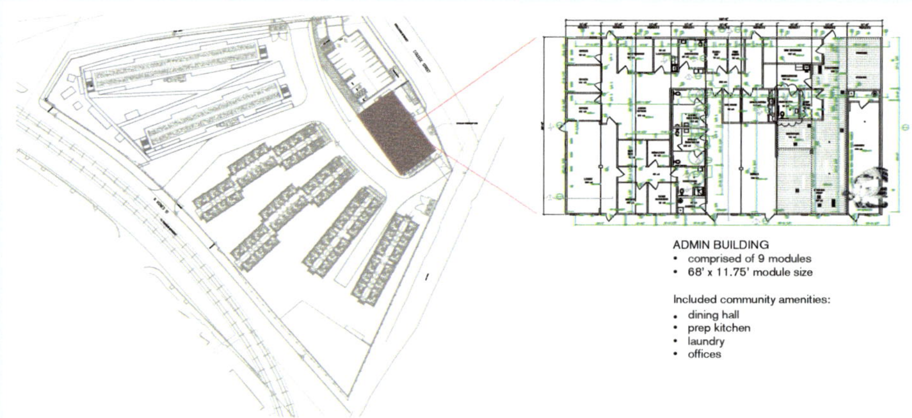


C

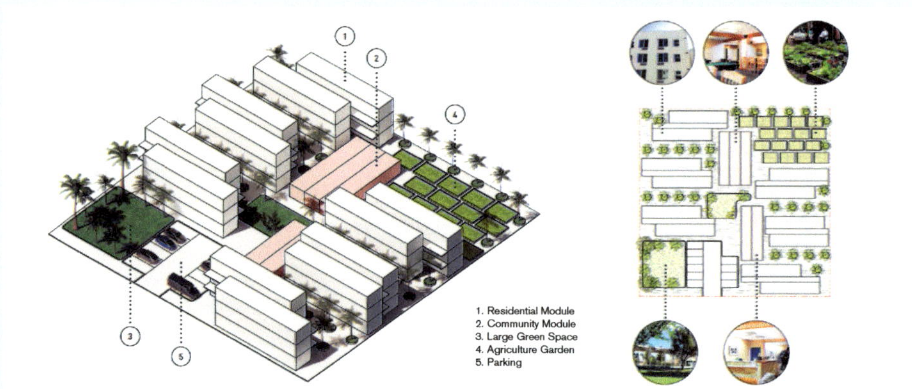

13 – MULTI-LEVEL SUPPORTIVE HOUSING MADE FROM SHIPPING CONTAINERS at Vignes Village by NAC Architecture, 2021, Downtown Los Angeles, California, USA: A Two buildings in situ and B Inner court view including access to stacked containers

A

B

## 14 – FOUR THREE-DIMENSIONAL PROJECTIONS OF A CUBE AND MEASURED AREA

A Axonometric, B Isometric, C Oblique and D Reverse angle axonometric

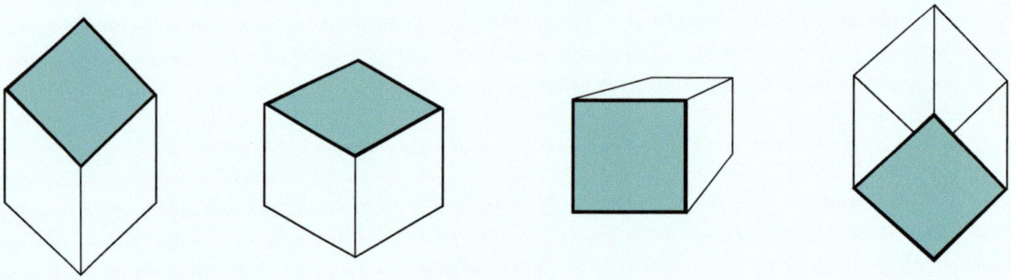

A B C D

## 15 – THREE PROJECTS BY PETER EISENMAN

A House VI of 1965 in Connecticut, USA, B House X of 1975 in Michigan, USA and C The Wexner Center for the Arts at Ohio State University of 1989 in Ohio, USA (axonometric and exterior)

A B C

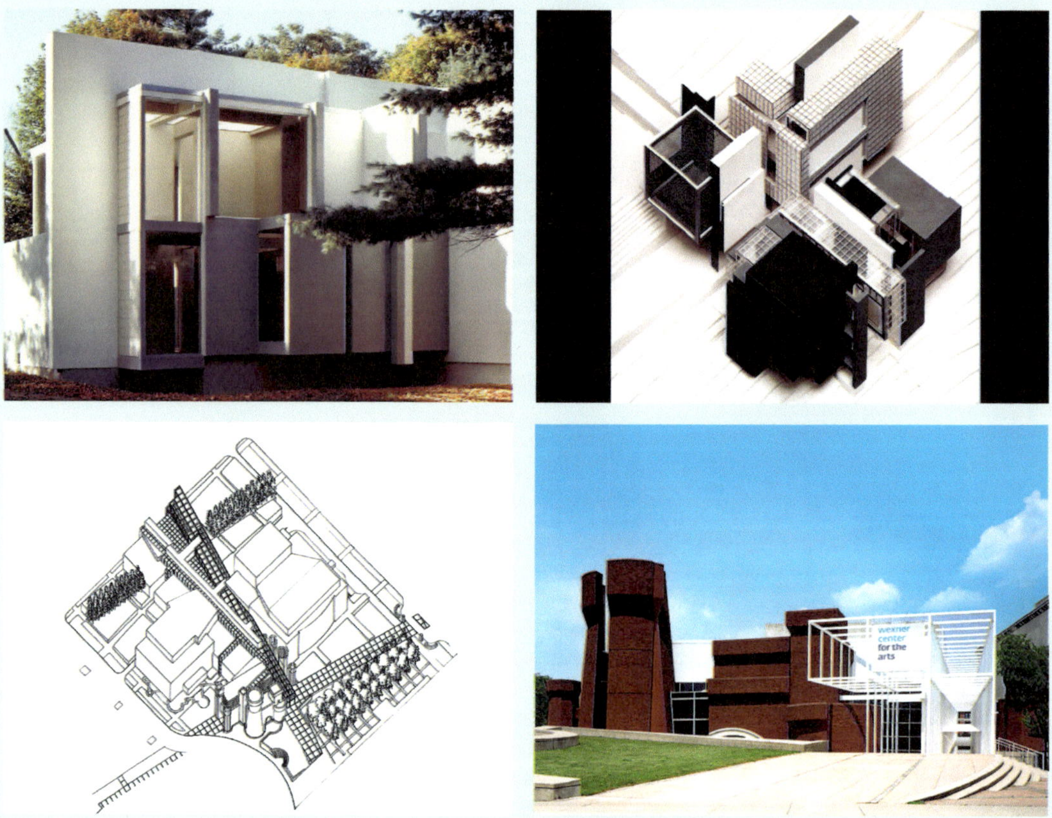

Earlier on, John Hejduk (1924–2000), a Czech-born American architect, theorist and educator, pursued a series of projects around primordial and elemental aspects of architecture, often with little concern for context or program but with emphasis on geometry and architectural language (Hays, 2010 and Lucas, 2019). Like Eisenman, his was a search for a non-referential architectural language. However, unlike Eisenman's contentiousness, Hejduk was oriented toward positive symbolic and narrative potentials (Hays, 2002). In his pursuit of expression rather than form, his work involved the onlooker through an encounter, one during which the gaze of the beholder was returned by the work. Similar to Gilles Deleuze's tensive notion of painting it was an encounter that was both actual and virtual simultaneously, involving both optic and haptic perception and also where the virtual is no less real than the actual (Deleuze, 1981). The arc of Hejduk's work began in the 1950s with the Seven Houses series and exploration of geometric conditions and moving then into tectonic realizations and on into allegorical representations where his architectural elements took on biomorphic qualities and became inhabited by mythical and other figures (Hays, 2002). The Seven Houses and Texas Houses series involved drawings that conformed to a regular nine-square composition. As shown in figure 16 this arrangement became imbued with fundamental positional meanings, such as perimeter, symmetry, fluidity and centrality. They could be and were projected into three dimensions, isometrically, to become a space. Moreover, Hejduk noted that these aspects of drawings involved a certain sensing by way of memory conditions, returning again to some of the cognitive discussion earlier in this volume and to Deleuze and his tensive conditions along with Jacques Lacan's idea of the 'gaze' also mentioned earlier. In this idea there is an intrinsic two-way interaction with an 'image-screen' in the middle and double articulation of viewer and object and object with viewer (Hays, 2002 and Lucas, 2019). These exercises were followed by the Diamond Houses from around 1963 through to 1967. There Hejduk observed that a drawing with two equal legs at right angles produced a square space. Moreover, an isometric projection of this square produced a diamond, even more primitive as a figure than a square. Further, if the diamond figure in plan was then projected isometrically it would result in a layering of squares spatially (Hays, 2010 and Lucas, 2019). From this the four different levels of the Diamond House could be articulated, as shown in figure 16. Eventually this led Hejduk to discover the Wall House that followed in 1964, or thereabouts, through into the 1970s. Conceptually, how this seems to have happened again through geometric manipulation, was through the flattening of the deep space implied by square plan on to the vertical square surface, effectively collapsing the figure into a wall, again illustrated in figure 16 (Hays, 2010). Later on, in 2001, some 28 years after it was originally designed in 1973, Wall House 2 was constructed. Originally intended for a client friend and meant to be built in Ridgefield, Connecticut, it was passed on to another client and built after Hejduk's death by a development company in the Netherlands, with an area of some 250 square meters (Svelven, 2012). It is organized into horizontal and vertical elements centered on a vertical wall. This prominent two-dimensional plane effectively disconnects its three levels of separate functions as well as grouping them together, shown in figure 16. Moreover, referring back to earlier discussion, the wall becomes occupiable, so to speak, and also allows experience of inside and outside and back to front. From around 1981 onwards Hejduk developed the idea of the 'image-screen' into *masques* of various kinds and produced 32 allegorical drawings in which angels and other bodies inhabited the flatness of walled space. Much like Rilke's *Book of Hours* written between 1881 and 1903 with poetry celebrating Saint Francis and the Christian search for God, Hejduk's Enclosures series poetically encompassed and celebrated the wall in architecture (Hays, 2002 and Rilke, 2009).

## Tales About Traditional Artisanal Architecture

Artisanal architecture is the product of an approach to design and construction and a concern for the art and craft of building. In most, if not all cultural settings it is also a historical continuum that tends to transcend mere fashion and vagueness of style through an emphasis on craftsmanship and the making of buildings usually by groups of differently skilled craftsmen. In these regards the development and deployment of wood technology in China since ancient times is a robust and impressive example of artisanal practice. Dating more or less from the time of the Zhou Dynasty (1026–256 BCE) bounded courtyard or quadrangular buildings emerged, primarily built of wood. Even earlier examples, such as the Erlitou structures are known archaeologically from the Bronze Age (Fletcher, 2009). The appeal of wood in China was due to several factors such as its abundance, its association with the 'Five Element Theory' and luckiness, and its ease of working with. Tectonically, it became associated with a number of features: These characteristics included the *dougong* joint system, construction of overhanging roofs, freestanding weight-bearing pillars, stamped earth foundations and screen or 'curtain' walls between pillars and columns. Technology also evolved over time beginning with the relatively simple early structures of the Zhou Dynasty and then on to more complex structures of the Qin and Han Dynasties (206 BCE–220 CE). And then on to the Tang and Song Dynasties (960–1279 CE). Certainly, by the Ming Dynasty (1268–1644) new components had been added and it reached what might be called a mature art and craft (Xujie, 2002, Guo and An, 2020 and Pang, 2021). During this evolution several manuals, standards and regulations were promulgated. These documents included the timber woodworking manual *Mu Jing* of the 10th century (Chinese Rare Book Collection, 1936); the notable *Yingzhao Fashi* of 1103 by Li Jie during the Song Dynasty (Guo, 1998); the *Lu Ban Jing* carpentry manual of 1537 or thereabouts (Ruitenbeek, 1993) and the Ming *King-cheng tso fa* of around the 1730s, as well as Liang Sicheng's version of the *Qingshi yingtsao li* of slightly later (Liang, 2004). Of these perhaps the most notable was the Song Dynasty *Yingzhao Fashi* certainly with regard to its historical resurrection in the 1920s by Zhu Qiqian (1872–1964), a Chinese patriot and former Minister of the Interior during the waning Qing Dynasty. In retirement he came upon a copy of the *Yingzhao Fashi* while visiting Nanjing and set about to have it published and augmented by a philological exercise in which components of the modular bracketing system, as well as other technological components were

## 16 – JOHN HEJDUK'S GEOMETRIES AND TECTONICS

A Qualities of the nine-square plan, B The Diagonal House, C Diamond to square isometric projection and flattening of the diamond-square plan to a vertical plane and D Wall House 2 of 2001 in Groningen, Netherlands

A

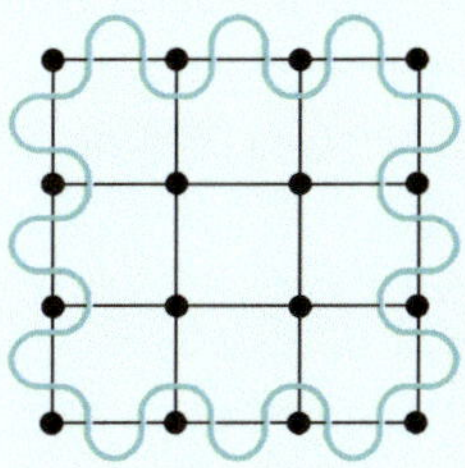

B

C

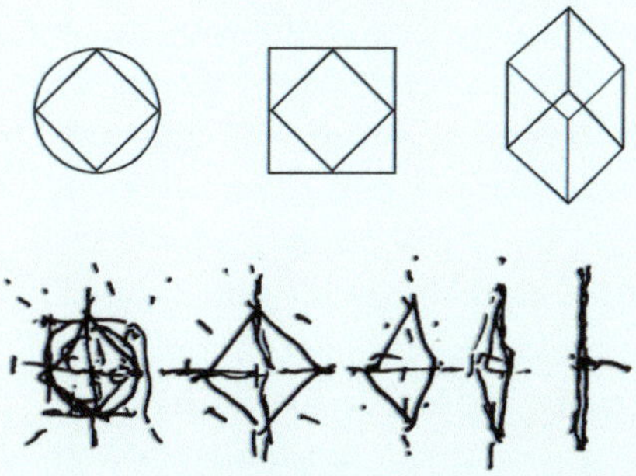

D

identified, as shown in figure 17. He did this because, while serving as Interior Minister, he had experienced the total lack of knowledge of artisans about what they were doing in conserving parts of Beijing's Forbidden City, which he regarded as a severe lapse and a matter of national strategic importance. Later he went on to form the Institute for Research in Chinese Architecture in 1930 that employed the likes of Liang Sicheng (Li, 2003). The modular system was devised to overcome two problems in overcrowded Song Dynasty Kaifeng at the time. The first was the matter of structural failures requiring more regulated and manners of robust building. The second was stemming graft and corruption by overcharging for building materials. In this regard the number of modules could be simply added up and used as an accurate proxy for building cost (Guo, 1998 and Li, 2003).

Nowadays, the artisanal approach to traditional architecture in China is largely in the hands of the *jiangpai* communities (artisan families or gangs), especially in the south. As discussed at some length in chapter 3 this is essentially a tool-based and calculation, data sifting and craftsman-driven approach. Its relative uniformity first really came into being during the Ming Dynasty and the construction of the Forbidden City under the Yongle Emperor between 1406 and 1420. Built on the back of *Dadu* from the late 13th century, this effort required the recruitment and governance of numerous craftsmen from north and south China (Li and Wang, 2013 and McClintock, 2014). By the 18th century, the artisan community was comprised of a matrix of building techniques and practices led primarily by carpenters. During the subsequent Qing Dynasty, the 'Eight Great Crafts' became recognized with conservation and enlargement of the Forbidden City at its peak before the decline with the fall of the Qing in the early 20th century. Since 1949, there have been several major renovations of the palace as a public museum (Guo, 2008). Also, as noted in chapter 3, the *zhanggan* or *gao-chi* method of design and construction by the *jiangpai* involved what amounted to a use of a 'pole-ruler', as shown in figure 14 of the earlier chapter, specifying the dimensions and other characteristics of important wooden building aspects of traditional architecture like the large overhanging roofs of houses and ancestral halls. As can be seen in figure 18, here it serves to measure part of that structure. It was also used to specify more complicated curvilinear roof supports and bracketing components again as shown in figure 18. The specific markings on a particular *jiangpai zhanggan* are usually a trade secret, as noted in chapter 3 (Yao, 2017). The core of the *jiangpai*'s construction expertise are three what might be called 'working drawing' components, which collectively address the major aspects of resolving a building from plan to structural details (Li, 2002). Further, these are not strictly drawings in the usual Western sense, for they involve combinations of instruments, actual notations and calculations representing a system of collective know-how (Zhang, 2010). The first of these components is the *dimian-tu* or literally the 'ground map'. Usually, it is a schematic sketch or simply worked out on the ground of the building site mainly as a matrix of points representing column locations. Remember traditional Chinese wooden architecture is usually columnar in form. However, within the know-how of the *dimian-tu* is also

## 17 – EXCERPTS FROM THE SONG DYNASTY *YINGZHAO FASHI* by Li Jie A Annotations of the modular bracketing system and B Specification of modular components

A

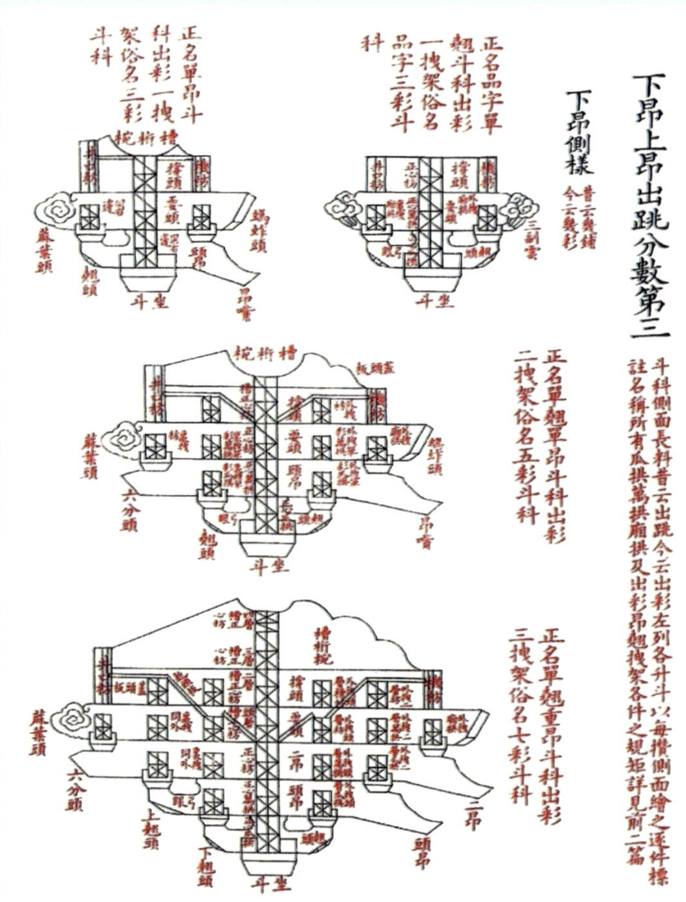


B

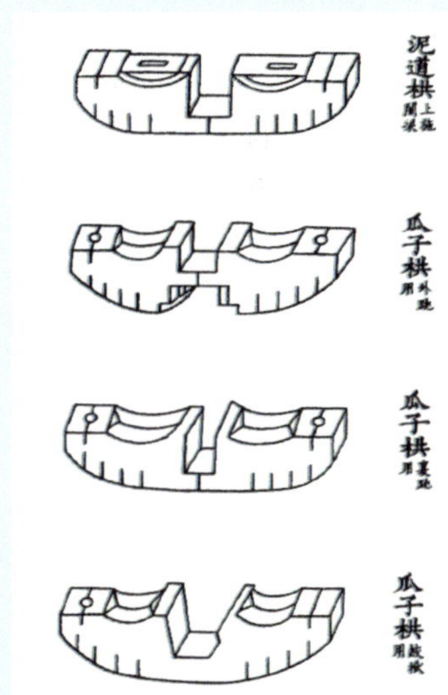

*feng shui* and other geomantic information concerning the orientation of a building, as well as conditions associated with auspicious and ominous numerology. The second component is the *shuigua-tu* or *shui-gua* diagrams which provide information about the shaping and making of building frameworks, more literally from 'who-hang charts' or sectional considerations closer to Western architectural language. Indeed, the *dimian-tu* and *shuigua-tu* aspects together define most of the *jiangpai* working techniques. Essentially the knowledge of the *shuigua-tu* includes a set of steps centrally involved with the determination of the shape of a roof to ensure both adequate drainage and technical stability. This shape, in turn, is given by the roof's curvature and supporting characteristics by taking into account the building layout, the grid of column spacings, interactions among beams and purlins, incorporation of ornamentation, and so on. Typically, it involves at least five steps. First, a determination is made of the number of beams needed in a roof and the distance between the front and rear eaves according to the building's plan layout. Second, the lowest part of the roof is determined, followed by step three, the drawing of a polyline diagram of the front and back ramps from the eaves to the ridge line. Fourth, given the overall inclination of the roof and elevation of the eave truss, the tuning, as it were, of purlins is made to produce an appropriate smooth curve to the roof. Finally, tuning of both ends regarding the building's main façade is made, allowing each beam's location and size to be determined (Zhang, 2010 and Yao, 2017). Arrival at *shuigua* knowledge also often requires reference to hexagram calculations and the screening of information regarding auspicious meanings and other traditional insights in order to be able to select appropriate elements and parts of construction (Yao, 2017). The third component is the making and using of the *gao-chi* or *zhang-gan* ('pole ruler') where the terms literally refer to long strip of wood used as a ruler. As noted earlier, its markings are also largely an amalgamation of the know-how of the first two components. Some of this process is illustrated here in the building of an ancestral hall in Fujian Province as shown in figure 18. In sum, *jiangpai* practices are strict calculation and selection processes from among building references and a variety of sources including past experience and geomantic traditions like *feng shui*. These practices are less about the final outcome or production of a design as an object as they are about the intricacies of the process of physically making architecture. Moreover, within the confines of know-how from both *dimian-tu* and *shuigua-tu* though seemingly confining and inevitable in outcome, there is adequate room for flexibility and improvisation.

In summary, these tales or stories reveal aspects of design thinking, at least in architecture, that are largely absent from other more cognitively based perspectives like those elaborated in chapters 2 and 5. First, these cases suggest strong connections between the idea of 'scenes' leading to stories and storytelling and through that to design strategies and resolutions. From a social science perspective, the value and analysis of 'scenescapes', as they are often referred to, has been well established, especially in revelation of the qualities of everyday places and how they shape social life (Silver and Clark, 2016). The broader concept of '*mise-en-scene*' as applied in

18 – THE JIANGPAI AT WORK ON AN ANCESTRAL HALL in Fujian Province, China (A) Image of an ancestral hall in Fujian Province, China, (B) A *zhanggan* or *gao-chi* in use on the building site, (C) Using the *zhanggan* to shape wooden components and (D) Curvilinear and bracket roof forms being made

A

B

C

D

the performing arts like cinema, also captures both the spirit and structure of these links. Simply put, '*mise-en-scene*' refers to the type of place and situation in which action happens, like design thinking in this case (Kawin, 1992). Second, often more complete and precise accounts of the way things are or 'knowing that' lead to clearer accounts of the way things should be and 'knowing how'. Fuller accounting, for instance, of all metabolic attributes of constructed environments allows fuller reconciliation to positive outcomes. Third, in work about the geometry and substance of the thingness of building, the positioning of onlookers by way of contrivances like image-screens and *masques* can be effective. Fourth, the apparent lock-step aspects of at least some traditional artisanal ways of making, or knowing how often involve more than simply narrative accounts around knowing that, by more fully embracing the tools, instruments and materials of making itself. Finally, techniques that readily convert the making of wicked problems into tame problems can improve the sheer quality of design thinking in architecture by making it more direct and efficient. As briefly noted, these four stories also reflect themes of current interest, at least in academic and related professional circumstances. Much like other times in the past alluded to throughout this text, specific themes, preoccupations, desires and essentially storylines are deemed of utmost importance, often at the expense of others waiting in the wings, as it were. The late 1960s and early 1970s, for instance, were influenced by keen interests in growth and change and design methods, while the discourse of hypermodernity followed more recently (Stein and Spreckelmeyer, 1999). It is almost as if the discipline of architecture, in many if not most quarters, can be likened to the *Neverending Story* in which the exploits of life in the other world of Fantastica through the eyes of Bastian Bux carry on perpetually (Ende, 1979). Nevertheless, work on the palpable thingness of architecture continues to be among preoccupations with the quality of design thinking that goes with it.

# References


Alberti, L. B. 1991 (1452). *On the Art of Building,* translated by Joseph Rykwert. Cambridge, MA: The MIT Press.

Alexander, C. 1964. *Notes on a Synthesis of Form.* Cambridge, MA: Harvard University Press.

Alexander, C. 1965. "A City is Not a Tree". *Architectural Forum.* April.

Alexander, C., S. Ishikawa and M. Silverstein. 1968. *A Pattern Language Which Generates Multi-Service Centers.* Berkeley: Center for Environmental Structure.

Althusser, L. 2008 (1971). *On Ideology,* translated by Ben Brewster. New York: Verso.

Anderson, J. R. 1983. *The Architecture of Cognition.* Cambridge, Mass.: Harvard University Press.

Anderson, J. R. and G. H. Bauer. 1973. *Human Associative Memory.* New York: V. N. Winston.

ArchDaily, 2011. "Pixel / Studio 505". *ArchDaily,* 14 December.

ArchDaily, 2013. "Angel Square / 3D Reid". *ArchDaily,* 27 February.

ArchDaily, 2014. "Suzlon One Earth Global Headquarters / Christopher Benninger". *ArchDaily,* 14 January.

ArchDaily, 2016. "Museum of Tomorrow / Santiago Calatrava". *ArchDaily,* 14 April.

ArchDaily, 2017. "Louvre Abu Dhabi / Ateliers Jean Nouvel". *ArchDaily,* 8 November.

Archer, L. B. 1968. *The Structure of Design Processes.* Doctoral Dissertation, Royal College of Art, London.

Arnaiz, C. and P. G. Rowe. 2020. *When Urbanization Comes to Ground.* Novato, CA: ORO Editions.

Arnold, J. E. 1959. "Creative Engineering". In P. Smith and W. Grotz, eds. *Creativity: An Examination of the Creative Process.* New York: Hastings House, pp. 33–46.

Asimow, M. 1962. *Introduction to Design.* Englewood Cliffs, NJ: Prentice Hall.

Bacini, P. and H. Brunner. 2012 (1991). *Metabolism of the Anthroposphere: Analysis, Evaluation and Design.* Cambridge, MA: The MIT Press.

Baldwin, E. 2010. "CopenHill: The Story of BIG's Iconic Waste-to-Energy Plant". *ArchDaily,* 7 October.

Baldwin, E. 2021. "Adaptive Reuse: Rethinking Carbon, Sustainability and Social Justice". *ArchDaily,* 2 November.

Banham, R. 1972. *Theory and Design of the First Machine Age.* London: Architectural Press.

Bartlett, F. C. 1932. *Remembering: A Study in Experimental and Social Psychology.* Cambridge: Cambridge University Press.

Batty, M. 2018. "Digital Twins". *Environmental Planning B: Urban Analytics and City Science,* vol. 45, no. 5, pp. 817–820.

Baumann, K., B. Caldwell, F. Bor et al. 2017. "Participatory Design Fiction: Community Storytelling for Speculative Urban Technologies". *Proceedings of the Conference on Human Factors in Computing Systems,* vol. 10.

Beck, H. and J. Cooper. 2002. *Glenn Murcutt: A Singular Practice.* Mulgrave: The Images Publishing Group.

Behera, R. K., P. K. Bala and A. Ray. 2021. "A Cognitive Chatbot for Personalised Contextual Customer Service: Behind the Scene and Beyond the Hype". *Information Systems Frontiers,* vol. 23, April.

Bersales, J. E. R. 2012. *San Pedro Calungsod: The Canonization Album.* Cebu: University of San Carlos Press.

Biljecki, F., J. Stoker, H. Ledoux et al. 2015. "Application of 3D City Models: State of the Art Review". *International Journal of Geoinformation,* vol. 4, no. 4, pp. 2842–2889.

Bizzell, P. and B. Herzberg, eds. 2001 (1984). *The Rhetorical Tradition: Readings from Classical Times to the Present.* New York: St. Martins.

Bleecker, J, 2009. *Design Fiction: A Short Essay on Design Science and Function.* Los Angeles: Near Future Laboratory.

Bleecker, J. 2014. *TBD Catalog.* Los Angeles: Near Future Laboratory.

Bohr, S. P. 2009. *Futurism's Incredible Journey.* Roseville, CA: Amazing Facts.

Bossi, L. 2009. "Chapel, Chosen Children Village Foundation". *Domus,* 22 April.

Broschart, D. and P. Zeile. 2015. "Architecture: Augmented Reality in Architecture and Urban Planning". *Proceedings of Digital Landscape Architecture,* pp. 111–118.

Brown, T. 2008. "Design Thinking". *Harvard Business Review,* June.

Brown, T. 2020. *On Design Thinking.* Boston: Harvard Business Review Press.

Bruner, J. S. 1986. *Actual Minds, Possible Worlds.* Cambridge, MA: Harvard University Press.

Buildmedia, 2021. *The Boundary: Wellington Digital Twin.* Wellington: Wellington City Council.

Busquets, J. 2022. *Modern Architecture and the City: A Quick Immersion.* New York: Tibidabo Press.

Butler, J. P. and G. C. Spivak. 2007. "Who Sings the National State". In *Language, Politics, Belonging.* London: Seagull Books.

Candy, S. and C. Potter. eds. 2019. *Design and Future.* Taipei: Tamking University Press.

Casini, M. 2022. "Extended Reality for Smart Building Operation and Maintenance". *Energies,* vol. 15, no. 10, pp. 3756 f.

Cassirer, E. 1953. *Language and Myth.* New York: Dover.

Cassirer, E. 1965. *The Philosophy of Symbolic Form.* New Haven: Yale University Press.

Celant, G., ed. 2003. *Prada Aoyama Tokyo, Herzog & de Meuron.* Milan: Projetto Prada Arts Series.

Charles, D. 2010. *Definition in Greek Philosophy.* London: Oxford University Press.

Chen, K. 2021. *Digital Twin.* London: Royal Collins Publishing Company.

Chen, M. 2019. "VR/AR Applications: Infrastructure and Urban Design". *Intermap,* October.

Chinese Rare Book Collection. 1936. *Mu Jing.* Cambridge, Mass.: Harvard University Yenching Library.

Chomsky, A. N. and M. Ronat. 1998. *On Language: Chomsky's Classic Works Language and Responsibility and Reflections on Language in One Volume.* New York: New Books.

Churchman, C. W. 1967. "Wicked Problems". *Management Sciences,* vol. 4, no. 14, pp. B-141 and B-142.

CNN Staff, 2022. "Green Buildings: 18 Examples of Sustainable Architecture Around the World". *CNNStyle,* 24 April.

Coates, N. 2012. *Narrative Architecture.* New York: John Wiley and Sons.

Cross, N. 1982. "Designerly Ways of Knowing". *Design Studies,* vol. 3, no. 4, pp. 221–227.

Da Costa Meyer, E. 1995. *The Work of Antonio Sant'Elia: Retreat into the Future.* New Haven: Yale University Press.

De Jouvenel, B. 2012 (1967). *The Art of Conjecture.* London: Routledge.

Deleuze, G. 1981. *Francis Bacon: The Logic of Sensation.* London: Bloomsbury.

Derakhshani, F., M. Mostafavi et al. 2021. *Hutong Metabolism: ZAO/ standardarchitecture.* Berlin: ArchiTangle.

Droste, M. 2019. *Bauhaus.* London: Taschen.

Dunne, A. and F. Raby. 2013. *Speculative Everything: Design Fiction and Social Dreaming.* Cambridge, MA: The MIT Press.

Eastman, C. M. 1975. *Spatial Synthesis in Computer-Aided Building Design.* New York: John Wiley and Sons.

Eisenman, P. 1989. "Blue Line Text". In A. Papadakis, C. Cooke and A. Benjamin, eds., *Deconstruction: Omnibus Volume.* New York: Rizzoli.

Eisenman, P. 2006. *The Formal Basis of Modern Architecture.* Zurich: Lars Müller Publishers.

Ende, M. 1979. *Die unendliche Geschichte.* Stuttgart: Thienemann Verlag.

Erickson, M. J. 1982. *Contemporary Options in Eschatology.* London: Baker House.

Etherington, R. 2012. "Galaxy Soho by Zaha Hadid Architects". *dezeen,* 29 October.

Fann, K. T. 2020 (1920). *Peirce's Theory of Abduction.* London: Routledge.

FC Bayern München, 2015. *A Brief History of the Alliance Arena.* Munich: FC Bayern München.

Faste, R. 1994. "Ambidextrous Thinking". *Innovations in Mechanical Engineering Curricula for the 1990s.* American Society of Mechanical Engineers, November.

Fauconnier, G. 1994 (1985). *Mental Spaces: Aspects of Memory Construction in Natural Language.* Cambridge: Cambridge University Press.

Fauconnier, G. and M. Turner. 2002. *The Way We Think: Conceptual Blending and the Mind's Hidden Complexities.* New York: Basic Books.

Fauconnier, G. and M. Turner. 2006. "Mental Spaces: Conceptual Integration Networks". In D. Geeraerts, ed., *Cognitive Linguistics: Basic Readings.* Berlin: Mouton de Gruyter.

Fernández-Galiano, L. 2020. *Herzog & de Meuron, 1978–2002.* Madrid: Aviva.

Fiederer, L. 2011. "Olympiastadion, Behnisch and Frei Otto". *AD Classics.* 11 February.

Fillmore, C. 1985. "Frames and the Semantics of Understanding". *Quaderni di Semantica,* vol. 6, no. 2, pp. 222–254.

Fletcher, Sir B. 1996. *A History of Architecture.* 20th edition. London: Routledge.

Fletcher, K. 2009. "Erlitou Culture". In *Encyclopedia Britannica.* 25 February.

Foster, J. 2021. "Homelessness Along the Los Angeles River". *River LA,* Department of Digital and Civic Engagement.

Frampton, K. 1980. *Modern Architecture: A Critical Introduction.* London: Thames and Hudson.

Frampton, K. 1983. "Towards a Critical Regionalism: Six Points for an Architecture of Resistance". In H. Foster, ed., *The Anti-Aesthetic: Essays on Postmodern Culture.* Seattle: Bay Press.

Fraser, F. 2015. "Navigating the Maze of Faith: 100 Walls Church by CAZA in Cebu City, Philippines". *Architecture Review,* 2 December.

Friedman, A. 2007. "Farming in Suburbia". *Open House International,* vol. 32, no. 1, pp. 7–15.

Fuller, B. R. 1982 (1975). *Synergetics: Explorations in the Geometry of Thinking.* New York: Macmillan.

Garcia, F. H. 2023. "City Prepares to Sweep Homeless Encampments Near River". *Long Beach Post News,* 23 March.

Gelernter, D. H. 1993. *Mirror Worlds or the Day Software Puts the Universe in a Shoebox.* New York: Oxford University Press.

Gero, J. S. 2011. "Computer-Aided Architectural Design – Past, Present and Future". *Architectural Science Review,* vol. 26, no. 1, pp. 21–46.

Gibbs, R. W. 2000. "Making Good Psychology Out of Blending Theory". *Cognitive Linguistics,* vol. 11, pp. 347–358.

Glazer, N. 1974. "Schools of the Minor Professions". *Minerva,* pp. 346–347.

Goldberger, P. 1989. "The Museum that Theory Built". *New York Times,* 5 November.

Goldberger, P. 2017. *Building Art: The Life and Work of Frank Gehry.* New York: Vintage.

Gongadze, S. and A. Maassen. 2023. "Paris' Vision for a '15 Minute City' Sparks a Global Movement". *World Resources Institute.* 25 January.

Goodman, N. 1976. *Languages of Art.* Cambridge, MA: Hackett Publishing Company.

Grieves, M. 2022. "Can the Digital Twin Transform Manufacturing". *World Economic Forum Emerging Technologies,* November 19.

Griffith, A. 2014. "CAZA's 100 Walls Church is Surrounded by Staggered Walls". *dezeen,* 25 February.

Guo, C. 2008. "The Qing Palace: From a Forbidden City to a Park Heritage". *Museum International,* vol. 60, no. 1, pp. 78–88.

Guo, D. and P. An. 2020. "The Technology of Chinese Wooden Structure Architecture". In I. Hua and I. Feng, eds., *Thirty Great Inventions of China.* Singapore: Springer.

Guo, Q. 1988. "Yingtsao Fashi: The Twelfth Century Chinese Building Manual". *Architectural History,* vol. 41, pp. 1–13.

Habermas, J. 1968. *Knowledge and Human Interests.* Boston: Beacon Press.

Habraken, N. J. 1998. *The Structure of the Ordinary.* Cambridge, MA: The MIT Press.

Hall, R. A. 1962. "The Changing Technical Act". *Technology and Culture,* vol. 3, pp. 501–515.

Hamblen, J. O., T. S. Hall and M. D. Furman, 2001. *Rapid Prototyping and Digital Systems: A Tutorial Approach.* New York: Springer.

Hart, V. H. P. 1996. *Sebastiano Serlio on Architecture. Volume One.* New Haven: Yale University Press.

Harvard Graduate School of Education. 2010. *The Nature of Scientific Thinking.* Cambridge, MA: President and Fellows of Harvard University.

Hassan, H., E. S. Silva, E. Unger, M. Tajmazinani and S. MacFeely. 2020. "Artificial Intelligence (AI) or Intelligence Augmentation (IA): What is the Future". *AI,* vol. 1, no. 2, pp. 143–155.

Hays, K. M. 2002. *Sanctuaries: The Last Works of John Hejduk.* New York: Whitney and Abrams.

Hays, K. M. 2010. *Architecture's Desire: Reading the Late Avant-garde.* Cambridge, MA: The MIT Press.

Heathcote, E., 2017. "The Gulf's Blockbuster New Louvre Arrives – and It's Utterly Original". *Financial Times,* 10 November.

Heidegger, M. 1967. *What is a Thing.* Chicago: Henry Regnery.

Hoffman, J. 2022. *Speculative Futures: Design Approaches to Navigate Change, Foster Resilience and Create the Cities We Need.* Berkeley: North Atlantic Books.

Homeless Initiative, 2022. "2022 Homeless Count Results". *Homeless Initiative,* 8 September.

Howard, E. 1902 (1898). *Garden Cities of Tomorrow: A Peaceful Path to Real Reform.* London: Sonnenschein & Co.

Howarth, D. 2016. "Calatrava's Oculus at the World Trade Center". *dezeen,* 21 August.

Hoyt, A. 2015. "Next Progressives: CAZA". *Next Progressives,* 17 February.

Hughes, R. 1991. *Shock of the New: The Hundred-Year History of Modern Art.* New York: Knopf.

IPIC, 2012. *Special Report: Managing the Risks of Extreme Events and Disasters to Advance Climate Change Adaption.* Cambridge: U.N. Intergovernmental Panel on Climate Change.

Iskander, N. 2018. "Design Thinking is Fundamentally Conservative and Preserves the Status Quo'". *Harvard Business Review,* 6 September.

Johnson, B. D. 2022 (2011). *Science Fiction Prototyping: Designing the Future with Science.* Heidelberg: Springer Nature.

Johnson, M. 1987. *The Body in the Mind: The Bodily Basis of Meaning, Juxtaposition and Reason.* Chicago: University of Chicago Press.

Julien, S. C. 2016. "Clichy Batignolles L'éco-Quartier – une référence de développement urbain durable à Paris". *L'excellence environnementale distinguée.*

Kain, R. J. P. and R. Allison. 1986. "Problems and Sources in Historical Geography: Agriculture in the Past". *Teaching Geography,* vol. 11, no. 2, pp. 58–63.

Kant, I. 1933. *Critique of Pure Reason,* 2nd edition, translated by Norman Kemp Smith. London: Macmillan.

Kant, I. 2000. *Critique of Pure Reason.* Cambridge: Cambridge University Press.

Kaufmann, A. 1968. *The Science of Decision Making.* New York: World University Press.

Kawin, B. 1992. *How Movies Work.* Berkeley: University of California Press.

Khan-Magomedov, S. 1988. *Pioneers of Soviet Architecture.* London: Thames and Hudson.

Kimbell, L. 2011. "Rethinking Design Thinking: Part 1". *Design and Culture* vol. 3, no. 8, pp. 285–306.

Koestler, A. 1964. *The Act of Creation.* New York: Macmillan.

Koolhaas, R. 1978. *Delirious New York: A Retroactive Manifesto for Manhattan.* New York: Oxford University Press.

Koolhaas, R. 1997. *Rem Koolhaas: Conversations with Students.* New York: Princeton Architectural Press.

Koolhaas, R. 2002. "Junkspace". *October,* no. 100, pp. 175–190.

Koolhaas, R. and C. Balmond with Arup. 2008. *Serpentine Gallery Pavilion 2006.* Cologne: Walter König.

Koolhaas, R., B. Mau and J. Sigler. 1995. *S. M. L. XL.* New York: Monacelli Press.

Kuhn, T. S. 1996 (1962) *The Structure of Scientific Revolutions.* Chicago: University of Chicago Press.

Lakoff, G. 1987. *Women, Fire, and Dangerous Things: What Categories Reveal About the Mind.* Chicago: University of Chicago Press.

Lakoff, G. and M. Johnson. 1980. *Metaphors We Live By.* Chicago: University of Chicago Press.

Langdon, D. 2014. "Wexner Center for the Arts / Peter Eisenman". *AD Classics. ArchDaily.* 12 October.

Lawson, B. 2005. *How Designers Think: The Design Process Demystified.* London: Routledge.

Le Corbusier 1985 (1923). *Towards a New Architecture,* translated by F. Etchells. New York: Dover Publications.

Levi, A. W. 1970. *The Humanities Today.* New York: Oxford University Press.

Levin, S. 2022. "Los Angeles County is Home to More than 69,000 Unhoused People, Count Finds". *The Guardian,* 8 September.

Li, Q. 2002 (1988). *A Study of Traditional Construction Craftsmanship.* Taipei: Yanlou Ancient Architecture Press.

Li, S. 2003. "Reconstructing Chinese Building Tradition: The Yingtsao Fashi in the Early Twentieth Century". *Journal of the Society of Architectural Historians,* vol. 62, no. 4, pp. 470–489.

Li, Y. and L. Wang. 2013. "The Last Craftsman of the Imperial Palace Techniques". *Zhongguo Wen Hua Yi Chan,* no. 3, pp. 24–33.

Liang, S. 2004. *Complete Works of Liang Sicheng.* Beijing: China Architecture and Building Press.

Loire, S. O. 2013. "Green Energy". *Irish Arts Review,* vol. 30, no. 2.

Lucas, R. 2019. *Drawing Parallels: Knowledge Production in Axonometric, Isometric and Oblique Drawings.* New York: Routledge.

MacEachren, A. M. 1995. *How Maps Work: Representation, Visualization and Design.* New York: The Guilford Press.

Mack, G. 2020. *Herzog & de Meuron, 2002–2004.* Basel: Birkhäuser.

Mahoney, M. S. 2011. *Histories of Computing.* Cambridge, MA: Harvard University Press.

Makridakis, S. 2017. "The Forthcoming Artificial Intelligence (AI) Revolution: Its Impact on Society and Firms". *Futures,* vol. 90, pp. 46–60.

Mallin, S. B. 1979. *Merleau-Ponty's Philosophy.* New Haven: Yale University Press.

Maltzan, M. 2016. "Social Transparency: Project on Housing". In J. Graham, ed. *Columbia Books on Architecture in the City.* New York: Columbia University Press.

Marinetti, F. T. 1909. "Declaration of Futurism". *Poesia,* vol. 5, no. 6, April.

Markov, V. 1968. *Russian Futurism.* Los Angeles: University of California Press.

Marshall, S. F. 1995. *Schemas in Problem Solving.* Cambridge: Cambridge University Press.

McCarthy, J. 1959. "Programs With Common Sense" *Proceedings of the Teddington Conference on the Mechanization of Thought Processes.* London: Her Majesty's Stationary Office, pp. 756–761.

McClintock, T. K. 2014. "The Conservation of Juanqiuzhai: A Prototype for Architectural Interiors in the Forbidden City". *Journal of the American Institute of Conservation,* vol. 53, no. 2, pp. 116–139.

McKnight, J. 2021. "Shipping Containers Used to Build LA Housing Complex for the Homeless". *dezeen,* 29 July.

Merleau-Ponty, M. 1962. *Phenomenology of Perception,* translated by Colin Smith. London: Routledge.

Middleton, R. 2003. *Architecture of the Nineteenth Century.* London: Phaidon.

Milgram, P. and F. Kishino. 1994. "A Taxonomy of Mixed Reality Visual Displays". *IECIE Transactions on Information and Systems,* vol. 70, pp. 1321–1329.

Milgram, P., H. Takemura, A. Utsumi and F. Kishino. 1995. "Augmented Reality: A Class of Displays on the Reality-Virtuality Continuum". *Proceedings SPIE vol. 2351 Telemanipulator and Telepresence Technologies,* pp. 282–292.

Miller, G. A. 1956. "The Magic Number Seven, Plus or Minus Two: Some Limits on Our Capacity for Processing Information". *Psychological Review,* vol. 63, pp. 81–97.

Minsky, M. 1975. "A Framework for Representing Knowledge". In P. H. Winston, ed., *The Psychology of Computer Vision.* New York: McGraw-Hill.

Mitchell, W. J. 1977. *Computer Aided Architectural Design.* New York: Petrocelli-Charter.

Moneo, R. 2004. *Theoretical Anxiety and Design Strategies in the Work of Eight Contemporary Architects.* Cambridge, MA: The MIT Press.

Moore, R. 2010. "Roadmap 2050 by Rem Koolhaas' OMA". *Guardian,* May 9.

Moore, W. 1970. *The Professions.* New York: Russell Sage Books.

Morgan, M. H. 1914. *Ten Books on Architecture.* Project Gutenberg.

Moussavi, F. and M. Kubo. 2008. *The Function of Ornament.* Barcelona: Actar.

Mumford, L. 2000 (1971). *Technics and Human Development: The Myth of the Machine.* New York: Mariner Books.

Murcutt, G. 2008. *Thinking Drawing.* Tokyo: Toto.

Needham, J. 1994. *The Shorter Science and Civilization of China.* Cambridge: Cambridge University Press.

Negroponte, N. 1972. *The Soft Architecture Machine.* Cambridge, MA: The MIT Press.

Newell, A.; J. C. Shaw and H. A. Simon. 1957. "Elements of a Theory of Problem Solving". *Rand Corporation Report. P-971,* March.

Newell, A., J. C. Shaw and H. A. Simon. 1967. "The Process of Creative Thinking". In H. Gruber, G. Terrell and M. Wertheimer, eds., *Contemporary Approaches to Creative Thinking.* New York: Atherton Press, pp. 33–119.

Newell, A. and H. A. Simon. 1972. *Human Problem Solving.* Englewood Cliffs, NJ: Prentice Hall.

Nickerson, C. 2021. "The Role of Schemata in Psychology". *Simply Psychology.* 6 December.

Northern Architecture, 2022. *Renaissance Architectural Treatises.* Northernarchiteture.us.

Nugent, C. 2020. "The Climate is Breaking Down: Architect Bjarke Ingels Has a Plan for That". *Time,* 21 October.

OMA. 1982. "Parc de la Villette". *OMA Office Work,* Rotterdam.

Orwell, G. 1984 (1949). *1984.* London: Signet Classic.

Palladio, A. 1570. *I quattro libiri dell'arcitettura.* Venice: Dominico de Franceschi.

Pang, K. 2021. "Chinese Wooden Architecture: Why Wood Was Used and How". *China Highlights,* 23 August.

Papadakis, A., C. Cooke and A. Benjamin, eds. 1989. *Deconstruction: Omnibus Volume.* New York: Rizzoli.

Pasternak, A. 2008. "National Stadium". *Architectural Record,* vol. 92, no. 9, July.

Perez, A. 2010. "AD Classics: House VI / Peter Eisenman". *ArchDaily,* 4 June.

Perkins, D. N. 1981. *The Mind's Best Work.* Cambridge, MA: Harvard University Press.

Piaget, J. 1952. *The Origins of Intelligence in Children.* New York: International Universities Press.

Piaget, J. 1970. *Structuralism.* New York: Basic Books.

Picon, A. 2010. *Digital Culture in Architecture: An Introduction for the Design Profession.* Basel: Birkhäuser.

Picon, A. 2013. *Ornament: The Politics of Architecture and Subjectivity.* New York: Wiley.

Picon, A. 2015. *Smart Cities: A Spatialized Intelligence.* New York: Wiley.

Pinker, S. 1990. "A Theory of Graph Comprehension". In R. Freedle, ed., *Artificial Intelligence and the Future of Testing.* Mahwah, NJ: LEA Publishers, pp. 73–126.

Pinker, S. 1997. *How the Mind Works.* New York: W. W. Norton.

Plato. 2012. *Meno.* New York: Empire Books.

Pollock, N. R. 2001. "Toyo Ito & Associates Mediatheque, Sendai, Japan". *Architectural Record,* May, pp. 189–190.

Polya, G. 1957. *How to Solve It.* London: Doubleday.

Polyani, M. 1966. *The Tacit Dimension.* New York: Anchor.

Porada, B. 2013. "The 'World's Greenest Commercial Building' Opens in Seattle Today". *ArchDaily,* 22 April.

Porter, M. E. and J. E. Heppelmann. 2017. "Why Every Organization Needs an Augmented Reality Strategy". *Harvard Business Review,* November, pp. 46–47.

Putnam, H. 1981. *Reason, Truth and History.* Cambridge: Cambridge University Press.

Richey, T. 2013. *Wicked Problems: Social Messes.* New York: Springer.

Rilke, R. M. 2009. *The Poetry of Rilke.* New York: North Point Press.

Ritchie, L. D. 2004. "Lost in Conceptual Space: Metaphors of Conceptual Integration". *Metaphors and Symbols,* vol. 19, pp. 31–50.

Rittel, H. W. J. and M. W. Webber. 1973. "Dilemmas in a General Theory of Planning". *Policy Sciences,* vol. 4, no. 2, pp. 155–169.

Rockström, J., J. Gupta, D. Qin et al. 2023. "Safe and Just Earth System Boundaries". *Nature,* 31 May.

Rossi, A. 1982 (1966). *The Architecture of the City.* Cambridge, MA: The MIT Press.

Rowe, C. and F. Koetter. 1984. *Collage City.* Cambridge, MA: The MIT Press.

Rowe, P. G. 1982. "A priori Knowledge and Heuristic Reasoning in Architectural Design". *Journal of Architectural Education,* vol. 30, no. 1, pp. 18–23.

Rowe, P. G. 1987. *Design Thinking.* Cambridge, MA: The MIT Press.

Rowe, P. G. 1992. *Making a Middle Landscape.* Cambridge, MA: The MIT Press.

Rowe, P. G. 1999. *Building Barcelona: A Second Renaissance.* Barcelona: Actar Press.

Rowe, P. G. 2011. *Emergent Architectural Territories in East Asian Cities.* Basel: Birkhäuser.

Rowe, P. G. 2017. *Design Thinking in the Digital Age.* Berlin: Steinberg Press.

Rowe, P. G. and B. Guo. 2023. "Environmental Resilience and the Metabolism of Peripheral Settlement in an American Metropolitan Area". *COJ Review & Research,* vol. 4, no. 5, pp.1–2.

Rowe, P. G., L. Wang and Z. Chen. 2022. *China Modern: Episodes Backward and Forward in Time.* Basel: Birkhäuser.

Rowe, P. G. and Y. Fu. 2022. *Southeast Asia Modern: From Roots to Contemporary Turns.* Basel: Birkhäuser

Rowe, P. G., Y. Fu and J. Song. 2021. *Korean Modern: The Matter of Identity.* Basel: Birkhäuser.

Rowland, I. 1999. *Vitruvius: Ten Books on Architecture.* Cambridge: Cambridge University Press.

Rubio, J. M. 2014. *Columbusplein.* Photographic Portfolio.

Rudin, J. and E. Pellegrino. 2022. *Out of Architecture.* London: Routledge.

Ruitenbeek, K. 1993. *Carpentry and Building in Late Imperial China: A Study of the Fifteenth Century Carpenter's Manual Lu Ban Jing.* Leiden: E. J. Brill.

Rumelhart, D. F. and A. Ortony, 1977. "The Representation of Knowledge in Memory". In D. C. Anderson, R. J. Spiro and W. E. Montague, eds., *Schooling and the Acquisition of Knowledge.* Hillsdale, NJ: Lawrence Erlbaum Associates, pp. 99–135.

Ryan, J. 2010. *A History of the Internet and the Digital Future.* London: Reaktion Books.

Ryan J., G. Dunford and S. Sellars, 2006. *Micronations: The Lonely Planet Guide to Home-Made Nations.* London: Lonely Planet.

Ryle, G. 1945. "Knowing How and Knowing That: The Presidential Address". *Proceedings of the Aristotelian Society, 1945–1946, New Series,* vol. 46, pp. 1–16.

Ryle, G. 1949. *The Concept of Mind.* Chicago: University of Chicago Press.

SAMSHA, 2023. "Results for the National Survey on Drug Use and Health: Key Substance Abuse and Mental Health Indicators in the United States". *U.S. Department of Health and Human Services.*

Schank, R. C. 1982. *Dynamic Memory.* Cambridge: Cambridge University Press.

Schank, R. C. and R. Abelson. 1977. *Scripts, Plans, Goals and Understanding.* Hilldale, NJ: Lawrence Erlbaum Associates.

Schein, E. 1972. *Professional Education: Some New Directions.* New York: McGraw-Hill.

Schmidt, M. 2008. "The Sankey Diagram in Energy and Material Flow Management". *Journal of Industrial Ecology,* vol. 12, no. 2, pp. 173–185.

Schön, D. A. 1983. *The Reflective Practitioner: How Professionals Think in Action.* New York: Basic Books.

Schön, D. A. 1991. *Educating the Reflective Practitioner: Toward a New Design for Teaching and Learning in the Professions.* New York: Wiley and Sons.

Schrotter, M. and C. Hüzeler. 2020. "The Digital Twin of the City of Zurich for Urban Planning". *Journal of Photogrammetry, Remote Sensing and Geoinformation Science,* vol. 88, pp. 99–112.

Scolari, M. 2012. *Oblique Drawing: A History of Anti-Perspective.* Cambridge, MA: The MIT Press.

Sepasgozar, S. M. E. 2022. *Digital Twin and Cities.* London: Palgrave Macmillan.

Serlio, S. 1584. *Tutte L'opera d'architettura.* Venice: Francesco de' Franceschi.

Sharp, S. 2021. "Container-Based Supportive Housing Opens in Chinatown". *Urbanize Los Angeles,* 15 July.

Shmurak, S. 2018. "Paris is Building the Eco-Community of the Future Right Now. Here's How". *Inspiration,* 25 January.

Silver, D. A. and T. N. Clark. 2016. *Scenescapes: How Qualities of Place Shape Social Life.* Chicago: University of Chicago Press.

Simon, H. A. 1969. *The Sciences of the Artificial.* Cambridge, MA: The MIT Press.

Simon, H. A. 1977. "Structure of Ill-Structured Problems". *Artificial Intelligence,* vol. 4, pp. 181–201.

Simon, H. A. 1995. "Machine as Mind". In P. Millican and A. Clark, eds., *Android Epistemology.* Cambridge, MA: The MIT Press.

Skid Row Housing Trust. 2023. "Homes, Supports, Services". *skidrow.org/about/our-mission values/.*

Small, H. 2013. *The Value of the Humanities.* New York: Oxford University Press.

Smith, D. 2021. "This L.A. Project Shows That Homeless Housing Can Be Done Quickly and Cheaply". *Los Angeles Times,* 18 January.

Smithson, A., ed. 1964. *Team Ten Primer.* Cambridge, MA: The MIT Press.

Spacey, J. 2016. "Design Thinking versus System Thinking". *Simpliable,* 22 August.

Stein, J. M. and K. F. Spreckelmeyer, eds. 1999. *Classic Readings in Architecture.* New York: McGraw-Hill.

Steinberg, R. 1999. *The Nature of Cognition.* Cambridge, MA: The MIT Press.

Stewart, L. D. 2022. "How Can Design Thinking Transform Diversity Initiatives of Architectural Trade Organizations Within the United States". PhD diss., National Louis University, Tampa, Florida.

Stirling, J. 1975. *James Stirling: Buildings and Projects, 1950–1975.* London: Oxford University Press.

Studio Guide, 2023. "Architecture Narratives – The Storytelling of Design". *Archisoup.*

Suzuki, E. 2020. "What is Parametric Design in Architecture, and How is it Shaping the Industry". *Transcend,* 15 December.

Svelven, M. 2012. "Wall House 2 / John Hejduk, Thomas Müller Ivan Reimann Architekten & Otonomo Architekten". *AD Classics, ArchDaily,* 6 February.

Tafuri, M. 1972. *Architecture and Utopia.* Cambridge, MA: The MIT Press.

Testa, P. 1996. *Álvaro Siza.* Basel: Birkhäuser.

Todorova, T. 2014. "Design Strategies in Parc de la Villette by Rem Koolhaas". RIBA Thesis, London.

Toffler, A. 1970. *Future Shock.* New York: Putnam Books.

Tolkien, J. R. R. 1954. *The Lord of the Rings.* New York: William Morrow.

Tschumi, B. 2014. *Notations: Diagrams and Sequences.* New York: Artifice Press.

Turing, A. M. 1950. "Computing Machines and Intelligence". *Mind,* vol. 49, no. 236, pp. 433–460.

Tzonis, A. and L. Lefaivre, 1981. "The Grid and Pathway: An Introduction to the Work of Dimitris and Suzana Antonakakis", *Architecture Greece,* vol. 15, pp. 254–277.

Veisdal, J. 2019. "The Birthplace of AI: The 1956 Dartmouth Workshop". *Cantors Paradise,* 12 September.

Venturi, R. C. 1966. *Complexity and Contradiction.* New York: The Museum of Modern Art Press.

Venturi, R. C., D. Scott-Brown and S. Izenour. 1972. *Learning From Las Vegas.* Cambridge, MA: The MIT Press.

Vinsel, L. 2018. "Design Thinking is a Boondoggle". *Chronicle of Higher Education,* 21 May.

Waite, R. 2021. "Farshid Moussavi Reveals Designs for the Houston Ismaili Center Complex". *Architecture Journal,* 16 November.

Walley, D. R. 1997. *Under Construction: The Role of Arts and Humanities.* Bloomington: Indiana University Press.

Wang, D. 2009. "Augmented Reality in Architecture and Design: Potential and Challenges for Applications". *International Journal of Architectural Computing,* vol. 7, no. 2, pp. 309–326.

Warren, H. C. 1921. *A History of the Association Psychology.* London: Charles Scribner's Sons.

Webber, M. W. 1964. *Explorations into Urban Structure.* Philadelphia: University of Pennsylvania Press.

Weber, N. F. 2008. *Le Corbusier: A Life.* New York: Alfred A. Knopf.

Wertheimer, M. 1938. "Gestalt Theory". In W. D. Ellis, ed., *A Source Book of Gestalt Psychology.* London: Routledge.

Wertheimer, M. 1945. *Productive Thinking.* New York: Harper.

Winstanley, T. 2011. "Institute du Monde Arabe". *AD Classics,* 2 October.

Witte, R., ed. 2002. *Toyo Ito: Sendai Mediatheque.* New York: Prestel.

Wittgenstein, L. 1953. *Philosophical Investigations.* London: Blackwell.

Wolman, A. 1965. "The Metabolism of Cities". *Scientific American,* vol. 213, pp. 179–190.

World Commission in Environment and Development, 1987. *Our Common Future.* New York: Oxford University Press.

Xujie, L. 2002. *Chinese Architecture: The Origins of Chinese Architecture.* New Haven: Yale University Press.

Yao, H. 2017. *Traditional Housing Construction Technology in Quanzhou.* Fujian: Wenbao.

Zambonini, H. 2020. "Heaven is Real: Speculative Critical Design as a Tool for Creating Participatory Fictions". PhD diss. Glasgow School of Art.

Zhang, Y. 2010. *Study of Traditional Carpentry Skills in Fujian.* Nanjing: Southeast University Press.

Zhang, Y. and G. Zhu. 2005. "A Study on the Penny Ruler Technique in Fujian". *Ancient Architecture and Garden Technology,* vol. 3.

Zhu, J., W. Chen and H. Li, eds. 2022. *Routledge Handbook of Chinese Architecture: Social Production of Buildings and Spaces in History.* London: Routledge.

Zumthor, P. 1998 (2010). *Thinking Architecture.* Basel: Birkhäuser.

Zwicky, F. 1962. "Morphology of Propulsive Power". *Monograph on Morphological Research,* no. 1.

# Illustration Credits

## Chapter 1

Fig. 1 A Drawn by authors based on Scientific Method, Wikipedia, 2021.
Fig. 1 B Peter G. Rowe, 1987, *Design Thinking*, The MIT Press, p. 22.
Fig. 2 Drawn by authors based on Tim Brown and IDEO's Design Thinking Diagram, 2008.

## Chapter 2

Fig. 1 Drawn by authors based on Lawson, 1980, Archer, 1964 and Asimow, 1962.
Fig. 2 Drawn by authors based on Alexander, 1965.
Fig. 3 Drawn by authors based on Alexander, 1968.
Fig. 4 Drawn by authors.
Fig. 5 Maxar, Google Earth Image, 2023.
Fig. 6 Copyright and courtesy of Stan Allen Architects.
Fig. 7 Drawn by authors based on Carlos Arnaiz Architects.
Fig. 8 Copyright and courtesy of Carlos Arnaiz Architects.
Fig. 9 Copyright and courtesy of Carlos Arnaiz Architects.

## Chapter 3

Fig. 1 A Drawn by authors based on Wood, Smith and Grossniklaus, 2001.
Fig. 1 B Drawn by authors.
Fig. 1 C Drawn by authors based on Yang and Rishe, 2006.
Fig. 2 A Drawn by authors based on Anderson, 1987.
Fig. 2 B Drawn by authors based on Minsky, 1975.
Fig. 3 Drawn by authors based on Lakoff, 1987.
Fig. 4 Drawn by authors based on Fauconnier, 1984.
Fig. 5 A Drawn by authors based on MacEachren, 1995.
Fig. 5 B Drawn by authors based on Pinker, 1990.
Fig. 6 Drawn by authors based on Simon, 1979.
Fig. 7 A Drawn by authors based on Schön, 1983.
Fig. 7 B Drawn by authors based on Schön, 1983.
Fig. 7 C Drawn by authors based on Schön, 1983.
Fig. 8 Public Domain, part of the series La Città Nuova, 1914.
Fig. 9 Copyright and courtesy of Jason Evans and Dunne and Raby, 2009.
Fig. 10 Copyright and courtesy of 21st Century Robot, Trossen Robotics, 2014.
Fig. 11 Public Domain, Nichelle Nichols, NASA, 1977.
Fig. 12 Copyright and courtesy of Stadsarchief Amsterdam.
Fig. 13 WARNER BROS, Allstar Picture Library Ltd, Alamy Stock Photo, 1982.
Fig. 14 White, Zink, Codeca and Clark, 2021.
Fig. 15 A Copyright and courtesy of Zhanliang Chen.
Fig. 15 B Copyright and courtesy of Zhanliang Chen
Fig. 15 C Copyright and courtesy of China.org.cn, 2007.

## Chapter 4

Fig. 1 A Copyright and courtesy of Office for Metropolitan Architecture.
Fig. 1 B Dietmar Rabich, Creative Commons, 2022.
Fig. 2 Ajay Suresh, Creative Commons, 2021.
Fig. 3 Chainwit, Creative Commons, 2019.
Fig. 4 Copyright and courtesy of Office for Metropolitan Architecture.
Fig. 5 Copyright and courtesy of Peter G. Rowe.
Fig. 6 Drawn by the author based on Archweb dwg of Toyo Ito & Associates, Architects.
Fig. 7 Metrocentric, Creative Commons/Flickr, 2006.
Fig. 8 Tiia Monto, Creative Commons, 2014.
Fig. 9 Peter G. Rowe, 2006. *Building Barcelona: A Second Renaixença*, Barcelona Regional, p. 118, Rosalia Vila and Dorote Boisot.
Fig. 10 Copyright and courtesy of Yoeun Chung.
Fig. 11 A Drawn by the author based on Zaha Hadid Architects, 2012.
Fig. 11 B Dingding, Creative Commons, 2020.
Fig. 12 A Copyright and courtesy of Jungwoo Lee.
Fig. 12 B Copyright and courtesy of Jungwoo Lee.
Fig. 13 Arthur Weidmann, Creative Commons, 2022 (top); Randi Hausken, Creative Commons, 2018 (left); Rictor Norton & David Allen, Creative Commons, 2016 (right).
Fig. 14 A Mia, Creative Commons/ Flickr, 2009.
Fig. 14 B Zprecech, Dreamstime.com.
Fig. 15 A Olga Slobodianiuk, Dreamstime.com (top); Saletomic, Dreamstime.com (bottom).
Fig. 15 B Copyright and courtesy of The Ateliers Jean Nouvel.
Fig. 16 A Copyright and courtesy of The Ateliers Jean Nouvel.
Fig. 16 B Ninoak, Dreamstime.com
Fig. 16 C and D Wirestock, Dreamstime.com
Fig. 17 A Copyright and courtesy of Farshid Moussavi Architecture.
Fig. 17 B Copyright and courtesy of Farshid Moussavi Architecture.
Fig. 18 A Copyright and courtesy of Peter G. Rowe.
Fig. 18 B Copyright and courtesy of Peter G. Rowe.
Fig. 18 C Copyright and courtesy of Peter G. Rowe.
Fig. 19 A Patrick Huebgen, Creative Commons, 2005.
Fig. 19 B Martin Falbisoner, Creative Commons, 2015.
Fig. 19 C Richard Bartz, Creative Commons, 2008.
Fig. 20 A Kakidai, Creative Commons, 2018.
Fig. 20 B Copyright and courtesy of Peter G. Rowe.
Fig. 20 C Roman Suzuki, Creative Commons, 2007.
Fig. 21 A Maxar, Google Earth Image, 2023.
Fig. 21 B Oliver Foerstner, Dreamstime.com.
Fig. 21 C John Stamets, Creative Commons, 2012.
Fig. 21 D Copyright and courtesy of 3D Reid Architects.
Fig. 22 A Copyright and courtesy of ZAO/standardarchitecture.
Fig. 22 B Copyright and courtesy of Peter G. Rowe.
Fig. 22 C Copyright and courtesy of He Shu and Trace Architecture Office.
Fig. 22 D Copyright and courtesy of DnA Design and Architecture.

## Chapter 5

Fig. 1 Drawn by authors based on Fauconnier and Turner, 2002.
Fig. 2 Drawn by authors.
Fig. 3 Copyright and courtesy of Carlos Arnaiz Architects.
Fig. 4 Copyright and courtesy of Carlos Arnaiz Architects.
Fig. 5 Drawn by authors.
Fig. 6 Public Domain.
Fig. 7 A Dagmarakowalik, Creative Commons, 2023.

Fig. 7 B Oregon State University, Creative Commons, 2020.
Fig. 7 C Copyright and courtesy of Jihun Kim, "Airflow Analysis and Design Optimization" by Dr. Jihun Kim of MASS FLOW LAB in Collaboration with MODU Architecture, 2014.
Fig. 7 D Images George Rex, Creative Commons, 2016.
Fig. 7 E Copyright and courtesy of Peter G. Rowe.
Fig. 8 A Public Domain.
Fig. 8 B Copyright and courtesy of Barry Pittendrigh and Purdue University.
Fig. 8 C Drawn by authors based on Precision Agricultural Research Group of UNE, 2016.
Fig. 9 Drawn by authors based on Milgram et al., 1995.
Fig. 10 Drawn by authors based on Milgram et al., 1995.
Fig. 11 A Alessi, Creative Commons, 2023 and "Ply Chair" by Jasper Morrison, 1988.
Fig. 11 B Public Domain, Vincent Van Gogh, 1886 and "Op-La Tray Table" by Jasper Morrison, 1988.
Fig. 12 Drawn by authors.

**Chapter 6**

Fig. 1 Copyright and courtesy of Paris en Commun.
Fig. 2 A Copyright and courtesy of Philippe Guignard, Air Images.
Fig. 2 B Copyright and courtesy of Philippe Guignard, Air Images.
Fig. 2 C Copyright and courtesy of Paris Métropole Aménagement.
Fig. 2 D Besopha, Creative Commons, 2016 (top); Guilhem Vellut, Creative Commons, 2016 (bottom).
Fig. 3 A Drawn by authors based on Polymago and Paris Batignolles Aménagement, 2015.
Fig. 3 B Drawn by authors based on Polymago and Paris Batignolles Aménagement, 2015.
Fig. 3 C Drawn by authors based on Polymago and Paris Batignolles Aménagement, 2015.
Fig. 3 D Drawn by authors based on Polymago and Paris Batignolles Aménagement, 2015.
Fig. 3 E Drawn by authors based on Polymago and Paris Batignolles Aménagement, 2015.
Fig. 4 A Drawn by authors.
Fig. 4 B Drawn by authors.
Fig. 4 C Drawn by authors.
Fig. 5 Drawn by authors.
Fig. 6 A Copyright and courtesy of Nancy Fyler, Neponset River Watershed Association.
Fig. 6 B Drawn by authors on top of Google Earth Image, 2023.
Fig. 7 A Copyright and courtesy of Ben Parker and Priyanka Kar.
Fig. 7 B Copyright and courtesy of Ben Parker and Priyanka Kar.
Fig. 7 C Copyright and courtesy of Ben Parker and Priyanka Kar.
Fig. 7 D Copyright and courtesy of Ben Parker and Priyanka Kar.
Fig. 8 A Copyright and courtesy of Michael Maltzan Architects.
Fig. 8 B Laurie Avocado, Creative Commons, 2014.
Fig. 8 C Copyright and courtesy of Michael Maltzan Architects.
Fig. 8 D Copyright and courtesy of Michael Maltzan Architects.
Fig. 9 ADrawn by authors based on Modufy.
Fig. 9 B Drawn by authors based on Modufy.
Fig. 9 C Drawn by authors based on Modufy.
Fig. 9 D Drawn by authors based on Modufy.
Fig. 10 A Drawn by authors based on Modufy.
Fig. 10 B Drawn by authors based on Modufy.
Fig. 10 C Drawn by authors based on Modufy.
Fig. 10 D Drawn by authors based on Modufy.
Fig. 11 Copyright and courtesy of NAC Architecture and Carlos Arnaiz Architects.
Fig. 12 A Copyright and courtesy of NAC Architecture.
Fig. 12 B Copyright and courtesy of NAC Architecture.
Fig. 13 A Copyright and courtesy of Modufy and Carlos Arnaiz Architects.
Fig. 13 B Copyright and courtesy of Modufy and Carlos Arnaiz Architects.
Fig. 13 C Copyright and courtesy of Modufy and Carlos Arnaiz Architects.
Fig. 14 Drawn by authors.
Fig. 15 Copyright and courtesy of Eisenman Architects.
Fig. 16 A Drawn by authors.
Fig. 16 B Edited by authors based on Nathaniel Barlam.
Fig. 16 C Drawn by authors based on K. Michael Hays, *Architecture's Desire*, The MIT Press 2009, p. 91.
Fig. 16 D Wenkbrauwalbatros, Creative Commons, 2009.
Fig. 17 A Li Jie, Public Domain.
Fig. 17 B Li Jie, Public Domain.
Fig. 18 A Copyright and courtesy of Zhanliang Chen.
Fig. 18 B Copyright and courtesy of Zhanliang Chen.
Fig. 18 C Copyright and courtesy of Zhanliang Chen.
Fig. 18 D Copyright and courtesy of Zhanliang Chen.

# Acknowledgments

This book metamorphized out of a felt need to address the shortcomings of an earlier publication, simply titled *Design Thinking* that was published in 1987, particularly with regard to the important role of 'schemata', especially those related to architectural design as a creative practice. This need was heightened over the years at Harvard by colleagues like Rafael Moneo, Michael Hays, Manuel de Solà-Morales, Carl Steinitz, Hashim Sarkis, Toshiko Mori, Mack Scogin, Homa Fajardi and François Vigier. More recently, working together with Ali Malkawi on a doctoral proseminar has helped shape thinking, as have periodic teaching encounters with Antoine Picon, Rahul Mehrotra, Joan Busquets and Yun Fu. Throughout, strong support and encouragement was given by Carlos Arnaiz, a practice partner and always amenable subject of some of the extended case study in this volume, as well as from Claire Doussard, our French colleague, especially around shared research interests and capacities. Numerous graduate students at Harvard left their mark and particularly most recently with the likes of Rolo Girodengo, Priyanka Kar, Kiki Cooper, Liang Wang, Tree Chen, Saad Boujane and the indefatigable and hugely talented Boya Guo. Then too there were the late Michael Sorkin and Lebbeus Woods whose visionary and moral positions have always been exemplary. Finally, a shout out must go to Roger Conover, formerly of The MIT Press, who got us into this subject in the first place and who has been a lifelong supporter, as well as to Andreas Müller and Ria Stein among the crew at Birkhäuser, and of course, Reinhard Steger whose talent and energy remains inexhaustible.

Peter G. Rowe and Yoeun Chung

# About the Authors

**Peter G. Rowe** is the Raymond Garbe Professor of Architecture and Urban Design at Harvard University's Graduate School of Design and also a Harvard University Distinguished Service Professor. He served for twelve years as Dean of the Faculty of Design at Harvard and prior to that as the Chairman of the Department of Urban Planning and Design as well as Director of the Urban Design Program. He is also currently the Founding Chairman of SURBA – the Studio for Urban Analyses in Brooklyn, New York. Born in New Zealand, Rowe is the holder of several honorary professorships in East Asia and the author, co-author and editor of numerous books and journal articles. He recently co-authored for Birkhäuser *Chinese Modern: Episodes Backward and Forward in Time, Southeast Asia Modern: From Roots to Contemporary Turns, Korean Modern: The Matter of Identity, Urban Intensities: Contemporary Housing Types and Territories,* and *China's Urban Communities.* In addition, he was the author of *Emergent Architectural Territories in East Asian Cities,* also with Birkhäuser, as well as the author of *Design Thinking* published by The MIT Press originally in 1987.

**Yoeun Chung** is a doctoral candidate at Harvard University's Graduate School of Design. She received her Bachelor of Architecture at Illinois Institute of Technology graduating cum laude, followed by a Master of Architecture in Urban Design at Harvard where she took on a multiple research projects and teaching assistant roles, including serving as a professional design assistant at Harvard GSD Extension Education School. Yoeun had previously worked as a designer for Skidmore Owings and Merrill and more recently at Grayscale Collaborative as an associate urban designer. Her current research interest lies in discovering the reciprocal relationship between inhabitants' lifestyle and physical built environment.

# Index

This publication was supported in part by the
Graduate School of Design, Harvard University

GRAPHIC DESIGN, LAYOUT
AND TYPESETTING
Proxi Design
Reinhard Steger
Maria Martí Vigil

PROOFREADING
Keonaona Peterson

PROJECT MANAGEMENT
Ria Stein

PRODUCTION
Anja Haering

LITHOGRAPHY
Oriol Rigat

PRINTING
Beltz Grafische Betriebe GmbH

LIBRARY OF CONGRESS
CONTROL NUMBER
2023945098

Bibliographic information published by the
German National Library
The German National Library lists this publication in the Deutsche Nationalbibliografie; detailed bibliographic data are available on the Internet at http://dnb.dnb.de.


ISBN 978-3-0356-2811-1
e-ISBN (PDF) 978-3-0356-2812-8


P.O. Box 44, 4009 Basel, Switzerland
Part of Walter de Gruyter GmbH, Berlin/Boston

Printed on acid-free paper produced from
chlorine-free pulp. TCF ∞

Printed in Germany

9 8 7 6 5 4 3 2 1

www.birkhauser.com